TOUCHSTONE

By Carlos Castaneda

Tales of Power

BY

CARLOS CASTANEDA

A TOUCHSTONE BOOK
PUBLISHED BY SIMON AND SCHUSTER

DESIGNED BY EVE METZ
MANUFACTURED IN THE UNITED STATES OF AMERICA

1 2 3 4 5 6 7 8 9 10

Library of Congress Cataloging in Publication Data
Castaneda, Carlos.

Tales of power.

1. Yaqui Indians — Religion and mythology. 2. Juan,
Don, 1891– 3. Hallucinogenic drugs and religious
experience. I. Title.

E99.Y3C295   299'.7   74–10601

ISBN 0–671–21858–1

ISBN 0-671-22144-2 pbk.

CONTENTS

The conditions of a solitary bird are five:
The first, that it flies to the highest point;
the second, that it does not suffer for company,
*   not even of its own kind;*
the third, that it aims its beak to the skies;
the fourth, that it does not have a definite color;
the fifth, that it sings very softly.

— San Juan de la Cruz, *Dichos de Luz y Amor*

PART ONE

A Witness to Acts of Power

AN APPOINTMENT WITH KNOWLEDGE

I had not seen don Juan for several months. It was the autumn of 1971. I had the certainty that he was at don Genaro's house in central Mexico and made the necessary preparations for a six- or seven-day drive to visit him. On the second day of my journey, however, on an impulse, I stopped at don Juan's place in Sonora in the midafternoon. I parked my car and walked a short distance to the house. To my surprise, I found him there.

"Don Juan! I didn't expect to find you here," I said.

He laughed; my surprise seemed to delight him. He was sitting on an empty milk crate by the front door. He appeared to have been waiting for me. There was an air of accomplishment in the ease with which he greeted me. He took off his hat and flourished it in a comical gesture. Then he put it on again and gave me a military salute. He was leaning against the wall, sitting on the crate as if it were a saddle.

"Sit down, sit down," he said in a jovial tone. "Good to see you again."

"I was going to go all the way to central Mexico for nothing," I said. "And then I would've had to drive back to Los Angeles. Finding you here has saved me days and days of driving."

"Somehow you would've found me," he said in a mysterious tone, "but let's say that you owe me the six days that you would've needed to get there, days which you should use in doing something more interesting than pressing down on the gas pedal of your car."

There was something engaging in don Juan's smile. His warmth was contagious.

"Where's your writing gear?" he asked.

I told him that I had left it in the car; he said that I looked unnatural without it and made me go back and get it.

"I have finished writing a book," I said.

He gave me a long, strange look that produced an itching in the pit of my stomach. It was as if he were pushing my middle section with a soft object. I felt like I was going to get ill, but then he turned his head to the side and I regained my original feeling of well-being.

I wanted to talk about my book but he made a gesture that indicated that he did not want me to say anything about it. He smiled. His mood was light and charming and he immediately engaged me in a casual conversation about people and current events. Finally I managed to steer the conversation onto the topic of my interest. I began by mentioning that I had reviewed my early notes and had realized that he had been giving me a detailed description of the sorcerers' world from the beginning of our association. In light of what he had said to me in those stages, I had begun to question the role of hallucinogenic plants.

"Why did you make me take those power plants so many times?" I asked.

He laughed and mumbled very softly, "'Cause you're dumb."

I heard him the first time, but I wanted to make sure and pretended I had not understood.

"I beg your pardon?" I asked.

"You know what I said," he replied and stood up.

He tapped me on the head as he walked by me. "You're rather slow," he said. "And there was no other way to jolt you."

"So none of that was absolutely necessary?" I asked.

"It was, in your case. There are other types of people, however, that do not seem to need them."

He stood next to me, staring at the top of the bushes by the left side of his house; then he sat down again and talked about Eligio, his other apprentice. He said that Eligio had taken psychotropic plants only once since he became his apprentice, and yet he was perhaps even more advanced than I was.

"To be sensitive is a natural condition of certain people," he said. "You are not. But neither am I. In the final analysis sensitivity matters very little."

"What's the thing that matters then?" I asked.

He seemed to search for an appropriate answer.

"What matters is that a warrior be impeccable," he finally said. "But that's only a way of talking, a way of beating around the bush. You have already accomplished some tasks of sorcery and I believe this is the time to mention the source of everything that matters. So I will say that what matters to a warrior is arriving at the totality of oneself."

"What is the totality of oneself, don Juan?"

"I said that I was only going to mention it. There are still a lot of loose ends in your life that you must tie together before we can talk about the totality of oneself."

He ended our conversation there. He made a gesture with his hands to signal that he wanted me to stop talking. Apparently there was something or somebody nearby. He tilted his head to the left, as if to listen. I could see the whites of his eyes as he focused on the bushes beyond the house to his left. He listened attentively for a few moments and then stood up, came to me and whispered in my ear that we had to leave the house and go for a walk.

"Is there something wrong?" I asked, also in a whisper.

"No. Nothing is wrong," he said. "Everything is rather right."

He led me into the desert chaparral. We walked for perhaps half an hour and then came to a small circular area free from vegetation, a spot about twelve feet in diameter where the reddish dirt was packed and perfectly flat. There were no signs, however, that machinery had cleared and flattened the area. Don Juan sat down in the center of it, facing the southeast. He pointed to a place about five feet away from him and asked me to sit there, facing him.

"What are we going to do here?" I asked.

"We have an appointment here tonight," he replied.

He scanned the surroundings with a quick glance, turning around on his seat until he was again facing the southeast.

His movements had alarmed me. I asked him who we had the appointment with.

"With knowledge," he said. "Let's say that knowledge is prowling around here."

He did not let me hook on to that cryptic answer. He quickly changed the subject and in a jovial tone he urged me to be natural, that is, to take notes and talk as we would have done at his house.

What was most pressing on my mind at that time was the vivid sensation I had had six months before, of "talking" to a coyote. That event meant to me that for the first time I had been capable of visualizing or apprehending, through my senses and in sober consciousness, the sorcerers' description of the world; a description in which communicating with animals through speech was a matter of course.

"We're not going to engage ourselves in dwelling on any experience of that nature," don Juan said upon hearing my question. "It is not advisable for you to indulge in focusing your attention on past events. We may touch on them, but only in reference."

"Why is that so, don Juan?"

"You don't have enough personal power yet to seek the sorcerers' explanation."

"Then there is a sorcerers' explanation!"

"Certainly. Sorcerers are men. We're creatures of thought. We seek clarifications."

"I was under the impression that my great flaw was to seek explanations."

"No. Your flaw is to seek convenient explanations, explanations that fit you and your world. What I object to is your reasonableness. A sorcerer explains things in his world too, but he's not as stiff as you."

"How can I arrive at the sorcerers' explanation?"

"By accumulating personal power. Personal power will make you slide with great ease into the sorcerers' explanation. The explanation is not what you would call an explanation; nevertheless, it makes the world and its mysteries, if not clear, at least less awesome. That should be the essence of an explanation, but that is not what you seek. You're after the reflection of your ideas."

I lost my momentum to ask questions. But his smile urged me to keep on talking. Another issue of great importance to me was his friend don Genaro and the extraordinary effect that his actions had had on me. Every time I had come into contact with him I had experienced the most outlandish sensory distortions.

Don Juan laughed when I voiced my question.

"Genaro is stupendous," he said. "But for the time being, there is no sense in talking about him or about what he does to you. Again, you don't have enough personal power to unravel that topic. Wait until you have it, then we will talk."

"What if I never have it?"

"If you never have it, we'll never talk."

"At the rate I'm going, will I ever have enough of it?" I asked.

"That's up to you," he replied. "I have given you all the information necessary. Now it's your responsibility to gain enough personal power to tip the scales."

"You're talking in metaphors," I said. "Give it to me straight. Tell me exactly what I should do. If you have already told me, let's say that I've forgotten it."

Don Juan chuckled and lay down, putting his arms behind his head.

"You know exactly what you need," he said.

I told him that sometimes I thought I knew, but that most of the time I had no self-confidence.

"I'm afraid that you are confusing issues," he said. "The self-confidence of the warrior is not the self-confidence of the average man. The average man seeks certainty in the eyes of the onlooker and calls that self-confidence. The warrior seeks impeccability in his own eyes and calls that humbleness. The average man is hooked to his fellow men, while the warrior is hooked only to himself. Perhaps you are chasing rainbows. You're after the self-confidence of the average man, when you should be after the humbleness of a warrior. The difference between the two is remarkable. Self-confidence entails knowing something for sure; humbleness entails being impeccable in one's actions and feelings."

"I've been trying to live in accordance with your suggestions," I said. "I may not be the best, but I'm the best of myself. Is that impeccability?"

"No. You must do better than that. You must push yourself beyond your limits, all the time."

"But that would be insane, don Juan. No one can do that."

"There are lots of things that you do now which would have seemed insane to you ten years ago. Those things themselves did not change, but your idea of yourself changed; what was impossible before is perfectly possible now and perhaps your total success in changing yourself is only a matter of time. In this affair the only possible course that a warrior has is to act consistently and without reservations. You know enough of the warrior's way to act accordingly, but your old habits and routines stand in your way."

I understood what he meant.

"Do you think that writing is one of the old habits I should change?" I asked. "Should I destroy my new manuscript?"

He did not answer. He stood up and turned to look at the edge of the chaparral.

I told him that I had received letters from various people telling me that it was wrong to write about my apprenticeship. They had cited as a precedent that the masters of Eastern esoteric doctrines demanded absolute secrecy about their teachings.

"Perhaps those masters are just indulging in being masters," don Juan said without looking at me. "I'm not a master, I'm only a warrior. So I really don't know what a master feels like."

"But maybe I'm revealing things I shouldn't, don Juan."

"It doesn't matter what one reveals or what one keeps to oneself," he said. "Everything we do, everything we are, rests on our personal power. If we have enough of it, one word uttered to us might be sufficient to change the course of our lives. But if we don't have enough personal power, the most magnificent piece of wisdom can be revealed to us and that revelation won't make a damn bit of difference."

He then lowered his voice as if he were disclosing a confidential matter to me.

"I'm going to utter perhaps the greatest piece of knowledge anyone can voice," he said. "Let me see what you can do with it.

"Do you know that at this very moment you are surrounded by eternity? And do you know that you can use that eternity, if you so desire?"

After a long pause, during which he urged me with a subtle movement of his eyes to make a statement, I said that I did not understand what he was talking about.

"There! Eternity is there!" he said, pointing to the horizon.

Then he pointed to the zenith. "Or there, or perhaps we can say that eternity is like this." He extended both arms to point to the east and west.

We looked at each other. His eyes held a question.

"What do you say to that?" he asked, coaxing me to ponder upon his words.

I did not know what to say.

"Do you know that you can extend yourself forever in any of the directions I have pointed to?" he went on. "Do you know that one moment can be eternity? This is not a riddle; it's a fact, but only if you mount that moment and use it to take the totality of yourself forever in any direction."

He stared at me.

"You didn't have this knowledge before," he said, smiling. "Now you do. I have revealed it to you, but it doesn't make a bit of difference, because you don't have enough personal power to utilize my revelation. Yet if you did have enough power, my words alone would serve as the means for you to round up the totality of yourself and to get the crucial part of it out of the boundaries in which it is contained."

He came to my side and poked my chest with his fingers; it was a very light tap.

"These are the boundaries I'm talking about," he said. "One can get out of them. We are a feeling, an awareness encased here."

He slapped my shoulders with both hands. My pad and pencil fell to the ground. Don Juan put his foot on the pad and stared at me and then laughed.

I asked him if he minded my taking notes. He said no in a reassuring tone and moved his foot away.

"We are luminous beings," he said, shaking his head rhythmically. "And for a luminous being only personal power matters. But if you ask me what personal power is, I have to tell you that my explanation will not explain it."

Don Juan looked at the western horizon and said that there were still a few hours of daylight left.

"We have to be here for a long time," he explained. "So, we either sit quietly or we talk. It is not natural for you to be silent, so let's keep on talking. This spot is a power place and it must become used to us before nightfall. You must sit here, as naturally as possible, without fear or impatience. It seems that the easiest way for you to relax is to take notes, so write to your heart's content.

"And now, suppose you tell me about your *dreaming*."

His sudden shift caught me unprepared. He repeated his request. There was a great deal to say about it. "Dreaming" entailed cultivating a peculiar control over one's dreams to the extent that the experiences undergone in them and those lived in one's waking hours acquired the same pragmatic valence. The sorcerers' allegation was that under the impact of "dreaming" the ordinary criteria to differentiate a dream from reality became inoperative.

Don Juan's praxis of "dreaming" was an exercise that consisted of finding one's hands in a dream. In other words, one had to deliberately dream that one was looking for and could find one's hands in a dream by simply dreaming that one lifted one's hands to the level of the eyes.

After years of unsuccessful attempts I had finally accomplished the task. Looking at it in retrospect, it had become evident to me that I had succeeded only after I had gained a degree of control over the world of my everyday life.

Don Juan wanted to know the salient points. I began telling him that the difficulty of setting up the command to look at my hands seemed to be, quite often, insurmountable. He had warned me that the early stage of the preparatory facet, which he called "setting up dreaming," consisted of a deadly game that one's mind played with itself, and that some part of myself was going to do everything it could to prevent the fulfillment of my task. That could include, don Juan had said, plunging me into a loss of meaning, melancholy, or even a suicidal depression. I did not go that far, however. My experience was rather on the light, comical side; nonetheless, the result was equally frustrating. Every time I was about to look at my hands in a dream something extraordinary would happen; I would begin to fly, or my dream would turn into a nightmare, or it would simply become a very pleasant experience of bodily excitation; everything in the dream would extend far beyond the "normal" in matters of vividness and, therefore, be terribly absorbing. My original intention of observing my hands was always forgotten in light of the new situation.

One night, quite unexpectedly, I found my hands in my dreams. I dreamt that I was walking on an unknown street in a foreign city and suddenly I lifted up my hands and placed them in front of my face. It was as if something within myself had given up and had permitted me to watch the backs of my hands.

Don Juan's instructions had been that as soon as the sight of my hands would begin to dissolve or change into something else, I had to shift my view from my hands to any other element in the surroundings of my dream. In that particular dream I shifted my view to a building at the end of the street. When the sight of the building began to dissipate I focused my attention on the other elements of the surroundings in my dream. The end result was an incredibly clear composite picture of a deserted street in some unknown foreign city.

Don Juan made me continue with my account of other experiences in "dreaming." We talked for a long time.

At the end of my report he stood up and went to the bushes. I also stood up. I was nervous. It was an unwarranted sensation since there was nothing precipitating fear or concern. Don Juan returned shortly. He noticed my agitation.

"Calm down," he said, holding my arm gently.

He made me sit down and put my notebook on my lap. He coaxed me to write. His argument was that I should not disturb the power place with unnecessary feelings of fear or hesitation.

"Why do I get so nervous?" I asked.

"It's natural," he said. "Something in you is threatened by your activities in *dreaming*. As long as you did not think about those activities, you were all right. But now that you have revealed your actions you're about to faint.

"Each warrior has his own way of *dreaming*. Each way is different. The only thing which we all have in common is that we play tricks in order to force ourselves to abandon the quest. The countermeasure is to persist in spite of all the barriers and disappointments."

He asked me then if I was capable of selecting topics for "dreaming." I said that I did not have the faintest idea of how to do that.

"The sorcerers' explanation of how to select a topic for *dreaming*," he said, "is that a warrior chooses the topic by deliberately holding an image in his mind while he shuts off his internal dialogue. In other words, if he is capable of not talking to himself for a moment and then holds the image or the thought of what he wants in *dreaming*, even if only for an instant, then the desired topic will come to him. I'm sure you've done that, although you were not aware of it."

There was a long pause and then don Juan began to sniff the air. It was as if he were cleaning his nose; he exhaled three or four times through his nostrils with great force. The muscles of his abdomen contracted in spasms, which he controlled by taking in short gasps of air.

"We won't talk about *dreaming* any more," he said. "You might become obsessed. If one is to succeed in anything, the success must come gently, with a great deal of effort but with no stress or obsession."

He stood up and walked to the edge of the bushes. He leaned forward and peered into the foliage. He seemed to be examining something in the leaves, without getting too close to them.

"What are you doing?" I asked, unable to contain my curiosity.

He turned to me, smiled and raised his brow.

"The bushes are filled with strange things," he said as he sat down again.

His tone was so casual that it scared me more than if he had let out a sudden yell. My notebook and pencil fell from my hands. He laughed and mimicked me and said that my exaggerated reactions were one of the loose ends that still existed in my life.

I wanted to raise a point but he would not let me talk.

"There's only a bit of daylight left," he said. "There are other things we ought to touch upon before the twilight sets in."

He then added that judging by my production in "dreaming" I must have learned how to stop my internal dialogue at will. I told him that I had.

At the beginning of our association don Juan had delineated another procedure: walking for long stretches without focusing the eyes on anything. His recommendation had been to not look at anything directly but, by slightly crossing the eyes, to keep a peripheral view of everything that presented itself to the eyes. He had insisted, although I had not understood at the time, that if one kept one's unfocused eyes at a point just above the horizon, it was possible to notice, at once, everything in almost the total 180-degree range in front of one's eyes. He had assured me that that exercise was the only way of shutting off the internal dialogue. He used to ask me for reports on my progress, and then he stopped inquiring about it.

I told don Juan that I had practiced the technique for years without noticing any change, but I had expected none anyway. One day, however, I had the shocking realization that I had just walked for about ten minutes without having said a single word to myself.

I mentioned to don Juan that on that occasion I also became cognizant that stopping the internal dialogue involved more than merely curtailing the words I said to myself. My entire thought processes had stopped and I had felt I was practically suspended, floating. A sensation of panic had ensued from that awareness and I had to resume my internal dialogue as an antidote.

"I've told you that the internal dialogue is what grounds us," don Juan said. "The world is such and such or so and so, only because we talk to ourselves about its being such and such or so and so."

Don Juan explained that the passageway into the world of sorcerers opens up after the warrior has learned to shut off the internal dialogue.

"To change our idea of the world is the crux of sorcery," he said. "And stopping the internal dialogue is the only way to accomplish it. The rest is just padding. Now you're in the position to know that nothing of what you've seen or done, with the exception of stopping the internal dialogue, could by itself have changed anything in you, or in your idea of the world. The provision is, of course, that that change should not be deranged. Now you can understand why a teacher doesn't clamp down on his apprentice. That would only breed obsession and morbidity."

He asked for details of other experiences I had had in shutting off the internal dialogue. I recounted everything that I could remember.

We talked until it became dark and I could no longer take notes in a comfortable manner; I had to pay attention to my writing and that altered my concentration. Don Juan became aware of it and began to laugh. He pointed out that I had accomplished another sorcery task, writing without concentrating. The moment he said it, I realized that I really did not pay attention to the act of taking notes. It seemed to be a separate activity I had nothing to do with. I felt odd. Don Juan asked me to sit by him in the center of the circle. He said it was too dark and I was no longer safe sitting so close to the edge of the chaparral. I felt a chill up my back and jumped to his side.

He made me face the southeast and asked me to command myself to be silent and without thoughts. I could not do it at first and had a moment of impatience. Don Juan turned his back to me and told me to lean on his shoulder for support. He said that once I had quieted down my thoughts, I should keep my eyes open, facing the bushes towards the southeast. In a mysterious tone he added that he was setting up a problem for me, and that if I resolved it I would be ready for another facet of the sorcerers' world.

I posed a weak question about the nature of the problem. He chuckled softly. I waited for his answer and then something in me was turned off. I felt I was suspended. My ears seemed to unplug and a myriad of noises in the chaparral became audible. There were so many that I could not distinguish them individually. I felt I was falling asleep and then all at once something caught my attention. It was not something which involved my thought processes; it was not a vision, or a feature of the environment either, yet my awareness had been engaged by something. I was fully awake. My eyes were focused on a spot on the edge of the chaparral, but I was not looking, or thinking, or talking to myself. My feelings were clear bodily sensations; they did not need words. I felt I was rushing through something indefinite. Perhaps what would have ordinarily been my thoughts were rushing; at any rate, I had the sensation that I had been caught in a landslide and something was avalanching, with me at the crest. I felt the rush in my stomach. Something was pulling me into the chaparral. I could distinguish the dark mass of the bushes in front of me. It was not, however, an undifferentiated darkness as it would ordinarily be. I could see every individual bush as if I were looking at them in a dark twilight. They seemed to be moving; the mass of their foliage looked like black skirts flowing towards me as if they were being blown by the wind, but there was no wind. I became absorbed in their mesmerizing movements; it was a pulsating ripple that seemed to draw them nearer and nearer to me. And then I noticed a lighter silhouette which seemed to be superimposed on the dark shapes of the bushes. I focused my eyes on a spot to the side of the lighter silhouette and I could make out a chartreuse glow on it. Then I looked at it without focusing and I had the certainty that the lighter silhouette was a man hiding in the underbrush.

I was, at that moment, in a most peculiar state of awareness. I was cognizant of the surroundings and of the mental processes that the surroundings engendered in myself, yet I was not thinking as I ordinarily think. For instance, when I realized that the silhouette superimposed on the bushes was a man, I recalled another occasion on the desert; I had noticed then, while don Genaro and I were walking in the chaparral at night, that a man was hiding in the bushes behind us, but the instant I had attempted to explain the phenomenon rationally I lost sight of the man. This time, however, I felt I had the upper hand and I refused to explain or to think anything at all. For a moment I had the impression that I could hold the man and force him to remain where he was. I then experienced a strange pain in the pit of my stomach. Something seemed to rip inside me and I could not hold the muscles of my midsection tense any longer. At the very moment I let go, the dark shape of an enormous bird, or some sort of flying animal, lurched at me from the chaparral. It was as if the shape of the man had turned into the shape of a bird. I had the clear conscious perception of fear. I gasped and then let out a loud yell and fell on my back.

Don Juan helped me up. His face was very close to mine. He was laughing.

"What was that?" I shouted.

He hushed me, putting his hand over my mouth. He put his lips to my ear and whispered that we had to leave the area in a calm and collected fashion, as if nothing had happened.

We walked side by side. His pace was relaxed and even. A couple of times he turned around quickly. I did the same and twice I caught sight of a dark mass that seemed to be following us. I heard a loud eerie shriek behind me. I experienced a moment of sheer terror; ripples ran through the muscles of my stomach; they came in spasms and grew in intensity until they simply forced my body to run.

The only way of talking about my reaction has to be in don Juan's terminology; and thus I can say that my body, due to the fright I was experiencing, was capable of executing what he had called "the gait of power," a technique he had taught me years before, consisting of running in the darkness without tripping or hurting oneself in any way.

I was not fully aware of what I had done or how I had done it. Suddenly I found myself again at don Juan's house. Apparently he had also run and we had arrived at the same time. He lit his kerosene lantern, hung it from a beam in the ceiling and casually asked me to sit down and relax.

I jogged on the same spot for a while until my nervousness became more manageable. Then I sat down. He forcefully ordered me to act as if nothing had happened and handed me my notebook. I had not realized that in my haste to leave the bushes I had dropped it.

"What happened out there, don Juan?" I finally asked.

"You had an appointment with knowledge," he said, pointing with a movement of his chin to the dark edge of the desert chaparral. "I took you there because I caught a glimpse of knowledge prowling around the house earlier. You might say that knowledge knew that you were coming and was waiting for you. Rather than meeting it here, I felt it was proper to meet it on a power spot. Then I set up a test to see if you had enough personal power to isolate it from the rest of the things around us. You did fine."

"Wait a minute!" I protested. "I saw the silhouette of a man hiding behind a bush and then I saw a huge bird."

"You didn't see a man!" he said emphatically. "Neither did you see a bird. The silhouette in the bushes and what flew to us was a moth. If you want to be accurate in sorcerers' terms, but very ridiculous in your own terms, you could say that tonight you had an appointment with a moth. Knowledge is a moth."

He looked at me piercingly. The light of the lantern created strange shadows on his face. I moved my eyes away.

"Perhaps you'll have enough personal power to unravel that mystery tonight," he said. "If not tonight, perhaps tomorrow; remember, you still owe me six days."

Don Juan stood up and walked to the kitchen in the back of the house. He took the lantern and set it against the wall on the short round stump that he used as a bench. We sat down on the floor opposite each other and served ourselves some beans and meat from a pot that he had placed in front of us. We ate in silence.

He gave me furtive glances from time to time and seemed on the verge of laughing. His eyes were like two slits. When he looked at me he would open them a bit and the moistness of the corneas reflected the light of the lantern. It was as if he were using the light to create a mirror reflection. He played with it, shaking his head almost imperceptibly every time he focused his eyes on me. The effect was a fascinating quiver of light. I became aware of his maneuvers after he had executed them a couple of times. I was convinced that he was acting with a definite purpose in mind. I felt compelled to ask him about it.

"I have an ulterior reason," he said reassuringly. "I'm soothing you with my eyes. You don't seem to be getting more nervous, do you?"

I had to admit that I felt quite at ease. The steady flicker in his eyes was not menacing and it had not scared or annoyed me in any way.

"How do you soothe me with your eyes?" I asked.

He repeated the imperceptible shake of his head. The corneas of his eyes were indeed reflecting the light of the kerosene lantern.

"Try to do it yourself," he said casually as he gave himself another serving of food. "You can soothe yourself."

I tried to shake my head; my movements were awkward.

"You won't soothe yourself bobbing your head like that," he said and laughed. "You'll give yourself a headache instead. The secret is not in the head shake but in the feeling that comes to the eyes from the area below the stomach. This is what makes the head shake."

He rubbed his umbilical region.

After I had finished eating I slouched against a pile of wood and some burlap sacks. I tried to imitate his head shake. Don Juan seemed to be enjoying himself immensely. He giggled and slapped his thighs.

Then a sudden noise interrupted his laughter. I heard a strange deep sound, like tapping on wood, that came from the chaparral. Don Juan jutted his chin, signaling me to remain alert.

"That's the little moth calling you," he said in an unemotional tone.

I jumped to my feet. The sound ceased instantaneously. I looked at don Juan for an explanation. He made a comical gesture of helplessness, shrugging his shoulders.

"You haven't fulfilled your appointment yet," he added.

I told him that I felt unworthy and that perhaps I should go home and come back when I felt stronger.

"You're talking nonsense," he snapped. "A warrior takes his lot, whatever it may be, and accepts it in ultimate humbleness. He accepts in humbleness what he is, not as grounds for regret but as a living challenge.

"It takes time for every one of us to understand that point and fully live it. I, for instance, hated the mere mention of the word 'humbleness.' I'm an Indian and we Indians have always been humble and have done nothing else but lower our heads. I thought humbleness was not in the warrior's way. I was wrong! I know now that the humbleness of a warrior is not the humbleness of a beggar. The warrior lowers his head to no one, but at the same time, he doesn't permit anyone to lower his head to him. The beggar, on the other hand, falls to his knees at the drop of a hat and scrapes the floor for anyone he deems to be higher; but at the same time, he demands that someone lower than him scrape the floor for him.

"That's why I told you earlier today that I didn't understand what masters felt like. I know only the humbleness of a warrior, and that will never permit me to be anyone's master."

We were quiet for a moment. His words had caused me a profound agitation. I was moved by them and at the same time I felt concerned with what I had witnessed in the chaparral. My conscious assessment was that don Juan was holding out on me and that he must have known what was really taking place.

I was involved in those deliberations when the same strange tapping noise jolted me out of my thoughts. Don Juan smiled and then began to chuckle.

"You like the humbleness of a beggar," he said softly. "You bow your head to reason."

"I always think that I'm being tricked," I said. "That's the crux of my problem."

"You're right. You are being tricked," he retorted with a disarming smile. "That cannot be your problem. The real crux of the matter is that you feel that I am deliberately lying to you, am I correct?"

"Yes. There is something in myself that doesn't let me believe that what's taking place is real."

"You're right again. Nothing of what is taking place is real."

"What do you mean by that, don Juan?"

"Things are real only after one has learned to agree on their realness. What took place this evening, for instance, cannot possibly be real to you, because no one could agree with you about it."

"Do you mean that you didn't see what happened?"

"Of course I did. But I don't count. I am the one who's lying to you, remember?"

Don Juan laughed until he coughed and choked. His laughter was friendly even though he was making fun of me.

"Don't pay too much attention to all my gibberish," he said reassuringly. "I'm just trying to relax you and I know that you feel at home only when you're muddled up."

His expression was deliberately comical and we both laughed. I told him that what he had just said made me feel more afraid than ever.

"You're afraid of me?" he asked.

"Not of you, but of what you represent."

"I represent the warrior's freedom. Are you afraid of that?"

"No. But I'm afraid of the awesomeness of your knowledge. There is no solace for me, no haven to go to."

"You're again confusing issues. Solace, haven, fear, all of them are moods that you have learned without ever questioning their value. As one can see, the black magicians have already engaged all your allegiance."

"Who are the black magicians, don Juan?"

"Our fellow men are the black magicians. And since you are with them, you too are a black magician. Think for a moment. Can you deviate from the path that they've lined up for you? No. Your thoughts and your actions are fixed forever in their terms. That is slavery. I, on the other hand, brought you freedom. Freedom is expensive, but the price is not impossible. So, fear your captors, your masters. Don't waste your time and your power fearing me."

I knew that he was right, and yet in spite of my genuine agreement with him I also knew that my lifelong habits would unavoidably make me stick to my old path. I did indeed feel like a slave.

After a long silence don Juan asked me if I had enough strength for another bout with knowledge.

"Do you mean with the moth?" I asked half in jest.

His body contorted with laughter. It was as if I had just told him the funniest joke in the world.

"What do you really mean when you say that knowledge is a moth?" I asked.

"I have no other meanings," he replied. "A moth is a moth. I thought that by now, with all your accomplishments, you would have had enough power to *see*. You caught sight of a man instead and that was not true *seeing*."

From the beginning of my apprenticeship, don Juan had depicted the concept of "seeing" as a special capacity that one could develop and which would allow one to apprehend the "ultimate" nature of things.

Over the years of our association I had developed a notion that what he meant by "seeing" was an intuitive grasp of things, or the capacity to understand something at once, or perhaps the ability to see through human interactions and discover covert meanings and motives.

"I should say that tonight, when you faced the moth, you were half looking and half *seeing*," don Juan proceeded. "In that state, although you were not altogether your usual self, you were still capable of being fully aware in order to operate your knowledge of the world."

Don Juan paused and looked at me. I did not know what to say at first.

"How was I operating my knowledge of the world?" I asked.

"Your knowledge of the world told you that in the bushes one can only find animals prowling or men hiding behind the foliage. You held that thought, and naturally you had to find ways to make the world conform to that thought."

"But I wasn't thinking at all, don Juan."

"Let's not call it thinking then. It is rather the habit of having the world always conform to our thoughts. When it doesn't, we simply make it conform. Moths as large as a man cannot be even a thought, therefore, for you, what was in the bushes had to be a man.

"The same thing happened with the coyote. Your old habits decided the nature of that encounter too. Something took place between you and the coyote, but it wasn't talk. I have been in the same quandary myself. I've told you that once I talked with a deer; now you've talked to a coyote, but neither you nor I will ever know what really took place at those times."

"What are you telling me, don Juan?"

"When the sorcerers' explanation became clear to me, it was too late to know what the deer did to me. I said that we talked, but that wasn't so. To say that we had a conversation is only a way of arranging it so I can talk about it. The deer and I did something, but at the time it was taking place I needed to make the world conform to my ideas, just like you did. I had been talking all my life, just like you, therefore my habits prevailed and were extended to the deer. When the deer came to me and did whatever it did, I was forced to understand it as talking."

"Is this the sorcerers' explanation?"

"No. This is my explanation for you. But it is not opposed to the sorcerers' explanation."

His statement threw me into a state of great intellectual excitation. For a while I forgot the prowling moth or even to take notes. I tried to rephrase his statements and we involved ourselves in a long discussion about the reflexive nature of our world. The world, according to don Juan, had to conform to its description; that is, the description reflected itself.

Another point in his elucidation was that we had learned to relate ourselves to our description of the world in terms of what he called "habits." I introduced what I thought was a more engulfing term, intentionality, the property of human consciousness whereby an object is referred to, or is intended.

Our conversation engendered a most interesting speculation. Examined in light of don Juan's explanation, my "talk" with the coyote acquired a new character. I had indeed "intended" the dialogue, since I have never known another avenue of intentional communication. I had also succeeded in conforming to the description that communication takes place through dialogue, and thus I made the description reflect itself.

I had a moment of great elation. Don Juan laughed and said that to be so moved by words was another aspect of my foolery. He made a comical gesture of talking without sounds.

"All of us go through the same shenanigans," he said after a long pause. "The only way to overcome them is to persist in acting like a warrior. The rest comes of itself and by itself."

"What is the rest, don Juan?"

"Knowledge and power. Men of knowledge have both. And yet none of them could tell how they got to have them, except that they had kept on acting like warriors and at a given moment everything changed."

He looked at me. He seemed undecided, then stood up and said that I had no other recourse but to keep my appointment with knowledge.

I felt a shiver; my heart began to pound fast. I got up. Don Juan moved around me as if he were examining my body from every possible angle. He signaled me to sit down and keep on writing.

"If you get too frightened you won't be able to keep your appointment," he said. "A warrior must be calm and collected and must never lose his grip."

"I'm really scared," I said. "Moth or whatever, there is something prowling around out there in the bushes."

"Of course there is!" he exclaimed. "My objection is that you insist on thinking that it is a man, just like you insist on thinking that you talked with a coyote."

A part of me fully understood his point; there was, however, another aspect of myself that would not let go and in spite of the evidence clung steadfast to "reason."

I told don Juan that his explanation did not satisfy my senses, although I was in complete intellectual agreement with it.

"That's the flaw with words," he said in an assuring tone. "They always force us to feel enlightened, but when we turn around to face the world they always fail us and we end up facing the world as we always have, without enlightenment. For this reason, a sorcerer seeks to act rather than to talk and to this effect he gets a new description of the world—a new description where talking is not that important, and where new acts have new reflections."

He sat down by me and gazed into my eyes and asked me to voice what I had really "seen" in the chaparral.

I was confronted at the moment with an absorbing inconsistency. I had seen the dark shape of a man, but I had also seen that shape turn into a bird. I had, therefore, witnessed more than my reason would allow me to consider possible. But rather than discarding my reason altogether, something in myself had selected parts of my experience, such as the size and general contour of the dark shape, and held them as reasonable possibilities, while it discarded other parts, such as the dark shape turning into a bird. And thus I had become convinced that I had seen a man.

Don Juan roared with laughter when I expressed my quandary. He said that sooner or later the sorcerers' explanation would come to my rescue and everything would then be perfectly clear, without having to be reasonable or unreasonable.

"In the meantime all I can do for you is to guarantee that that was not a man," he said.

Don Juan's gaze became quite unnerving. My body shivered involuntarily. He made me feel embarrassed and nervous.

"I'm looking for marks on your body," he explained. "You may not know it, but this evening you had quite a bout out there."

"What kind of marks are you looking for?"

"Not actual physical marks on your body but signs, indications in your luminous fibers, areas of brightness. We are luminous beings and everything we are or everything we feel shows in our fibers. Humans have a brightness peculiar only to them. That's the only way to tell them apart from other luminous living beings.

"If you would have *seen* tonight, you would have noticed that the shape in the bushes was not a luminous living being."

I wanted to ask more but he put his hand on my mouth and hushed me. He then put his mouth to my ear and whispered that I should listen and try to hear a soft rustling, the gentle muffled steps of a moth on the dry leaves and branches on the ground.

I could not hear anything. Don Juan stood up abruptly, picked up the lantern and said that we were going to sit under the ramada by the front door. He led me through the back and around the house, on the edge of the chaparral rather than going through the room and out the front door. He explained that it was essential to make our presence obvious. We half circled around the house on the left side. Don Juan's pace was extremely slow. His steps were weak and vacillating. His arm shook as he held the lantern.

I asked him if there was something wrong with him. He winked at me and whispered that the big moth that was prowling around had an appointment with a young man, and that the slow gait of a feeble old man was an obvious way of showing who was the appointee.

When we finally arrived at the front of the house, don Juan hooked the lantern on a beam and made me sit with my back against the wall. He sat to my right.

"We're going to sit here," he said, "and you are going to write and talk to me in a very normal manner. The moth that lurched at you today is around, in the bushes. After a while it'll come closer to look at you. That's why I've put the lantern on a beam right above you. The light will guide the moth to find you. When it gets to the edge of the bushes, it will call you. It is a very special sound. The sound by itself may help you."

"What kind of sound is it, don Juan?"

"It is a song. A haunting call that moths produce. Ordinarily it cannot be heard, but the moth out there in the bushes is a rare moth; you will hear its call clearly and, providing that you are impeccable, it will remain with you for the rest of your life."

"What is it going to help me with?"

"Tonight, you're going to try to finish what you've started earlier. *Seeing* happens only when the warrior is capable of stopping the internal dialogue.

"Today, you stopped your talk at will, out there in the bushes. And you *saw*. What you *saw* was not clear. You thought that it was a man. I say it was a moth. Neither of us is correct, but that's because we have to talk. I still have the upper hand because I *see* better than you and because I'm familiar with the sorcerers' explanation; so I know, although it's not altogether accurate, that the shape you *saw* tonight was a moth.

"And now, you're going to remain silent and thoughtless and let that little moth come to you again."

I could hardly take notes. Don Juan laughed and urged me to keep on writing as if nothing bothered me. He touched my arm and said that writing was the best protective shield that I had.

"We've never talked about moths," he went on. "The time was not right until now. As you already know, your spirit was unbalanced. To counteract that I taught you to live the warrior's way. Well, a warrior starts off with the certainty that his spirit is off balance; then by living in full control and awareness, but without hurry or compulsion, he does his ultimate best to gain this balance.

"In your case, as in the case of every man, your imbalance was due to the sum total of all your actions. But now your spirit seems to be in the proper light to talk about moths."

"How did you know that this was the right time to talk about moths?"

"I caught a glimpse of the moth prowling around when you arrived. It was the first time it was friendly and open. I had *seen* it before in the mountains around Genaro's house, but only as a menacing figure reflecting your lack of order."

I heard a strange sound at that moment. It was like a muffled creaking of a branch rubbing against another, or like the sputtering of a small motor heard from a distance. It changed scales, like a musical tone, creating an eerie rhythm. Then it stopped.

"That was the moth," don Juan said. "Perhaps you've already noticed that, although the light of the lantern is bright enough to attract moths, there isn't a single one flying around it."

I had not paid attention to it, but once don Juan made me aware of it, I also noticed an incredible silence in the desert around the house.

"Don't get jumpy," he said calmly. "There is nothing in this world that a warrior cannot account for. You see, a warrior considers himself already dead, so there is nothing for him to lose. The worst has already happened to him, therefore he's clear and calm; judging him by his acts or by his words, one would never suspect that he has witnessed everything."

Don Juan's words, and above all his mood, were very soothing to me. I told him that in my day-to-day life I no longer experienced the obsessive fear I used to, but that my body entered into convulsions of fright at the thought of what was out there in the dark.

"Out there, there is only knowledge," he said in a factual tone. "Knowledge is frightening, true; but if a warrior accepts the frightening nature of knowledge he cancels out its awesomeness."

The strange sputtering noise happened again. It seemed closer and louder. I listened carefully. The more attention I paid to it the more difficult it was to determine its nature. It did not seem to be the call of a bird or the cry of a land animal. The tone of each sputter was rich and deep; some were produced in a low key, others in a high one. They had a rhythm and a specific duration; some were long, I heard them like a single unit of sound; others were short and happened in a cluster, like the staccato sound of a machine gun.

"The moths are the heralds or, better yet, the guardians of eternity," don Juan said after the sound had stopped. "For some reason, or for no reason at all, they are the depositories of the gold dust of eternity."

The metaphor was foreign to me. I asked him to explain it.

"The moths carry a dust on their wings," he said. "A dark gold dust. That dust is the dust of knowledge."

His explanation had made the metaphor even more obscure. I vacillated for a moment trying to find the best way of wording my question. But he began to talk again.

"Knowledge is a most peculiar affair," he said, "especially for a warrior. Knowledge for a warrior is something that comes at once, engulfs him, and passes on."

"What does knowledge have to do with the dust on the wings of moths?" I asked after a long pause.

"Knowledge comes floating like specks of gold dust, the same dust that covers the wings of moths. So, for a warrior, knowledge is like taking a shower, or being rained on by specks of dark gold dust."

In the most polite manner I was capable of, I mentioned that his explanations had confused me even more. He laughed and assured me that he was making perfect sense, except that my reason would not allow me to be at ease.

"The moths have been the intimate friends and helpers of sorcerers from time immemorial," he said. "I had not touched upon this subject before, because of your lack of preparation."

"But how can the dust on their wings be knowledge?"

"You'll see."

He put his hand over my notebook and told me to close my eyes and become silent and without thoughts. He said that the call of the moth in the chaparral was going to aid me. If I paid attention to it, it would tell me of imminent events. He stressed that he did not know how the communication between the moth and myself was going to be established, neither did he know what the terms of the communication would be. He urged me to feel at ease and confident and trust my personal power.

After an initial period of impatience and nervousness I succeeded in becoming silent. My thoughts diminished in number until my mind was perfectly blank. The noises of the desert chaparral seemed to have been turned on as I became more calm.

The strange sound that don Juan said was made by a moth occurred again. It registered as a feeling in my body and not as a thought in my mind. It occurred to me that it was not threatening or malevolent at all. It was sweet and simple. It was like a child's call. It brought back the memory of a little boy that I once knew. The long sounds reminded me of his round blond head, the short staccato sounds of his laughter. The most anguishing feeling oppressed me, and yet there were no thoughts in my mind; I felt the anguish in my body. I could no longer remain sitting and slid to the floor on my side. My sadness was so intense that I began to think. I assessed my pain and sorrow and suddenly found myself in the midst of an internal debate about the little boy. The sputtering sound had ceased. My eyes were closed. I heard don Juan standing up and then I felt him helping me to sit up. I did not want to speak. He did not say a word. I heard him moving by me. I opened my eyes; he had knelt in front of me and was examining my face, holding the lantern close to me. He ordered me to put my hands over my stomach. He stood up, went to the kitchen and brought me some water. He splashed some on my face and gave me the rest to drink.

He sat down next to me and handed me my notes. I told him that the sound had involved me in the most painful reverie.

"You are indulging beyond your limits," he said dryly.

He seemed to immerse himself in thought, as if he were searching for an appropriate suggestion to make.

"The problem for tonight is *seeing* people," he finally said. "First you must stop your internal dialogue, then you must bring up the image of the person that you want to *see*; any thought that one holds in mind in a state of silence is properly a command, since there are no other thoughts to compete with it. Tonight, the moth in the bushes wants to help you, so it will sing for you. Its song will bring the golden specks and then you will *see* the person you've selected."

I wanted to have more details, but he made an abrupt gesture and signaled me to proceed.

After struggling for a few minutes to stop my internal dialogue I was thoroughly silent. And then I deliberately held the brief thought of a friend of mine. I kept my eyes closed for what I believed to be just an instant and then I became aware that someone was shaking me by the shoulders. It was a slow realization. I opened my eyes and found myself lying on my left side. I had apparently fallen asleep so deeply that I did not remember having slumped to the ground. Don Juan helped me to sit up again. He was laughing. He imitated my snoring and said that if he had not witnessed it himself he would not believe that anyone could fall asleep so fast. He said that it was a treat for him to be around me whenever I had to do something that my reason did not understand. He pushed my notebook away from me and said that we had to start all over.

I followed the necessary steps. The strange sputtering sound happened again. This time, however, it did not come from the chaparral; rather it seemed to happen inside of me, as if my lips, or legs, or arms were producing it. The sound soon engulfed me. I felt like soft balls were being sputtered out from or against me; it was a soothing, exquisite feeling of being bombarded by heavy cotton puffs. Suddenly I heard a door blown open by a gust of wind and I was thinking again. I thought that I had ruined another chance. I opened my eyes and found myself in my room. The objects on my desk were as I had left them. The door was open; there was a strong wind outside. The thought crossed my mind that I should check the water heater. I then heard a rattling on the sliding windows that I had put up myself and which did not fit well on the window frame. It was a furious rattling as if someone wanted to enter. I experienced a jolt of fright. I stood up from my chair. I felt something pulling me. I screamed.

Don Juan was shaking me by the shoulders. I excitedly gave him an account of my vision. It had been so vivid that I was shivering. I felt that I had just been at my desk, in my full corporeal form.

Don Juan shook his head in disbelief and said that I was a genius in tricking myself. He did not seem impressed by what I had done. He discarded it flatly and ordered me to start again.

I then heard the mysterious sound again. It came to me, as don Juan had suggested, in the form of a rain of golden specks. I did not feel that they were flat specks or flakes, as he had described them, but rather spherical bubbles. They floated towards me. One of them burst open and revealed a scene to me. It was as if it had stopped in front of my eyes and opened up, disclosing a strange object. It looked like a mushroom. I was definitely looking at it, and what I was experiencing was not a dream. The mushroomlike object remained unchanged within my field of "vision" and then it popped, as though the light that was shining on it had been turned off. An interminable darkness followed it. I felt a tremor, a very unsettling jolt, and then I had the abrupt realization that I was being shaken. All at once my senses were turned on. Don Juan was shaking me vigorously, and I was looking at him. I must have just opened my eyes at that moment.

He sprinkled water on my face. The coldness of the water was very appealing. After a moment's pause he wanted to know what had happened.

I recounted every detail of my vision.

"But what did I *see*?" I asked.

"Your friend," he retorted.

I laughed and patiently explained that I had "seen" a mushroomlike figure. Although I had no criteria to judge dimensions, I had had the feeling that it was about a foot long.

Don Juan emphasized that feeling was all that counted. He said that my feelings were the gauge that assessed the state of being of the subject that I was "seeing."

"From your description and your feelings I must conclude that your friend must be a very fine man," he said.

I was baffled by his words.

He said that the mushroomlike formation was the essential shape of human beings when a sorcerer was "seeing" them from far away, but when a sorcerer was directly facing the person he was "seeing," the human quality was shown as an egglike cluster of luminous fibers.

"You were not facing your friend," he said. "Therefore, he appeared like a mushroom."

"Why is that so, don Juan?"

"No one knows. That simply is the way men appear in this specific type of *seeing*."

He added that every feature of the mushroomlike formation had a special significance, but that it was impossible for a beginner to accurately interpret that significance.

I then had an intriguing recollection. Some years before, in a state of nonordinary reality elicited by the intake of psychotropic plants, I had experienced or perceived, while I was looking at a water stream, that a cluster of bubbles floated towards me, engulfing me. The golden bubbles I had just envisioned had floated and engulfed me in exactly the same manner. In fact, I could say that both clusters had had the same structure and the same pattern.

Don Juan listened to my commentaries without interest.

"Don't waste your power on trifles," he said. "You are dealing with that immensity out there."

He pointed towards the chaparral with a movement of his hand.

"To turn that magnificence out there into reasonableness doesn't do anything for you. Here, surrounding us, is eternity itself. To engage in reducing it to a manageable nonsense is petty and outright disastrous."

He then insisted that I should attempt to "see" another person from my realm of acquaintances. He added that once the vision had terminated I should strive to open my eyes by myself and surface to the full awareness of my immediate surroundings.

I succeeded in holding the view of another mushroomlike form, but while the first one had been yellowish and small, the second one was whitish, larger and contorted.

By the time we had finished talking about the two shapes I had "seen," I had forgotten the "moth in the bushes," which had been so overwhelming a little while before. I told don Juan that it amazed me that I had such a facility for discarding something so truly uncanny. It was as if I were not the person I knew myself to be.

"I don't see why you make such a fuss out of this," don Juan said. "Whenever the dialogue stops, the world collapses and extraordinary facets of ourselves surface, as though they had been kept heavily guarded by our words. You are like you are, because you tell yourself that you are that way."

After a short rest, don Juan urged me to continue "calling" friends. He said that the point was to attempt to "see" as many times as possible, in order to establish a guideline for feeling.

I called thirty-two persons in succession. After each attempt, he demanded a careful and detailed rendition of everything I had perceived in my vision. He changed that procedure, however, as I became more proficient in my performance, judging by my stopping the internal dialogue in a matter of seconds, by my being capable of opening my eyes by myself at the end of each experience, and by my resuming ordinary activities without any transition. I noticed this change while we were discussing the coloration of the mushroomlike formations. He had already made the point that what I called coloration was not a hue but a glow of different intensities. I was about to describe a yellowish glow that I had envisioned when he interrupted me and accurately described what I had "seen." From that point on he discussed the content of each vision, not as if he had understood what I had said, but as if he had "seen" it himself. When I called him to comment on it he flatly refused to talk about it.

By the time I had finished calling the thirty-two persons, I had realized that I had "seen" a variety of mushroomlike shapes, and glows, and I had had a variety of feelings towards them, ranging from mild delight to sheer disgust.

Don Juan explained that men were filled with configurations that could be wishes, problems, sorrows, worries, and so on. He asserted that only a profoundly powerful sorcerer could untangle the meaning of those configurations, and that I had to be content with viewing only the general shape of men.

I was very tired. There was something indeed fatiguing about those strange shapes. My overall sensation was one of queasiness. I had not liked them. They had made me feel trapped and doomed.

Don Juan commanded me to write in order to dispel the sensation of somberness. And after a long silent interval during which I could not write anything, he asked me to call on people that he himself would select.

A new series of forms emerged. They were not mushroomlike, but looked more like Japanese cups for sake, turned upside down. Some of them had a headlike formation, just like the foot of sake cups; others were more round. Their shapes were appealing and peaceful. I sensed that there was some inherent feeling of happiness about them. They bounced, as opposed to the earthbound heaviness that the previous batch had exhibited. Somehow, the mere fact that they were there eased my fatigue.

Among the persons he had selected was his apprentice Eligio. When I summoned the vision of Eligio I got a jolt that shook me out of my visionary state. Eligio had a long white shape that jerked and seemed to leap at me. Don Juan explained that Eligio was a very talented apprentice and that he, no doubt, had noticed that someone was "seeing" him.

Another of don Juan's selections was Pablito, don Genaro's apprentice. The jolt that the vision of Pablito gave me was even greater than Eligio's.

Don Juan laughed so hard that tears rolled down his cheeks.

"Why are those people shaped differently?" I asked.

"They have more personal power," he replied. "As you might have noticed, they are not pegged down to the ground."

"What has given them that lightness? Were they born that way?"

"We all are born that light and bouncy, but we become earthbound and fixed. We make ourselves that way. So perhaps we may say that these people are shaped differently because they live like warriors. That's not important though. What's of value is that you are at the edge now. You've called forty-seven people, and there is only one more left in order for you to complete the original forty-eight."

I remembered at that moment that years before he had told me, while discussing corn sorcery and divination, that the number of corn kernels that a sorcerer possessed was forty-eight. He had never explained why.

I asked him again, "Why forty-eight?"

"Forty-eight is our number," he said. "That's what makes us men. I don't know why. Don't waste your power in idiotic questions."

He stood up and stretched his arms and legs. He told me to do the same. I noticed that there was a tinge of light in the sky towards the east. We sat down again. He leaned over and put his mouth to my ear.

"The last person you're going to call is Genaro, the real McCoy," he whispered.

I felt a surge of curiosity and excitation. I breezed through the required steps. The strange sound from the edge of the chaparral became vivid and acquired new strength. I had almost forgotten about it. The golden bubbles engulfed me and then in one of them I saw don Genaro himself. He was standing in front of me, holding his hat in his hand. He was smiling. I hurriedly opened my eyes and was about to speak to don Juan, but before I could say a word my body stiffened like a board; my hair stood on end and for a long moment I did not know what to do or say. Don Genaro was standing right in front of me. In person!

I turned to don Juan; he was smiling. Then both of them broke into a giant laugh. I also tried to laugh. I could not. I stood up.

Don Juan handed me a cup of water. I drank it automatically. I thought he was going to sprinkle water on my face. Instead, he refilled my cup.

Don Genaro scratched his head and hid a grin.

"Aren't you going to greet Genaro?" don Juan asked.

It took an enormous effort for me to organize my thoughts and my feelings. I finally mumbled some greetings to don Genaro. He took a bow.

"You called me, didn't you?" he asked, smiling.

I muttered my amazement at having found him standing there.

"He did call you," don Juan interjected.

"Well, here I am," don Genaro said to me. "What can I do for you?"

Slowly my mind seemed to become organized and finally I had a sudden insight. My thoughts were crystal clear and I "knew" what had really taken place. I figured that don Genaro had been visiting with don Juan, and that as soon as they had heard my car approaching, don Genaro had slipped into the bushes and had remained in hiding until it got dark. I believed the evidence was convincing. Don Juan, since he had no doubt engineered the entire affair, gave me clues from time to time, thus guiding its development. At the appropriate time, don Genaro had made me notice his presence, and when don Juan and I were walking back to the house, he followed us in the most obvious manner in order to arouse my fear. Then he had waited in the chaparral and made the strange sound whenever don Juan had signaled him. The final signal to come out from behind the bushes must have been given by don Juan while my eyes were closed after he had asked me to "call" don Genaro. Then don Genaro must have walked to the ramada and waited until I opened my eyes and then scared me out of my wits.

The only incongruencies in my logical explanatory scheme were that I had actually seen the man hiding in the bushes turn into a bird, and that I had first visualized don Genaro as an image in a golden bubble. In my vision he had been dressed exactly as he was in person. Since there was no logical way for me to explain those incongruencies, I assumed, as I have always done in similar circumstances, that the emotional stress may have played an important role in determining what I "believed I saw."

I began to laugh quite involuntarily at the thought of their preposterous trick. I told them about my deductions. They laughed uproariously. I honestly believed that their laughter was the giveaway.

"You were hiding in the bushes, weren't you?" I asked don Genaro.

Don Juan sat down and held his head in both hands.

"No. I wasn't hiding," don Genaro said patiently. "I was far from here and then you called, so I came to see you."

"Where were you, don Genaro?"

"Far away."

"How far?"

Don Juan interrupted me and said that don Genaro had showed up as an act of deference to me, and that I could not ask where he had been, because he had been nowhere.

Don Genaro came to my defense and said that it was all right to ask him anything.

"If you were not hiding around the house, where were you, don Genaro?" I asked.

"I was at my house," he said with great candor.

"In central Mexico?"

"Yes! It's the only house I've got."

They looked at each other and again broke into laughter. I knew that they were kidding me, but I decided not to contest the point any further. I thought they must have had a reason for engaging themselves in such an elaborate production. I sat down.

I felt that I was truthfully cut in two; some part of me was not shocked at all and could accept any of don Juan or don Genaro's acts at their face value. But there was another part of me that flatly refused; it was my strongest part. My conscious assessment was that I had accepted don Juan's sorcery description of the world merely on an intellectual basis, while my body as a whole entity refused it, thus my dilemma. But then over the course of the years of my association with don Juan and don Genaro I had experienced extraordinary phenomena and those had been bodily experiences, not intellectual ones. Earlier that very night I had executed the "gait of power," which, from the point of view of my intellect, was an inconceivable accomplishment; and best of all, I had had incredible visions through no other means than my own volition.

I explained to them the nature of my painful and at the same time bona fide perplexity.

"This guy is a genius," don Juan said to don Genaro, shaking his head in disbelief.

"You're a huge genius, Carlitos," don Genaro said as if he were relaying a message.

They sat down on either side of me, don Juan to my right and don Genaro to my left. Don Juan observed that soon it was going to be morning. At that instant I again heard the moth's call. It had moved. The sound was coming from the opposite direction. I looked at both of them, holding their gaze. My logical scheme began to disintegrate.

The sound had a mesmerizing richness and depth. Then I heard muffled steps, soft feet crushing the dry underbrush. The sputtering sound came closer and I huddled against don Juan. He dryly ordered me to "see" it. I made a supreme effort, not so much to please him as to please myself. I had been sure that don Genaro was the moth. But don Genaro was sitting with me; what, then, was in the bushes? A moth?

The sputtering sound echoed in my ears. I could not stop my internal dialogue altogether. I heard the sound but I could not feel it in my body as I had done earlier. I heard definite steps. Something was creeping in the dark. There was a loud cracking noise, as if a branch had been snapped in two, and suddenly a terrifying memory seized me. Years before I had spent a dreadful night in the wilderness and had been harassed by something, something very light and soft that had stepped on my neck over and over while I crouched on the ground. Don Juan had explained the event as an encounter with "the ally," a mysterious force that a sorcerer learned to perceive as an entity.

I leaned closer to don Juan and whispered what I had remembered. Don Genaro crawled on all fours to get closer to us.

"What did he say?" he asked don Juan in a whisper.

"He said that there is an ally out there," don Juan replied in a low voice.

Don Genaro crawled back and sat down. Then he turned to me and said in a loud whisper, "You're a genius."

They laughed quietly. Don Genaro pointed towards the chaparral with a movement of his chin.

"Go out there and grab it," he said. "Take off your clothes and scare the devil out of that ally."

They shook with laughter. The sound in the meantime had ceased. Don Juan ordered me to stop my thoughts but to keep my eyes open, focused on the edge of the chaparral in front of me. He said that the moth had changed positions because don Genaro was there, and that if it were going to manifest itself to me, it would choose to come from the front.

After a moment's struggle to quiet my thoughts, I perceived the sound again. It was richer than ever. I heard first the muffled steps on dry twigs and then I felt them on my body. At that instant I distinguished a dark mass directly in front of me, at the edge of the chaparral.

I felt I was being shaken. I opened my eyes. Don Juan and don Genaro were standing above me and I was kneeling, as if I had fallen asleep in a crouching position. Don Juan gave me some water and I sat down again with my back against the wall.

A short while later it was dawn. The chaparral seemed to wake up. The morning cold was crisp and invigorating.

The moth had not been don Genaro. My rational structure was falling apart. I did not want to ask any more questions, nor did I want to remain quiet. I finally had to talk.

"But if you were in central Mexico, don Genaro, how did you get here?" I asked.

Don Genaro made some ludicrous and utterly hilarious gestures with his mouth.

"I'm sorry," he said to me, "my mouth doesn't want to talk."

He then turned to don Juan and said, grinning, "Why don't you tell him?"

Don Juan vacillated. Then he said that don Genaro, as a consummate artist of sorcery, was capable of prodigious deeds.

Don Genaro's chest swelled as if don Juan's words were inflating it. He seemed to have inhaled so much air that his chest looked twice its normal size. He appeared to be on the verge of floating. He leaped in the air. I had the impression that the air inside his lungs had forced him to jump. He paced back and forth on the dirt floor until he apparently got his chest under control; he patted it and with great force ran the palms of his hands from his pectoral muscles to his stomach as if he were deflating the inner tube of a tire. He finally sat down.

Don Juan was grinning. His eyes were shining with sheer delight.

"Write your notes," he ordered me softly. "Write, write or you'll die!"

Then he remarked that even don Genaro no longer felt that my taking notes was so outlandish.

"That's right!" don Genaro retorted. "I've been thinking of taking up writing myself."

"Genaro is a man of knowledge," don Juan said dryly. "And being a man of knowledge, he's perfectly capable of transporting himself over great distances."

He reminded me that once, years before, the three of us had been in the mountains, and that don Genaro, in an effort to help me overcome my stupid reason, had taken a prodigious leap to the peaks of the Sierras, ten miles away. I remembered the event, but I also remembered that I could not even conceive that he had jumped.

Don Juan added that don Genaro was capable of performing extraordinary feats at certain times.

"Genaro at certain times is not Genaro but his double," he said.

He repeated it three or four times. Then both of them watched me as if waiting for my impending reaction.

I had not understood what he meant by "his double." He had never mentioned that before. I asked for a clarification.

"There is another Genaro," he explained.

All three of us looked at one another. I became very apprehensive. Don Juan urged me with a movement of his eyes to keep on talking.

"Do you have a twin brother?" I asked, turning to don Genaro.

"Of course," he said. "I have a twin."

I could not determine whether or not they were putting me on. They both giggled with the abandon of children that were pulling a prank.

"You may say," don Juan went on, "that at this moment Genaro is his twin."

That statement brought both of them to the ground with laughter. But I could not enjoy their mirth. My body shivered involuntarily.

Don Juan said in a severe tone that I was too heavy and self-important.

"Let go!" he commanded me dryly. "You know that Genaro is a

sorcerer and an impeccable warrior. So he's capable of performing deeds that would be unthinkable for the average man. His double, the other Genaro, is one of those deeds."

I was speechless. I could not conceive that they were just teasing me.

"For a warrior like Genaro," he went on, "to produce the other is not such a farfetched enterprise."

After pondering for a long time what to say next, I asked, "Is the other like the self?"

"The other is the self," don Juan replied.

His explanation had taken an incredible turn, and yet it was not really more incredible than anything else they did.

"What's the other made of?" I asked don Juan after minutes of indecision.

"There is no way of knowing that," he said.

"Is it real or just an illusion?"

"It's real of course."

"Would it be possible then to say that it is made of flesh and blood?" I asked.

"No. It would not be possible," don Genaro answered.

"But if it is as real as I am . . ."

"As real as you?" don Juan and don Genaro interjected in unison.

They looked at each other and laughed until I thought they were going to get ill. Don Genaro threw his hat on the floor and danced around it. His dance was agile and graceful and, for some inexplicable reason, utterly funny. Perhaps the humor was in the exquisitely "professional" movements he executed. The incongruency was so subtle and at the same time so remarkable that I doubled up with laughter.

"The trouble with you, Carlitos," he said as he sat down again, "is that you're a genius."

"I have to know about the double," I said.

"There's no way of knowing whether he's flesh and blood," don Juan said. "Because he is not as real as you. Genaro's double is as real as Genaro. Do you see what I mean?"

"But you have to admit, don Juan, that there must be a way to know."

"The double is the self; that explanation should suffice. If you would *see*, however, you'd know that there is a great difference between Genaro and his double. For a sorcerer who *sees*, the double is brighter."

I felt I was too weak to ask any more questions. I put my writing pad down and for a moment I thought I was going to pass out. I had tunnel vision; everything around me was dark with the exception of a round spot of clear scenery in front of my eyes.

Don Juan said that I had to get some food. I was not hungry. Don Genaro announced that he was famished, stood up and went to the back of the house. Don Juan also stood up and signaled me to follow. In the kitchen, don Genaro gave himself a serving of food and then became involved in the most comical mimicking of a person who wants to eat but can't swallow. I thought that don Juan was going to die; he roared, kicked, cried, coughed and choked with laughter. I thought I too was going to split my sides. Don Genaro's antics were priceless.

He finally gave up and looked at don Juan and me in succession; he had shiny eyes and a beaming smile.

"It doesn't work," he said, shrugging his shoulders.

I ate a huge amount of food, and so did don Juan; then all of us returned to the front of the house. The sunlight was brilliant, the sky was clear and the morning breeze sharpened the air. I felt happy and strong.

We sat in a triangle facing one another. After a polite silence I decided to ask them to clarify my dilemma. I felt that I was again in top form and wanted to exploit my strength.

"Tell me more about the double, don Juan," I said.

Don Juan pointed at don Genaro and don Genaro bowed.

"There he is," don Juan said. "There is nothing to tell. He's here for you to witness him."

"But he's don Genaro," I said in a feeble attempt to guide the conversation.

"Surely I'm Genaro," he said and perked his shoulders.

"What is a double then, don Genaro?" I asked.

"Ask him," he snapped, pointing to don Juan. "He's the one who talks. I'm dumb."

"A double is the sorcerer himself, developed through his *dreaming*," don Juan explained. "A double is an act of power to a sorcerer but only a tale of power to you. In the case of Genaro, his double is indistinguishable from the original. That's because his impeccability as a warrior is supreme; thus, you've never noticed the difference yourself. But in the years that you've known him, you've been with the original Genaro only twice; every other time you've been with his double."

"But this is preposterous!" I exclaimed.

I felt an anxiety building up in my chest. I became so agitated that I dropped my writing pad, and my pencil rolled out of sight. Don Juan and don Genaro practically dove to the ground and began the most farcical search for it. I had never seen a more astonishing performance of theatrical magic and sleight of hand. Except that there was no stage, or props, or any type of gadgetry, and most likely the performers were not using sleight of hand.

Don Genaro, the head magician, and his assistant, don Juan, produced in a matter of minutes the most astounding, bizarre and outlandish collection of objects which they found underneath, or behind, or above every object within the periphery of the ramada.

In the style of stage magic, the assistant set up the props, which in this case were the few items on the dirt floor—rocks, burlap sacks, pieces of wood, a milk crate, a lantern and my jacket—then the magician, don Genaro, would proceed to find an object, which he would throw away as soon as he had attested that it was not my pencil. The collection of objects found included pieces of clothing, wigs, eyeglasses, toys, utensils, pieces of machinery, women's underwear, human teeth, sandwiches, and religious objects. One of them was outright disgusting. It was a piece of compact human excrement that don Genaro took from underneath my jacket. Finally, don Genaro found my pencil and handed it to me after dusting it off with the tail of his shirt.

They celebrated their clowning with yells and chuckles. I found myself watching, unable to join them.

"Don't take things so seriously, Carlitos," don Genaro said with a tone of concern. "Otherwise you're going to bust a . . ."

He made a ludicrous gesture that could have meant anything.

After their laughter subsided I asked don Genaro what a double did, or what a sorcerer did with the double.

Don Juan answered. He said that the double had power, and that it was used to accomplish feats that would be unimaginable under ordinary terms.

"I've told you time and time again that the world is un-fathomable," he said to me. "And so are we, and so is every being that exists in this world. It is impossible, therefore, to reason out the double. You've been allowed to witness it, though, and that should be more than enough."

"But there must be a way to talk about it," I said. "You yourself have told me that you explained your conversation with the deer in order to talk about it. Can't you do the same with the double?"

He was quiet for a moment. I pleaded with him. The anxiety I was experiencing was beyond anything I had ever gone through.

"Well, a sorcerer can double up," don Juan said. "That's all one can say."

"But is he aware that he is doubled?"

"Of course he's aware of it."

"Does he know that he is in two places at once?"

Both of them looked at me and then they exchanged a glance.

"Where is the other don Genaro?" I asked.

Don Genaro leaned towards me and stared into my eyes.

"I don't know," he said softly. "No sorcerer knows where his other is."

"Genaro is right," don Juan said. "A sorcerer has no notion that he is in two places at once. To be aware of that would be the equivalent of facing his double, and the sorcerer that finds himself face to face with himself is a dead sorcerer. That is the rule. That is the way power has set things up. No one knows why."

Don Juan explained that by the time a warrior had conquered

"dreaming" and "seeing" and had developed a double, he must have also succeeded in erasing personal history, self-importance, and routines. He said that all the techniques which he had taught me and which I had considered to be empty talk were, in essence, means for removing the impracticality of having a double in the ordinary world, by making the self and the world fluid, and by placing them outside the bounds of prediction.

"A fluid warrior can no longer make the world chronological," don Juan explained. "And for him, the world and himself are no longer objects. He's a luminous being existing in a luminous world. The double is a simple affair for a sorcerer because he knows what he's doing. To take notes is a simple affair for you, but you still scare Genaro with your pencil."

"Can an outsider, looking at a sorcerer, see that he is in two places at once?" I asked don Juan.

"Certainly. That would be the only way to know it."

"But can't one logically assume that the sorcerer would also notice that he has been in two places?"

"Aha!" don Juan exclaimed. "For once you've got it right. A sorcerer may certainly notice afterwards that he has been in two places at once. But this is only bookkeeping and has no bearing on the fact that while he's acting he has no notion of his duality."

My mind boggled. I felt that if I did not keep on writing I would explode.

"Think of this," he went on. "The world doesn't yield to us directly, the description of the world stands in between. So, properly speaking, we are always one step removed and our experience of the world is always a recollection of the experience. We are perennially recollecting the instant that has just happened, just passed. We recollect, recollect, recollect."

He turned his hand over and over to give me the feeling of what he meant.

"If our entire experience of the world is recollection, then it's not so outlandish to conclude that a sorcerer can be in two places at once. This is not the case from the point of view of his own perception, because in order to experience the world, a sorcerer, like every other man, has to recollect the act he has just performed, the event he has just witnessed, the experience he has just lived. In his awareness there is only a single recollection. But for an outsider looking at the sorcerer it may appear as if the sorcerer is acting two different episodes at once. The sorcerer, however, recollects two separate single instants, because the glue of the description of time is no longer binding him."

When don Juan had finished talking I was sure I was running a temperature.

Don Genaro examined me with curious eyes.

"He's right," he said. "We're always one jump behind."

He moved his hand as don Juan had done; his body started to jerk and he jumped back on his seat. It was as if he had the hiccups and the hiccups were forcing his body to jump back. He began to move backwards, jumping on his seat, and went all the way to the end of the ramada and back.

The sight of don Genaro leaping backwards on his buttocks, instead of being funny as it should have been, threw me into an attack of fear so intense that don Juan had to strike me repeatedly on the top of my head with his knuckles.

"I just can't grasp all this, don Juan," I said.

"I can't either," don Juan retorted, shrugging his shoulders.

"Neither can I, dear Carlitos," don Genaro added.

My fatigue, the bulk of my sensory experience, the mood of lightness and humor that prevailed, and don Genaro's clowning were too much for my nerves. I could not stop the agitation in my stomach muscles.

Don Juan made me roll on the ground until I had regained my calmness, then I sat down facing them again.

"Is the double solid?" I asked don Juan after a long silence.

They looked at me.

"Does the double have corporealness?" I asked.

"Certainly," don Juan said. "Solidity, corporealness are memories. Therefore, like everything else we feel about the world, they are memories we accumulate. Memories of the description. You have the memory of my solidity, the same way you have the memory of communicating through words. Thus, you talked with a coyote and you feel me as being solid."

Don Juan put his shoulder next to mine and nudged me lightly. "Touch me," he said.

I patted him and then I embraced him. I was close to tears.

Don Genaro stood up and came closer to me. He looked like a small child with shiny mischievous eyes. He puckered up his lips and looked at me for a long moment.

"What about me?" he asked, trying to hide a smile. "Aren't you going to embrace me too?"

I stood up and extended my arms to touch him; my body seemed to freeze on the spot. I had no power to move. I tried to force my arms to reach him, but my struggle was in vain.

Don Juan and don Genaro stood by, watching me. I felt my body contorting under an unknown pressure.

Don Genaro sat down and pretended to sulk because I had not embraced him; he pouted and hit the ground with his heels, then both of them exploded into more roaring laughter.

The muscles of my stomach trembled, making my whole body shake. Don Juan pointed out that I was moving my head the way he had recommended earlier, and that that was the chance to soothe myself by reflecting a beam of light on the cornea of my eyes. He forcefully dragged me from under the roof of his ramada to the open field and manipulated my body into position so that my eyes would catch the eastern sunlight; but by the time he had put my body in place, I had stopped shivering. I noticed that I was clutching my notebook only after don Genaro said that the weight of the sheets was giving me the shivers.

I told don Juan that my body was pulling me to leave. I waved my hand to don Genaro. I did not want to give them time to make me change my mind.

"Good-by, don Genaro," I yelled. "I have to go now."

He waved back at me.

Don Juan walked a few yards with me towards my car.

"Do you also have a double, don Juan?" I asked.

"Of course!" he exclaimed.

I had at that moment a maddening thought. I wanted to discard it and leave in a hurry but something in myself kept on needling me. Over the course of the years of our association, it had become customary for me that every time I wanted to see don Juan I would just go to Sonora or central Mexico and I would always find him waiting for me. I had learned to take that for granted and it had never occurred to me until then to think anything of it.

"Tell me something, don Juan," I said, half in jest. "Are you yourself or are you your double?"

He leaned over towards me. He was grinning.

"My double," he whispered.

My body leaped in the air as if I had been propelled by a formidable force. I ran to my car.

"I was just kidding," don Juan said in a loud voice. "You can't go yet. You still owe me five more days."

Both of them ran towards my car as I was backing up. They were laughing and jumping up and down.

"Carlitos, call me any time!" don Genaro shouted.

THE DREAMER AND THE DREAMED

I drove to don Juan's house and arrived there in the early morning. I had spent the night in a motel on the way down so I would get to his house before noon.

Don Juan was in the back and came to the front when I called him. He gave me a warm greeting and the impression that he was pleased to see me. He made a comment that I thought was intended to put me at ease but produced the opposite effect.

"I heard you coming," he said as he grinned. "And I ran to the back. I was afraid that if I had stayed here you would've been frightened."

He casually remarked that I was somber and heavy. He said that I reminded him of Eligio, who was morbid enough to be a good sorcerer but too morbid to become a man of knowledge. He added that the only way to counteract the devasting effect of the sorcerers' world was to laugh at it.

He was right in his assessment of my mood. I was indeed worried and frightened. We went for a long walk. It took hours for my feelings to ease up. Walking with him made me feel better than if he had attempted to talk me out of my somberness.

We returned to his house in the late afternoon. I was famished. After eating we sat under his ramada. The sky was clear. The afternoon light made me feel complacent. I wanted to talk.

"I've felt uneasy for months," I said. "There was something truly awesome in what you and don Genaro said and did the last time I was here."

Don Juan did not say anything. He got up and moved around the ramada.

"I've got to talk about this," I said. "It obsesses me and I can't stop pondering upon it."

"Are you afraid?" he asked.

I was not afraid but baffled, overwhelmed by what I had heard and witnessed. The loopholes in my reason were so gigantic that either I had to repair them or I had to dispose of my reason altogether.

My comments made him laugh.

"Don't throw away your reason yet," he said. "It's not time for it. It'll happen though, but I don't think that now is the moment."

"Should I try to find an explanation for what happened, then?" I asked.

"Certainly!" he retorted. "It's your duty to put your mind at ease. Warriors do not win victories by beating their heads against walls but by overtaking the walls. Warriors jump over the walls; they don't demolish them."

"How can I jump over this one?" I asked.

"First of all, I think it's deadly wrong for you to regard anything in such a serious fashion," he said as he sat down by my side. "There are three kinds of bad habits which we use over and over when confronted with unusual life situations. First, we may disregard what's happening or has happened and feel as if it had never occurred. That one is the bigot's way. Second, we may accept everything at its face value and feel as if we know what's going on. That's the pious man's way. Third, we may become obsessed with an event because either we cannot disregard it or we cannot accept it wholeheartedly. That's the fool's way. Your way? There is a fourth, the correct one, the warrior's way. A warrior acts as if nothing had ever happened, because he doesn't believe in anything, yet he accepts everything at its face value. He accepts without accepting and disregards without disregarding. He never feels as if he knows, neither does he feel as if nothing had ever happened. He acts as if he is in control, even though he might be shaking in his boots. To act in such a manner dissipates obsession."

We were quiet for a long time. Don Juan's words were like a balm to me.

"Can I talk about don Genaro and his double?" I asked.

"It depends on what you want to say about him," he replied. "Are you going to indulge in being obsessed?"

"I want to indulge in explanations," I said. "I'm obsessed because I haven't dared come to see you and I haven't been able to talk about my qualms and doubts with anyone."

"Don't you talk with your friends?"

"I do, but how could they help me?"

"I never thought that you needed help. You must cultivate the feeling that a warrior needs nothing. You say you need help. Help for what? You have everything needed for the extravagant journey that is your life. I have tried to teach you that the real experience is to be a man, and that what counts is being alive; life is the little detour that we are taking now. Life in itself is sufficient, self-explanatory and complete.

"A warrior understands this and lives accordingly; therefore, one may say without being presumptuous that the experience of experiences is being a warrior."

He seemed to wait for me to say something. I hesitated for a moment. I wanted to select my words carefully.

"If a warrior needs solace," he went on, "he simply chooses anyone and expresses to that person every detail of his turmoil. After all, the warrior is not seeking to be understood or helped; by talking he's merely relieving himself of his pressure. That is, providing that the warrior is given to talking; if he's not, he tells no one. But you're not living like a warrior altogether. Not yet anyway. And the pitfalls that you encounter must be truly monumental. You have all my sympathy."

He was not being facetious. Judging by the concern in his eyes, he seemed to be one who had been there himself. He stood up and patted me on the head. He walked back and forth the length of the ramada and looked casually to the chaparral around the house. His movements evoked a sensation of restlessness in me.

In order to relax I began to talk about my dilemma. I felt that it was inherently too late for me to pretend to be an innocent by-stander. Under his guidance I had trained myself to achieve strange perceptions, such as "stopping the internal dialogue," and controlling my dreams. Those were instances that could not be faked. I had followed his suggestions, although never to the letter, and had par-tially succeeded in disrupting daily routines, assuming responsibility for my acts, erasing personal history and had finally arrived at a point which years before I had dreaded; I was capable of being alone without disrupting my physical or emotional well-being. That was perhaps my single most astounding triumph. From the point of view of my former expectations and moods, to be alone and not "go out of my mind" was an inconceivable state. I was keenly aware of all the changes that had taken place in my life and in my view of the world, and I was also aware that it was somehow superfluous to be affected so profoundly by don Juan and don Genaro's revelation about the "double."

"What's wrong with me, don Juan?" I asked.

"You indulge," he snapped. "You feel that indulging in doubts and tribulations is the sign of a sensitive man. Well, the truth of the mat-ter is that you're the farthest thing from being sensitive. So why pre-tend? I told you the other day, a warrior accepts in humbleness what he is."

"You make it sound as if I were confusing myself deliberately," I said.

"We do confuse ourselves deliberately," he said. "All of us are aware of our doings. Our puny reason deliberately makes itself into the monster it fancies itself to be. It's too little for such a big mold, though."

I explained to him that my dilemma was perhaps more complex than what he was making it out to be. I said that as long as he and don Genaro were men like myself their superior control made them models for my own behavior. But if they were in essence men drastically different than I, then I could not conceive of them any longer as models, but as oddities, which I could not possibly aspire to emulate.

"Genaro is a man," don Juan said in a reassuring tone. "He's no longer a man like yourself, true. But that's his accomplishment and it shouldn't give rise to fear on your part. If he's different, the more reason to admire him."

"But his difference is not a human difference," I said.

"And what do you think it is? The difference between a man and a horse?"

"I don't know. But he's not like me."

"He was at one time, though."

"But can his change be understood by me?"

"Of course. You yourself are changing."

"Do you mean that I will develop a double?"

"No one develops a double. That's only a way of talking about it. You, for all the talking you do, are a sap for words. You get trapped by their meanings. Now you think that one develops a double through evil means, I suppose. All of us luminous beings have a double. All of us! A warrior learns to be aware of it, that's all. There are seemingly insurmountable barriers protecting that awareness. But that's expected; those barriers are what makes arriving at that awareness such a unique challenge."

"Why am I so afraid of it, don Juan?"

"Because you're thinking that the double is what the word says, a double, or another you. I chose those words in order to describe it. The double is oneself and cannot be faced in any other way."

"What if I don't want to have it?"

"The double is not a matter of personal choice. Neither is it a matter of personal choice who is selected to learn the sorcerers' knowledge that leads to that awareness. Have you ever asked yourself, why you in particular?"

"All the time. I've asked you that question hundreds of times but you've never answered it."

"I didn't mean that you should ask it as a question that begs an answer, but in the sense of a warrior's pondering on his great fortune, the fortune of having found a challenge.

"To make it into an ordinary question is the device of a conceited ordinary man who wants to be either admired or pitied for it. I have no interest in that kind of question, because there is no way of answering it. The decision of picking you was a design of power; no one can discern the designs of power. Now that you've been selected, there is nothing that you can do to stop the fulfillment of that design."

"But you yourself told me, don Juan, that one can always fail."

"That's true. One can always fail. But I think that you are referring to something else. You want to find a way out. You want to have the freedom to fail and quit on your own terms. Too late for that. A warrior is in the hands of power and his only freedom is to choose an impeccable life. There is no way to fake triumph or defeat. Your reason may want you to fail altogether in order to obliterate the totality of yourself. But there is a countermeasure which will not permit you to declare a false victory or defeat. If you think that you can retreat to the haven of failure, you're out of your mind. Your body will stand guard and will not let you go either way."

He began to chuckle softly.

"Why do you laugh?" I asked.

"You're in a terrible spot," he said. "It's too late for you to retreat but too soon to act. All you can do is witness. You're in the miserable position of an infant who cannot return to the mother's womb, but neither can he run around and act. All an infant can do is witness and listen to the stupendous tales of action being told to him. You are at that precise point now. You cannot go back to the womb of your old world, but you cannot act with power either. For you there is only witnessing acts of power and listening to tales, tales of power.

"The double is one of those tales. You know that, and that's why your reason is so taken by it. You are beating your head against a wall if you pretend to understand. All that I can say about it, by way of explanation, is that the double, although it is arrived at through *dreaming*, is as real as it can be."

"According to what you've told me, don Juan, the double can perform acts. Can the double then . . .?"

He did not let me continue with my line of reasoning. He reminded me that it was inappropriate to say that he had told me about the double, when I could say that I had witnessed it.

"Obviously the double can perform acts," I said.

"Obviously!" he replied.

"But can the double act in behalf of the self?"

"It is the self, damn it!"

I found it very difficult to explain myself. I had in mind that if a sorcerer could perform two actions at once, his capacity for utilitarian production had to double. He could work two jobs, be in two places, see two persons, and so on, at once.

Don Juan listened patiently.

"Let me put it this way," I said. "Hypothetically, can don Genaro kill someone hundreds of miles away by letting his double do it?"

Don Juan looked at me. He shook his head and moved his eyes away.

"You're filled with tales of violence," he said. "Genaro cannot kill anyone, simply because he no longer has any interest in his fellow men. By the time a warrior is capable of conquering *seeing* and *dreaming* and having the awareness of his luminosity, there is no such interest left in him."

I pointed out that at the beginning of my apprenticeship he had made the statement that a sorcerer, aided by his "ally," could be transported over hundreds of miles to deliver a blow to his enemies.

"I am responsible for your confusion," he said. "But you must remember that on another occasion I told you that, with you, I was not following the steps my own teacher prescribed. He was a sorcerer and I should've properly plunged you into that world. I didn't, because I am no longer concerned with the ups and downs of my fellow men. Yet, my teacher's words stuck with me. I talked to you many times in the manner he himself would have talked.

"Genaro is a man of knowledge. The purest of them all. His actions are impeccable. He's beyond ordinary men, and beyond sorcerers. His double is an expression of his joy and his humor. Thus, he cannot possibly use it to create or resolve ordinary situations. As far as I know, the double is the awareness of our state as luminous beings. It can do anything, and yet it chooses to be unobtrusive and gentle.

"It was my error to mislead you with borrowed words. My teacher was not capable of producing the effects Genaro does. For my teacher, unfortunately, certain things were, as they are for you, only tales of power."

I was compelled to defend my point. I said that I was speaking in a hypothetical sense.

"There is no hypothetical sense when you speak about the world of men of knowledge," he said. "A man of knowledge cannot possibly act towards his fellow men in injurious terms, hypothetically or otherwise."

"But, what if his fellow men are plotting against his security and well-being? Can he then use his double to protect himself?"

He clicked his tongue in disapproval.

"What incredible violence in your thoughts," he said. "No one can plot against the security and well-being of a man of knowledge. He *sees*, therefore he would take steps to avoid anything like that. Genaro, for example, has taken a calculated risk in joining you. But there is nothing that you could do to endanger his security. If there is anything, his *seeing* will let him know. Now, if there is something about you that is inherently injurious to him and his *seeing* cannot reach it, then it is his fate, and neither Genaro nor anyone else can avoid that. So, you see, a man of knowledge is in control without controlling anything."

We were quiet. The sun was about to reach the top of the heavy tall bushes on the west side of the house. There were about two hours of daylight left.

"Why don't you call Genaro?" don Juan said casually.

My body jumped. My initial reaction was to drop everything and run for my car. Don Juan broke into a belly laugh. I told him that I did not have to prove anything to myself, and that I was perfectly content to talk to him. Don Juan could not stop laughing. Finally he said that it was a shame that don Genaro was not there to enjoy a great scene.

"Look, if you're not interested in calling Genaro, I am," he said in a resolute tone. "I like his company."

I had a terrible sour taste on the roof of my mouth. Beads of perspiration ran down from my brow and my upper lip. I wanted to say something but there was really nothing to say.

Don Juan gave me a long, scrutinizing look.

"Come on," he said. "A warrior is always ready. To be a warrior is not a simple matter of wishing to be one. It is rather an endless struggle that will go on to the very last moment of our lives. Nobody is born a warrior, in exactly the same way that nobody is born a reasonable being. We make ourselves into one or the other.

"Pull yourself together. I don't want Genaro to see you shivering like this."

He stood up and paced back and forth on the clean floor of the ramada. I could not remain impassive. My nervousness was so intense that I could not write any more and I jumped to my feet.

Don Juan made me jog on the spot, facing the west. He had made me perform the same movements before on various occasions. The idea was to draw "power" from the impending twilight by raising one's arms to the sky with the fingers stretched, like a fan, and then clasp them forcefully when the arms were in the mid point between the horizon and the zenith.

The exercise worked and I became almost instantly calm and collected. I could not avoid wondering, however, what had happened to the old "me" that could never have relaxed so completely by performing those simple and idiotic movements.

I wanted to focus all my attention on the procedure that don Juan was doubtlessly going to follow to call don Genaro. I anticipated some portentous acts. Don Juan stood on the edge of the ramada facing the southeast, cupped his hands around his mouth, and yelled, "Genaro! Come here!"

A moment later don Genaro emerged from the chaparral. Both of them were beaming. They practically danced in front of me.

Don Genaro greeted me effusively and then sat down on the milk crate.

There was something dreadfully wrong with me. I was calm, unruffled. Some incredible state of indifference and aloofness had taken over my entire being. It was almost as if I were watching myself from a hiding place. In a very nonchalant manner I proceeded to tell don Genaro that during my last visit he had nearly scared me to death, and that not even during my experiences with psychotropic plants had I been in such a complete state of chaos. Both of them celebrated my statements as if they were meant to be funny. I laughed with them.

They obviously were aware of my state of emotional numbness. They watched me and humored me as if I were drunk.

There was something inside me that fought desperately to turn the situation into something familiar. I wanted to be concerned and afraid.

Don Juan finally splashed some water on my face and urged me to sit down and take notes. He said, as he had done before, that either I took notes or I died. The mere act of putting down some words brought back my familiar mood. It was as if something became crystal clear again, something that a moment before had been opaque and numb.

The advent of my usual self also meant the advent of my usual fears. Strangely enough I was less afraid of being afraid than of being unafraid. The familiarity of my old habits, no matter how unpleasant they were, was a delightful respite.

I fully realized then that don Genaro had just emerged from the chaparral. My usual processes were beginning to function. I started by refusing to think or speculate about the event. I made the resolution of not asking him anything. I was going to be a silent witness this time.

"Genaro has come again, exclusively for you," don Juan said.

Don Genaro was leaning against the wall of the house, resting his back against it while he sat on a tilted milk crate. He looked as if he were riding on horseback. His hands were in front of him, giving the impression that he was holding the reins of a horse.

"That's right, Carlitos," he said and brought the milk crate to rest on the ground.

He dismounted, whirling his right leg over an imaginary neck of a horse, and then jumped to the ground. His movements were so perfectly executed that he gave me the unquestionable sensation that he had arrived on horseback. He came to my side and sat down to my left.

"Genaro has come because he wants to tell you about the other," don Juan said.

He made a gesture of giving don Genaro the floor. Don Genaro bowed. He turned slightly to face me. "What would you like to know, Carlitos?" he asked in a high-pitched voice.

"Well, if you're going to tell me about the double, tell me everything," I said, feigning casualness.

Both of them shook their heads and glanced at each other.

"Genaro is going to tell you about the dreamer and the dreamed," don Juan said.

"As you know, Carlitos," don Genaro said with the air of an orator warming up, "the double begins in *dreaming*."

He gave me a long look and smiled. His eyes swept from my face to my notebook and pencil.

"The double is a dream," he said, scratched his arms and then stood up.

He walked to the edge of the ramada and stepped out into the chaparral. He stood by a bush showing three fourths of his profile to us; he was apparently urinating. After a moment I noticed that there seemed to be something wrong with him. He appeared to be trying desperately to urinate but could not. Don Juan's laughter was the clue that don Genaro was clowning again. Don Genaro contorted his body in such a comical fashion that he had don Juan and me practically in hysterics.

Don Genaro came back to the ramada and sat down. His smile radiated a rare warmth.

"When you can't, you just can't," he said and shrugged his shoulders.

Then after a moment's pause he added, sighing, "Yes, Carlitos, the double is a dream."

"Do you mean that he's not real?" I asked.

"No. I mean that he is a dream," he retorted.

Don Juan intervened and explained that don Genaro was referring to the first emergence of the awareness that we are luminous beings.

"Each one of us is different, and thus the details of our struggles are different," don Juan said. "The steps that we follow to arrive at the double are the same, though. Especially the beginning steps, which are muddled and uncertain."

Don Genaro agreed and made a comment on the uncertainty that a sorcerer had at that stage.

"When it first happened to me, I didn't know it had happened," he explained. "One day I had been picking plants in the mountains. I had gone into a place that was worked by other herb collectors. I had two huge sacks of plants. I was ready to go home, but before I did I decided to take a moment's rest. I lay down on the side of the trail in the shade of a tree and I fell asleep. I heard then the sound of people coming down the hill and woke up. I hurriedly ran for cover and hid behind some bushes a short distance across the road from where I had fallen asleep. While I hid there I had the nagging impression I had forgotten something. I looked to see if I had my two sacks of plants. I didn't have them. I looked across the road to the place where I had been sleeping and I nearly dropped my pants with fright. I was still there asleep! It was me! I touched my body. I was myself! By that time the people that were coming down the hill were upon the me that was asleep, while the me that was fully awake looked helplessly from my hiding place. Damn it to hell! They were going to find me there and take my sacks away. But they went by me as if I were not there at all.

"My vision had been so vivid that I went wild. I screamed and then I woke up again. Damn it! It had been a dream!"

Don Genaro stopped his account and looked at me as if waiting for a question or a comment.

"Tell him where you woke up the second time," don Juan said.

"I woke up by the road," don Genaro said, "where I had fallen asleep. But for one moment I didn't quite know where I really was. I can almost say that I was still looking at myself waking up, then something pulled me to the side of the road and I found myself rubbing my eyes."

There was a long pause. I did not know what to say.

"And what did you do next?" don Juan asked.

I realized, when both of them began to laugh, that he was teasing me. He was imitating my questions.

Don Genaro went on talking. He said that he was stunned for a moment and then went to check everything.

"The place where I had hid was there exactly as I had seen it," he said. "And the people who had walked by me were down the road, a short distance away. I know it because I ran downhill after them. They were the same people I had seen. I followed them until they got to town. They must have thought I was mad. I asked them if they had seen my friend sleeping by the side of the road. They all said they hadn't."

"You see," don Juan said, "all of us go through the same doubts. We are afraid of being mad; unfortunately for us, of course, all of us are already mad."

"You are a tinge madder than us, though," don Genaro said to me and winked. "And more suspicious."

They teased me about my suspiciousness. And then don Genaro began to talk again.

"All of us are dense beings," he said. "You're not the only one, Carlitos. I was a bit shook up by my dream for a couple of days, but then I had to work for my living and take care of too many things and really had no time for pondering upon the mystery of my dreams. So I forgot about it in no time at all. I was very much like you.

"But one day, a few months later, after a terribly tiring day, I fell asleep like a log in midafternoon. It had just started to rain and a leak in the roof woke me up. I jumped out of bed and climbed on top of the house to fix the leak before it began to pour. I felt so fine and strong that I finished in one minute and I didn't even get wet. I thought that the snooze I had taken had done me a lot of good. When I was through I went back into the house to get something to eat and I realized that I could not swallow. I thought I was sick. I mashed some roots and leaves and wrapped them around my neck and went to my bed. And then again when I got to my bed I nearly dropped my pants. I was there in bed asleep! I wanted to shake myself and wake me up, but I knew that that was not the thing one should do. So I ran out of the house. I was panic-stricken. I roamed around the hills aimlessly. I had no idea where I was going and although I had lived all my life there I got lost. I walked in the rain and didn't even feel it. It seemed that I couldn't think. Then the lightning and thunder became so intense that I woke up again."

He paused for a moment.

"Do you want to know where I woke up?" he asked me.

"Certainly," don Juan answered.

"I woke up in the hills in the rain," he said.

"But how did you know that you had woken up?" I asked.

"My body knew it," he replied.

"That was a stupid question," don Juan interjected. "You yourself know that something in the warrior is always aware of every change. It is precisely the aim of the warrior's way to foster and maintain that awareness. The warrior cleans it, shines it, and keeps it running."

He was right. I had to admit to them that I knew that there was something in me that registered and was aware of everything I did. And yet it had nothing to do with the ordinary awareness of myself. It was something else which I could not pin down. I told them that perhaps don Genaro could describe it better than I.

"You're doing very well yourself," don Genaro said. "It's an inner voice that tells you what's what. And at that time, it told me that I had woken up a second time. Of course, as soon as I woke up I became convinced that I must have been *dreaming*. Obviously it had not been an ordinary dream, but it hadn't been *dreaming* proper either. So I settled for something else: walking in my sleep, half awake, I suppose. I could not understand it in any other way."

Don Genaro said that his benefactor had explained to him that what he had gone through was not a dream at all, and that he should not insist on regarding it as walking in his sleep.

"What did he tell you that it was?" I asked.

They exchanged a glance.

"He told me it was the bogeyman," don Genaro replied, affecting the tone of a small child.

I explained to them that I wanted to know if don Genaro's benefactor explained things in the same way they themselves did.

"Of course he did," don Juan said.

"My benefactor explained that the dream in which one was watching oneself asleep," don Genaro went on, "was the time of the double. He recommended that rather than wasting my power in wondering and asking myself questions, I should use the opportunity to act, and that when I had another chance I should be prepared.

"My next chance took place at my benefactor's house. I was helping him with the housework. I had lain down to rest and as usual I fell sound asleep. His house was definitely a place of power for me and helped me. I was suddenly aroused by a loud noise and awakened. My benefactor's house was large. He was a wealthy man and had many people working for him. The noise seemed to be the sound of a shovel digging in gravel. I sat up to listen and then I stood up. The noise was very unsettling to me but I couldn't figure out why. I was pondering whether to go and check it out when I noticed that I was asleep on the floor. This time I knew what to expect and what to do and I followed the noise. I walked to the back of the house. There was no one there. The noise seemed to come from beyond the house. I kept on following it. The more I followed it the quicker I could move. I ended up at a distant place, witnessing incredible things."

He explained that at the time of those events he still was in the beginning stages of his apprenticeship and had done very little in the realm of "dreaming," but that he had an uncanny facility to dream that he was looking at himself.

"Where did you go, don Genaro?" I asked.

"That was the first time that I had really moved in *dreaming*," he said. "I knew enough about it to behave correctly, though. I didn't look at anything directly and ended up in a deep ravine where my benefactor had some of his power plants."

"Do you think it works better if one knows very little about *dreaming*?" I asked.

"No!" don Juan interjected. "Each of us has a facility for something in particular. Genaro's knack is for *dreaming*."

"What did you see in the ravine, don Genaro?" I asked.

"I saw my benefactor doing some dangerous maneuvers with people. I thought I was there to help him and hid behind some trees. Yet I couldn't have known how to help. I was not dumb, though, and I realized that the scene was there for me to watch, not to act in."

"When and how and where did you wake up?"

"I don't know when I woke up. It must have been hours later. All I know is that I followed my benefactor and the other men, and when they were about to reach my benefactor's house the noise that they made, because they were arguing, woke me up. I was at the place where I had seen myself asleep.

"Upon waking up, I realized that whatever I had seen and done was not a dream. I had actually gone some distance away, guided by the sound."

"Was your benefactor aware of what you were doing?"

"Certainly. He had been making the noise with the shovel to help me accomplish my task. When he walked into the house he pretended to scold me for falling asleep. I knew that he had *seen* me. Later on, after his friends had left, he told me that he had noticed my glow hiding behind the trees."

Don Genaro said that those three instances set him off on the path of "dreaming," and that it took him fifteen years to have his next chance.

"The fourth time was a more bizarre and a more complete vision," he said. "I found myself asleep in the middle of a cultivated field. I saw myself lying there on my side sound asleep. I knew that it was *dreaming*, because I had set myself to do *dreaming* every night. Usually, every time I had seen myself asleep, I was at the site where I had gone to sleep. This time I was not in my bed, and I knew I had gone to bed that night. In this *dreaming* it was daytime. So, I began to explore. I moved away from the place where I was lying and oriented myself. I knew where I was. I was actually not too far from my house, perhaps a couple of miles away. I walked around looking at every detail of the place. I stood in the shade of a big tree a short distance away and peered across a flat strip of land to some corn fields on the side of a hill. Something quite unusual struck me then; the details of the surroundings did not change or vanish no matter how long I peered at them. I got scared and ran back to where I was sleeping. I was still there exactly as I had been before. I began to watch myself. I had an eerie feeling of indifference towards the body I was watching.

"Then I heard the sound of people approaching. People always seemed to be around for me. I ran up ahead to a small hill and carefully watched from there. There were ten people coming to the field where I was. They were all young men. I ran back to where I was lying and went through one of the most agonizing times of my life, while I faced myself, lying there snoring like a pig. I knew that I had to awaken me but I had no idea how. I also knew that it was deadly for me to awaken myself. But if those young men were to find me there they were going to be very upset. All those deliberations that were going through my mind were not really thoughts. They were more appropriately scenes in front of my eyes. My worrying, for instance, was a scene in which I looked at myself while I had the sensation of being boxed in. I call that worrying. It has happened to me a number of times after that first time.

"Well, since I didn't know what to do I stood looking at myself, waiting for the worst. A bunch of fleeting images went past me in front of my eyes. I hung on to one in particular, the sight of my house and my bed. The image became very clear. Oh, how I wished to be back in my bed! Something shook me then; it felt like someone was hitting me and I woke up. I was on my bed! Obviously, I had been *dreaming*. I jumped out of bed and ran to the place of my *dreaming*. It was exactly as I had seen it. The young men were working there. I watched them for a long time. They were the same ones I had seen.

"I came back to the same place at the end of the day after everybody had gone and stood at the very spot where I had seen myself asleep. Someone had lain there. The weeds were crumpled."

Don Juan and don Genaro were observing me. They looked like two strange animals. I felt a shiver in my back. I was on the verge of indulging in the very rational fear that they were not really men like myself, but don Genaro laughed.

"In those days," he said, "I was just like you, Carlitos. I wanted to check everything. I was as suspicious as you are."

He paused, raised his finger and shook it at me. Then he faced don Juan.

"Weren't you as suspicious as this guy?" he asked.

"Not a chance," don Juan said. "He's the champ."

Don Genaro turned to me and made a gesture of apology.

"I think I was wrong," he said. "I was not as suspicious as you."

They chuckled softly as if they did not want to make noise. Don Juan's body convulsed with muffled laughter.

"This is a place of power for you," don Genaro said in a whisper. "You've written your fingers off right where you are sitting. Have you ever done some heavy *dreaming* here?"

"No, he hasn't," don Juan said in a low voice. "But he's done some heavy writing."

They doubled up. It seemed that they did not want to laugh out loud. Their bodies shook. Their soft laughter was like a rhythmical cackle.

Don Genaro sat up straight and slid closer to me. He patted me on the shoulder repeatedly, saying that I was a rascal, then he pulled my left arm with great force towards him. I lost my balance and fell forward. I almost hit my face on the hard ground. I automatically put my right arm in front and buffered my fall. One of them held me down by pressing on my neck. I was not sure who. The hand that was holding me felt like don Genaro's. I had a moment of devastating panic. I felt I was fainting, perhaps I did. The pressure in my stomach was so intense that I vomited. My next clear perception was that somebody was helping me to sit up. Don Genaro was squatting in front of me. I turned around to look for don Juan. He was nowhere in sight. Don Genaro had a beaming smile. His eyes were shiny. They were looking fixedly at mine. I asked him what he had done to me and he said that I was in pieces. His tone was reproachful and he seemed to be annoyed or dissatisfied with me. He repeated various times that I was in pieces and that I had to come together again. He tried to feign a severe tone but he laughed in the middle of his harangue. He was telling me that it was just terrible that I was spread all over the place, and that he would have to use a broom to sweep all my pieces into one heap. Then he added that I might get the pieces in the wrong places and end up with my penis where my thumb should be. He cracked up at that point. I wanted to laugh and had a most unusual sensation. My body fell apart! It was as if I had been a mechanical toy that simply broke up into pieces. I had no physical feelings whatever, and neither had I any fear or concern. Coming apart was a scene that I witnessed from the point of view of the perceiver, and yet I did not perceive anything from a sensorial point of reference.

The next thing I became aware of was that don Genaro was manipulating my body. I then had a physical sensation, a vibration so intense that it made me lose sight of everything around me.

I felt once more that someone was helping me to sit up. I again saw don Genaro squatting in front of me. He pulled me up by my armpits and helped me walk around. I could not figure out where I was. I had the feeling I was in a dream, and yet I had a complete sense of sequential time. I was keenly aware that I had just been with don Genaro and don Juan in the ramada of don Juan's house.

Don Genaro walked with me, propping me by holding my left armpit. The scenery I was watching changed constantly. I could not determine, however, the nature of what I was observing. What was in front of my eyes was rather like a feeling or a mood; and the center from where all those changes radiated was definitely in my stomach. I had made that connection not as a thought or a realization but as a bodily sensation that suddenly became fixed and predominant. The fluctuations around me came from my stomach. I was creating a world, an endless run of feelings and images. Everything I knew was there. That in itself was a feeling, not a thought or a conscious assessment.

I tried to keep tabs for a moment because of my nearly invincible habit of assessing everything, but at a certain instant my processes of bookkeeping ceased and a nameless something enveloped me, feelings and images of every sort.

At one point something in me began again the tabulation and I noticed that one image kept on repeating itself: don Juan and don Genaro, who were trying to reach me. The image was fleeting, it passed by me fast. It was something comparable to seeing them from the window of a fast-moving vehicle. They seemed to be trying to catch me as I went by. The image became clearer and it lasted longer as it kept on recurring. I consciously realized at one point that I was deliberately isolating it from among a myriad of other images. I sort of breezed through the rest to come to that particular scene. Finally I was capable of sustaining it by thinking about it. Once I had begun to think, my ordinary processes took over. They were not as defined as in my ordinary activities but clear enough to know that the scene or feeling I had isolated was that don Juan and don Genaro were in the ramada of don Juan's house and were holding me by the armpits. I wanted to keep on fleeing through other images and feelings, but they would not let me. I struggled for a moment. I felt bouncy and happy. I knew that I liked both of them and I also knew then that I was not afraid of them. I wanted to joke with them; I did not know how and I kept on laughing and patting them on their shoulders. I had another peculiar awareness. I was certain that I was "dreaming." If I focused my eyes on anything, it immediately became blurry.

Don Juan and don Genaro were talking to me. I could not keep their words straight and I could not distinguish which of them was talking. Don Juan then turned my body around and pointed to a lump on the ground. Don Genaro pulled me closer to it and made me go around it. The lump was a man lying on the ground. He was lying on his stomach, his face turned to his right. They kept on pointing out the man to me as they spoke. They pulled me and twisted me around him. I could not focus my eyes on him at all, but finally I had a feeling of quietness and sobriety and I looked at the man. I had a slow awakening into the realization that the man lying on the ground was me. My realization did not bring any terror or discomfort. I simply accepted it without emotion. At that moment I was not completely asleep, but neither was I completely awake and in sober consciousness. I also became more aware of don Juan and don Genaro and could tell them apart when they talked to me. Don Juan said that we were going to go to the round power place in the chaparral. As soon as he said it the image of the place popped in my mind. I saw the dark masses of bushes around it. I turned to my right; don Juan and don Genaro were also there. I had a jolt and the feeling that I was afraid of them. Perhaps because they looked like two menacing shadows. They came closer to me. As soon as I saw their features my fears vanished. I liked them again. It was as if I were drunk and did not have a firm grip on anything. They grabbed me by the shoulders and shook me in unison. They ordered me to wake up. I could hear their voices clearly and separately. I had then a unique moment. I held two images in my mind, two dreams. I felt that something in me was deeply asleep and was waking up and I found myself lying on the floor of the ramada with don Juan and don Genaro shaking me. But I also was at the power place and don Juan and don Genaro were still shaking me. There was one crucial instant in which I was neither in one place nor the other, but I was rather in both places as an observer seeing two scenes at once. I had the incredible sensation that at that instant I could have gone either way. All I had to do at that moment was to change perspective and rather than watch either scene from the outside feel it from the point of view of the subject.

There was something very warm about don Juan's house. I preferred that scene.

I next had a terrifying seizure, so shocking that my entire ordinary awareness came back to me at once. Don Juan and don Genaro were pouring buckets of water on me. I was in the ramada of don Juan's house.

Hours later we sat in the kitchen. Don Juan had insisted that I had to proceed as if nothing had happened. He gave me some food and said that I had to eat a great deal to compensate for my expenditure of energy.

It was after nine in the evening when I looked at my watch after we had sat down to eat. My experience had lasted several hours. From the point of view of my recollection, however, it seemed that I had just fallen asleep for a short while.

Even though I was completely myself, I still was numb. It was not until I had begun to write in my notebook that I regained my usual awareness. It was a surprise to me that taking notes could bring about instantaneous sobriety. The moment I was myself again a barrage of reasonable thoughts immediately came to my mind; they purported to explain the phenomenon I had experienced. I "knew" on the spot that don Genaro had hypnotized me the moment he pinned me down on the ground, but I did not attempt to figure out how he had done it.

They both laughed hysterically when I expressed my thoughts. Don Genaro examined my pencil and said that the pencil was the key to wind up my mainspring. I felt quite belligerent. I was tired and irritable. I found myself practically yelling at them while their bodies shook with laughter.

Don Juan said that it was permissible to miss the boat, but not by such a wide margin, and that don Genaro had come exclusively to help me and show me the mystery of the dreamer and the dreamed.

My irritability came to a peak. Don Juan signaled don Genaro with a movement of his head. Both of them stood and took me around the house. There don Genaro demonstrated his great repertoire of animal grunts and cries. He asked me to choose one and he taught me how to reproduce it.

After hours of practice I got to the point where I could imitate it quite well. The end result was that they themselves had enjoyed my clumsy attempts and laughed until they were practically weeping, and I had released my tension by reproducing the loud cry of an animal. I told them that there was something truly awesome in my imitation. The relaxation of my body was unequaled. Don Juan said that if I would perfect the cry I could turn it into an affair of power, or

I could simply use it to relieve my tension whenever I needed to. He suggested I should go to sleep. But I was afraid to fall asleep. I sat with them by the kitchen fire for a while and then, quite unintentionally, I fell into a deep sleep.

I woke up at dawn. Don Genaro was sleeping by the door. He seemingly woke up at the same time I did. They had covered me up and folded my jacket as a pillow. I felt very calm and rested. I commented to don Genaro that I had felt exhausted the night before. He said that so had he. He whispered as if he were confiding in me and told me that don Juan was even more exhausted because he was older.

"You and I are young," he said with a glint in his eyes. "But he's old. He must be about three hundred now."

I sat up hurriedly. Don Genaro covered his face with his blanket and roared with laughter. Don Juan came into the room at that moment.

I had a feeling of completeness and peace. For once, nothing really mattered. I was so at ease that I wanted to weep.

Don Juan said that the night before I had begun to be aware of my luminosity. He admonished me not to indulge in the sense of well-being I was having, because it would turn into complacency.

"At this moment," I said, "I don't want to explain anything. It doesn't matter what don Genaro did to me last night."

"I didn't do anything to you," don Genaro retorted. "Look, it's me, Genaro. Your Genaro! Touch me!"

I embraced don Genaro and we both laughed like two children.

He asked me if I thought it was strange that I could embrace him then when last time I had seen him there I had been unable to touch him. I assured him that those issues were no longer pertinent to me.

Don Juan's comment was that I was indulging in being broad-minded and good.

"Watch out!" he said. "A warrior never lets his guard down. If you keep on being so happy you're going to drain the little power you have left."

"What should I do?" I asked.

"Be yourself," he said. "Doubt everything. Be suspicious."

"But I don't like to be that way, don Juan."

"It is not a matter of whether you like it or not. What matters is, what can you use as a shield? A warrior must use everything available to him to close his mortal gap once it opens. So, it's of no importance that you really don't like to be suspicious or ask questions. That's your only shield now.

"Write, write. Or you'll die. To die with elation is a crappy way of dying."

"How should a warrior die, then?" don Genaro asked in exactly my own tone of voice.

"A warrior dies the hard way," don Juan said. "His death must struggle to take him. A warrior does not give himself to it."

Don Genaro opened his eyes to an enormous size and then blinked.

"What Genaro showed you yesterday is of utmost importance," don Juan went on. "You can't slough it off with piousness. Yesterday you told me that you had been driven wild with the idea of the double. But look at you now. You don't care any more. That's the trouble with people that go wild, they go wild both ways. Yesterday you were all questions, today you are all acceptance."

I pointed out that he always found a flaw in what I did, regardless of how I did it.

"That's not true!" he exclaimed. "There is no flaw in the warrior's way. Follow it and your acts cannot be criticized by anyone. Take yesterday as an example. The warrior's way would have been, first, to ask questions without fear and without suspicion and then let Genaro show you the mystery of the dreamer, without fighting him, or draining yourself. Today, the warrior's way would be to assemble what you've learned, without presumptuousness and without piousness. Do that and no one can find flaws in it."

I thought by his tone that don Juan must have been terribly annoyed with my blunderings. But he smiled at me and then giggled as if his own words had made him laugh.

I told him that I was just holding back, not wanting to burden them with my probes. I was indeed overwhelmed by what don Genaro had done. I had been convinced—although it no longer mattered — that don Genaro had been waiting in the bushes for don Juan to call him. Then later on he had cashed in on my fright and used it to stun me. After being held forcibly on the ground, I must have undoubtedly passed out, and then don Genaro must have mesmerized me.

Don Juan argued that I was too strong to be subdued that easily.

"What took place then?" I asked him.

"Genaro came to see you to tell you something very exclusive," he said. "When he came out of the bushes, he was Genaro the double. There is another way to talk about this that would explain it better, but I can't use it now."

"Why not, don Juan?"

"Because you are not ready yet to talk about the totality of oneself. For the time being I can only say that this Genaro here is not the double now."

He pointed to don Genaro with a movement of his head. Don Genaro blinked repeatedly.

"The Genaro of last night was the double. And as I told you already, the double has inconceivable power. He showed you a most important issue. In order to do that he had to touch you. The double simply tapped you on the neck, on the same spot the ally walked over you years ago. Naturally, you went out like a light. And naturally too, you indulged like a son of a bitch. It took us hours to round you up. Thus, you dissipated your power and when the time came for you to accomplish a warrior's feat you did not have enough sap."

"What was that warrior's feat, don Juan?"

"I told you that Genaro came to show you something, the mystery of luminous beings as dreamers. You wanted to know about the double. It begins in dreams. But then you asked, 'What is the double?' And I said the double is the self. The self dreams the double. That should be simple, except that there is nothing simple about us. Perhaps the ordinary dreams of the self are simple, but that doesn't mean that the self is simple. Once it has learned to dream the double, the self arrives at this weird crossroad and a moment comes when one realizes that it is the double who dreams the self."

I had written down everything he had said. I had also paid attention to what he was saying but had failed to understand him.

Don Juan repeated his statements.

"The lesson last night, as I told you, was about the dreamer and the dreamed, or who dreams whom."

"I beg your pardon," I said.

Both of them broke into laughter.

"Last night," don Juan proceeded, "you almost chose to wake up at the power place."

"What do you mean, don Juan?"

"That would have been the feat. If you had not indulged in your stupid ways, you would have had enough power to tip the scales, and you would've, no doubt, scared yourself to death. Fortunately or unfortunately, as the case may be, you did not have enough power. In fact, you wasted your power in worthless confusion to the point that you almost didn't have enough to survive.

"So, as you may very well understand, to indulge in your little quirks is not only stupid and wasteful but also injurious. A warrior that drains himself cannot live. The body is not an indestructible affair. You might have gotten gravely ill. You didn't, simply because Genaro and I deviated some of your crap."

The full impact of his words was beginning to take hold of me.

"Last night Genaro guided you through the intricacies of the double," don Juan went on. "Only he can do that for you. And it was not a vision or a hallucination when you saw yourself lying on the ground. You could have realized that with infinite clarity if you had not gotten lost in your indulging, and you could have known then that you yourself are a dream, that your double is dreaming you, in the same fashion that you dreamed him last night."

"But how can that be possible, don Juan?"

"No one knows how it happens. We only know that it does happen. That's the mystery of us as luminous beings. Last night you had two dreams and you could have awakened in either one, but you didn't have enough power even to understand that."

They looked at me fixedly for a moment.

"I think he understands," don Genaro said.

THE SECRET OF THE LUMINOUS BEINGS

Don Genaro delighted me for hours with some preposterous instructions on how to manage my daily world. Don Juan said that I should be very careful and serious-minded about the recommendations made by don Genaro because, although they were funny, they were not a joke.

Around noon don Genaro stood up and without saying a word walked into the bushes. I was also going to get up but don Juan gently held me down and in a solemn voice announced that don Genaro was going to try one more thing with me.

"What's he up to?" I asked. "What is he going to do to me?"

Don Juan assured me that I did not have to worry.

"You are approaching a crossroad," he said. "A certain crossroad that every warrior comes to."

I had the idea that he was talking about my death. He seemed to anticipate my question and signaled me not to say anything.

"We won't discuss this matter," he said. "Suffice it to say that the crossroad I'm referring to is the sorcerers' explanation. Genaro believes you're ready for it."

"When are you going to tell me about it?"

"I don't know when. You are the recipient, therefore it is up to you. You will have to decide when."

"What's wrong with right now?"

"To decide doesn't mean to choose an arbitrary time," he said. "To decide means that you have trimmed your spirit impeccably, and that you have done everything possible to be worthy of knowledge and power.

"Today, however, you must solve a little riddle for Genaro. He's gone ahead of us and he'll be waiting somewhere in the chaparral. No one knows the spot where he'll be, or the specific time to go to him. If you're capable of determining the right time to leave the house, you will also be capable of guiding yourself to where he is."

I told don Juan that I could not imagine anyone being able to solve such a riddle.

"How can leaving the house at a specific time guide me to where don Genaro is?" I asked.

Don Juan smiled and began to hum a tune. He seemed to enjoy my agitation.

"That's the problem which Genaro has set up for you," he said. "If you have enough personal power you will decide with absolute certainty the right time to leave the house. How leaving at the precise time will guide you is something that no one knows. And yet, if you have enough power, you yourself will attest that this is so."

"But how am I going to be guided, don Juan?"

"No one knows that either."

"I think don Genaro is pulling my leg."

"You better watch out then," he said. "If Genaro is pulling your leg he's liable to yank it out."

Don Juan laughed at his own joke. I could not join him. My fear about the inherent danger of don Genaro's manipulations was too real.

"Can you give me some clues?" I asked.

"There are no clues!" he said cuttingly.

"Why does don Genaro want to do this?"

"He wants to test you," he replied. "Let's say that it is very important for him to know whether you can take the sorcerers' explanation. If you solve the riddle, the implication will be that you have stored enough personal power and you're ready. But if you flub it, it'll be because you don't have enough power and in that case the sorcerers' explanation won't make any sense to you. I think that we should give you the explanation regardless of whether you understand it or not; that's my idea. Genaro is a more conservative warrior; he wants things in their proper order and he won't give in until he thinks you're ready."

"Why don't you just tell me about the sorcerers' explanation your-self?"

"Because Genaro must be the one who helps you."

"Why is that so, don Juan?"

"Genaro doesn't want me to tell you why," he said. "Not yet."

"Would it hurt me to know the sorcerers' explanation?" I asked.

"I don't think so."

"Please, don Juan, tell me then."

"You must be joking. Genaro has precise ideas on this matter and we must honor and respect them."

He made an imperative gesture to quiet me.

After a long unnerving pause I ventured a question. "But how can I solve this riddle, don Juan?"

"I really don't know that, thus I can't advise you what to do," he said. "Genaro is most efficient. He designed the riddle just for you. Since he's doing this for your benefit, he's attuned to you alone, therefore only you can pick the precise time to leave the house. He will call you himself and guide you by means of his call."

"What will his call be like?"

"I don't know. His call is for you, not for me. He'll be tapping your *will* directly. In other words, you must use your *will* in order to know the call.

"Genaro feels that he must make sure, at this point, that you have stored sufficient personal power to enable you to turn your *will* into a functioning unit."

"Will" was another concept which don Juan had delineated with great care but without making it clear. I had gathered from his expla-nations that "will" was a force that emanated from the umbilical region through an unseen opening below the navel, an opening he had called the "gap." "Will" was allegedly cultivated only by sorcer-ers. It came to the practitioners veiled in mystery and purportedly gave them the capacity to perform extraordinary acts.

I remarked to don Juan that there was no chance that anything so vague could ever be a functioning unit in my life.

"That's where you're wrong," he said. "The *will* develops in a warrior in spite of every opposition of the reason."

"Can't don Genaro, being a sorcerer, know whether I'm ready or not, without testing me?" I asked.

"He certainly can," he said. "But that knowledge won't be of any value or consequence, because it has nothing to do with you. You are the one who's learning, therefore you yourself must claim knowledge as power, not Genaro. Genaro is not concerned with his knowing as much as with your knowing. You must find out whether or not your *will* works. This is a very difficult point to make. In spite of what Genaro or I know about you, you must prove to yourself that you are in the position to claim knowledge as power. In other words, you yourself have to be convinced that you can exercise your *will*. If you're not, then you must become convinced today. If you cannot perform this task, then Genaro's conclusion will be that regardless of what he might *see* about you, you're not ready yet."

I experienced an overwhelming apprehension.

"Is all this necessary?" I asked.

"It's Genaro's request and must be obeyed," he said in a firm but friendly tone.

"But what does don Genaro have to do with me?"

"You may find that out today," he said and smiled.

I pleaded with don Juan to get me out of that intolerable situation and explain all the mysterious talk. He laughed and patted my chest and made a joke about a Mexican weight lifter who had enormous pectoral muscles but could not do heavy physical labor because his back was weak.

"Watch those muscles," he said. "They shouldn't be just for show."

"My muscles have nothing to do with what you're talking about," I said in a belligerent mood.

"They do," he replied. "The body must be perfection before the *will* is a functioning unit."

Don Juan had again deviated the direction of my probing. I felt restless and frustrated.

I stood up and went to the kitchen and drank some water. Don Juan followed me and suggested that I should practice the animal cry that don Genaro had taught me. We walked to the side of the house;

I sat on a pile of wood and involved myself in reproducing it. Don Juan made some corrections and gave me some pointers about my breathing; the end result was a state of complete physical relaxation.

We returned to the ramada and sat down again. I told him that sometimes I felt irked with myself because I was so helpless.

"There is nothing wrong with the feeling of being helpless," he said. "All of us are most familiar with it. Remember that we have spent an eternity as helpless infants. I have already told you that at this very moment you are like an infant who can't get out of the crib by himself, much less act on his own. Genaro gets you out of your crib, let's say, by picking you up. But an infant wants to act and since he can't, he complains. There is nothing wrong with that, but to indulge in protesting and complaining is another matter."

He demanded that I keep myself relaxed; he suggested that I ask him questions for a while, until I was in a better frame of mind.

For a moment I was at a loss and could not decide what to ask.

Don Juan unrolled a straw mat and told me to sit on it. Then he filled a large gourd with water and put it in a carrying net. He seemed to be preparing for a journey. He sat down again and urged me with a movement of his eyebrows to begin my questions.

I asked him to tell me more about the moth.

He gave me a long scrutinizing look and chuckled.

"That was an ally," he said. "You know that."

"But what actually is an ally, don Juan?"

"There is no way of saying what exactly an ally is, just as there is no way of saying what exactly a tree is."

"A tree is a living organism," I said.

"That doesn't tell me much," he said. "I can also say that an ally is a force, a tension. I've told you that already, but that doesn't say much about an ally.

"Just like in the case of a tree, the only way to know what an ally is, is by experiencing it. Over the years I have struggled to prepare you for the momentous encounter with an ally. You may not realize this, but it took you years of preparation to meet tree. To meet ally is no different. A teacher must acquaint his disciple with ally little by little, piece by piece. You have, over the course of the years, stored a great amount of knowledge about it and now you are capable of putting that knowledge together to experience ally the way you experience tree."

"I have no idea that I'm doing that, don Juan."

"Your reason is not aware of it, because it cannot accept the possibility of ally to begin with. Fortunately, it is not the reason which puts ally together. It is the body. You have perceived ally in many degrees and on many occasions. Each of those perceptions was stored in your body. The sum of those pieces is the ally. I don't know any other way of describing it."

I said that I could not conceive that my body was acting by itself as if it were an entity separate from my reason.

"It isn't, but we have made it so," he said. "Our reason is petty and it is always at odds with our body. This, of course, is only a way of talking, but the triumph of a man of knowledge is that he has joined the two together. Since you're not a man of knowledge, your body does things now that your reason cannot comprehend. The ally is one of those things. You were not mad, neither were you dreaming when you perceived the ally that night, right here."

I asked him about the frightening idea, which he and don Genaro had implanted in me, that the ally was an entity waiting for me at the edge of a small valley in the mountains of northern Mexico. They had told me that sooner or later I had to keep my appointment with the ally and wrestle with it.

"Those are ways of talking about mysteries for which there are no words," he said. "Genaro and I said that at the edge of that plain the ally was waiting for you. That statement was true, but it doesn't have the meaning that you want to give it. The ally is waiting for you, that's for sure, but it is not at the edge of any plain. It is right here, or there, or in any other place. The ally is waiting for you, just like death is waiting for you, everywhere and nowhere."

"Why is the ally waiting for me?"

"For the same reason that death waits for you," he said, "because you were born. There is no possibility of explaining at this point what is meant by that. You must first experience the ally. You must perceive it in its full force, then the sorcerers' explanation may throw light upon it. So far you've had enough power to clarify at least one point, that the ally is a moth.

"Some years ago you and I went to the mountains and you had a bout with something. I had no way of telling you then what was taking place; you saw a strange shadow flying back and forth in front of the fire. You yourself said that it looked like a moth; although you didn't know what you were talking about, you were absolutely correct, the shadow was a moth. Then, on another occasion, something frightened you out of your wits, after you had fallen asleep, again in front of a fire. I had warned you not to fall asleep, but you disregarded my warning; that act left you at the mercy of the ally and the moth stepped on your neck. Why you survived will always be a mystery to me. You didn't know then but I had given you up for dead. Your blunder was that serious.

"From then on every time we've been in the mountains or in the desert, even if you didn't notice it, the moth always followed us. All in all then, we can say that for you the ally is a moth. But I cannot say that it is really a moth, the way we know moths. Calling the ally a moth is again only a way of talking, a way of making that immensity out there understandable."

"Is the ally a moth for you too?" I asked.

"No. The way one understands the ally is a personal matter," he said.

I mentioned that we were back where we had started; he had not told me what an ally really was.

"There's no need to be confused," he said. "Confusion is a mood one enters into, but one can also get out of it. At this point there is no way of clarifying anything. Perhaps later on today we'll be able to consider these matters in detail; it's up to you. Or rather, it's up to your personal power."

He refused to say one more word. I became quite upset with the fear that I was going to fail the test. Don Juan took me to the back of his house and made me sit on a straw mat at the edge of an irrigation ditch. The water moved so slowly that it almost seemed stagnant. He commanded me to sit quietly, shut off my internal dialogue and look at the water. He said that years before he had discovered that I had a certain affinity for bodies of water, a feeling that was most convenient for the endeavors I was involved in. I remarked that I was not particularly fond of bodies of water, but neither did I dislike them. He said that that was precisely why water was beneficial for me, I was indifferent towards it. Under conditions of stress water could not trap me, but neither could it reject me.

He sat slightly behind me to my right and admonished me to let go and not be afraid, because he was there to help me if there was any need.

I had a moment of fear. I looked at him, waiting for further instructions. He forcibly turned my head towards the water and ordered me to proceed. I had no idea what he wanted me to do so I simply relaxed. As I looked at the water I caught sight of the reeds on the opposite side. Unconsciously I rested my unfocused eyes on them. The slow current made them quiver. The water had the color of the desert dirt. I noticed that the ripples around the reeds looked like furrows or crevices on a smooth surface. At one instant the reeds became gigantic, the water was a smooth flat ocher surface, and then in a matter of seconds I was sound asleep; or perhaps I entered into a perceptual state for which I had no parallel. The closest way of describing it would be to say that I went to sleep and had a portentous dream.

I felt that I could have gone on with it indefinitely if I had wanted to, but I deliberately ended it by engaging myself in a conscious self-dialogue. I opened my eyes. I was lying on the straw mat. Don Juan was a few feet away. My dream had been so magnificent that I began to recount it to him. He signaled me to be quiet. With a long twig he pointed to two long shadows that some dry branches of desert chaparral cast on the ground. The tip of his twig followed the outline of one of the shadows as if it were drawing it, then it jumped to the other and did the same with it; the shadows were about a foot long and over an inch wide; they were from five to six inches apart from each other. The movement of the twig forced my eyes out of focus and I found myself looking with crossed eyes at four long shadows; suddenly the two shadows in the middle merged into one and created an extraordinary perception of depth. There was some inexplicable roundness and volume in the shadow thus formed. It was almost like a transparent tube, a round bar of some unknown substance. I knew that my eyes were crossed and yet they seemed to be focused on one spot; the view there was crystal clear. I could move my eyes without dispelling the image.

I continued watching but without letting my guard down. I experienced a curious compulsion to let go and immerse myself in the scene. Something in what I was observing seemed to pull me; but something in myself surfaced and I began a semiconscious dialogue; almost instantly I became aware of my surroundings in the world of everyday life.

Don Juan was watching me. He appeared to be puzzled. I asked him if there was something wrong. He did not answer. He helped me to sit up. It was only then that I realized that I had been lying on my back, looking at the sky, and don Juan had been leaning over my face.

My first impulse was to tell him that I had actually seen the shadows on the ground while I had been looking at the sky, but he put his hand over my mouth. We sat in silence for a while. I had no thoughts. I experienced an exquisite sense of peace, and then quite abruptly I had an unyielding urge to get up and go into the chaparral to look for don Genaro.

I made an attempt to speak to don Juan; he jutted his chin and twisted his lips as a silent command not to talk. I tried to assess my predicament in a rational manner; I was enjoying my silence so much, however, that I did not want to bother with logical considerations.

After a moment's pause, I again felt the imperious need to walk into the bushes. I followed a trail. Don Juan tagged along behind me as if I were the leader.

We walked for about an hour. I succeeded in remaining without any thoughts. Then we came to a hillside. Don Genaro was there, sitting near the top of a rock wall. He greeted me effusively and had to yell his words; he was about fifty feet above the ground. Don Juan made me sit down and then sat next to me.

Don Genaro explained that I had found the place where he had been waiting because he had guided me with a sound he had been making. As he voiced his words, I realized that I had indeed been hearing a peculiar sound I thought to be a buzzing in my ears; it had seemed to be more of an internal affair, a bodily condition, a feeling of sound so undetermined that it was beyond the realm of conscious assessment and interpretation.

I believed that don Genaro had a small instrument in his left hand. From where I sat I could not distinguish it clearly. It looked like a jew's-harp; with it he produced a soft eerie sound which was practically indiscernible. He kept on playing it for a moment, as if allowing me time to fully realize what he had just said. Then he showed me his left hand. There was nothing in it; he was not holding any instrument. It had appeared to me that he was playing some instrument because of the manner in which he had put his hand to his mouth; actually, the sound was being produced with his lips and the edge of his left hand, between the thumb and index finger.

I turned to don Juan to explain to him that I had been fooled by don Genaro's movements. He made a quick gesture and told me not to talk and to pay close attention to what don Genaro was doing. I turned back to look at don Genaro, but he was no longer there. I thought that he must have climbed down. I waited a few moments for him to emerge from behind the bushes. The rock he had been standing on was a peculiar formation; it was more like a huge ledge on the side of a larger rock wall. I must have taken my eyes away from him for only a couple of seconds. If he had climbed up I would have caught sight of him before he had reached the top of the rock wall, and if he had climbed down he would also have been visible from where I was sitting.

I asked don Juan about don Genaro's whereabouts. He replied that he still was standing on the rock ledge. As far as I could judge, there was no one there, but don Juan maintained over and over again that don Genaro was still standing on the rock.

He did not seem to be joking. His eyes were steady and fierce. He said in a cutting tone that my senses were not the proper avenue to appraise what don Genaro was doing. He ordered me to shut off my internal dialogue. I struggled for a moment and began to close my eyes. Don Juan lurched at me and shook me by the shoulders. He whispered that I had to keep my view on the rock ledge.

I had a sensation of drowsiness and heard don Juan's words as if they were coming from far away. I automatically looked at the ledge. Don Genaro was there again. That did not interest me. I noticed semiconsciously that it was very difficult for me to breathe, but before I could have a thought about it, don Genaro jumped to the ground. That act did not catch my interest either. He came over to me and helped me stand up, holding me by the arm; don Juan held my other arm. They propped me up between the two of them. Then it was only don Genaro who was helping me walk. He whispered something in my ear that I could not understand and suddenly I felt that he had pulled my body in some strange way; he grabbed me, in a manner of speaking, by the skin of my stomach and pulled me up to the ledge, or perhaps onto another rock. I knew that for an instant I was on a rock. I could have sworn that it was the rock ledge; the image was so fleeting, however, that I could not evaluate it in detail. Then I felt that something in me faltered and I fell backwards. I had a faint feeling of anguish or perhaps physical discomfort. The next thing I knew don Juan was talking to me. I could not understand him. I concentrated my attention on his lips. The sensation I had was dreamlike; I was trying to rip from the inside an enveloping filmlike sheet that encased me, while don Juan tried to rip it from the outside. Finally, it actually popped and don Juan's words became audible and their meaning crystal clear. He was commanding me to surface by myself. I struggled desperately to gain my sobriety; I had no success. I quite consciously wondered why I was having so much trouble. I fought to talk to myself.

Don Juan seemed to be aware of my difficulty. He urged me to try harder. Something out there was preventing me from engaging myself in my familiar internal dialogue. It was as if a strange force were making me drowsy and indifferent.

I fought against it until I began to lose my breath. I heard don Juan talking to me. My body contorted involuntarily with the tension. I felt as if I were embraced and locked in mortal combat with something that was keeping me from breathing. I did not have fear, but rather some uncontrollable fury possessed me. My wrath mounted to such heights that I growled and screamed like an animal. Then my body was taken by a seizure; I had a jolt that stopped me instantly. I could again breathe normally and then I realized that don Juan had poured his gourd of water over my stomach and neck, soaking me.

He helped me sit up. Don Genaro was standing on the ledge. He called my name and then jumped to the ground. I saw him plummeting down from a height of fifty feet or so and I experienced an unbearable sensation around my umbilical region; I had had the same sensation in dreams of falling.

Don Genaro came to me and asked me, smiling, if I had liked his leap. I tried unsuccessfully to say something. Don Genaro called my name again.

"Carlitos! Watch me!" he said.

He swung his arms at his sides four or five times as if to get momentum and then jumped out of sight, or I thought he did. Or perhaps he did something else for which I had no description. He was five or six feet away from me and then he vanished as if he had been sucked away by an uncontrollable force.

I felt aloof and tired. I had a sense of indifference and did not want to think or talk to myself. I was not afraid, but inexplicably sad. I wanted to weep. Don Juan hit me repeatedly with his knuckles on the top of my head and laughed as if everything that had happened were a joke. He then demanded that I talk to myself because that was the time when the internal dialogue was desperately needed. I heard him ordering me, "Talk! Talk."

I had an involuntary spasm in the muscles of my lips. My mouth moved without sounds. I remembered don Genaro moving his mouth in a similar way when he was clowning and I wished I could have said, as he had, "My mouth doesn't want to talk." I tried to voice the words and my lips contorted in a painful way. Don Juan seemed to be on the verge of collapsing with laughter. His enjoyment was contagious and I also laughed. Finally, he helped me to stand up. I asked him if don Genaro was coming back. He said that don Genaro had had enough of me for the day.

*   *   *

"You almost made it," don Juan said.

We had been sitting near the fire in the earth stove. He had insisted that I eat. I was not hungry, or tired. An unusual melancholy had overtaken me; I felt removed from all the events of the day. Don Juan handed me my writing pad. I made a supreme effort to recapture my usual state. I jotted down some comments. Little by little, I brought myself back into my old pattern. It was as if a veil were being lifted; suddenly I was again involved in my familiar attitude of interest and bewilderment.

"Good, good," don Juan said, patting my head. "I've told you that the true art of a warrior is to balance terror and wonder."

Don Juan's mood was unusual. He seemed almost nervous, anxious. He appeared to be willing to speak on his own accord. I believed that he was preparing me for the sorcerers' explanation and I became quite anxious myself. His eyes had a strange glimmer that I had seen only a few times before. After I told him what I thought of his unusual attitude he said that he was happy for me, that as a warrior he could rejoice in the triumphs of his fellow men, if they were triumphs of the spirit. He added that unfortunately I was not yet ready for the sorcerers' explanation, in spite of the fact that I had successfully solved don Genaro's riddle. His contention was that when he had poured water over my body I had actually been dying and my whole achievement had been canceled out by my incapacity to fend off the last of don Genaro's onslaughts.

"Genaro's power was like a tide that engulfed you," he said.

"Did don Genaro want to hurt me?" I asked.

"No," he said. "Genaro wants to help you. But power can be met only with power. He was testing you and you failed."

"But I solved his riddle, didn't I?"

"You did fine," he said. "So fine that Genaro had to believe that you were capable of a complete warrior's feat. You almost made it. What floored you this time was not indulging, though."

"What was it then?"

"You're too impatient and violent; instead of relaxing and going with Genaro you began to fight him. You can't win against him; he's stronger than you."

Don Juan then volunteered some advice and suggestions about my personal relations with people. His remarks were a serious sequel to what don Genaro had jokingly said to me earlier. He was in a talkative mood and without any coaxing on my part he began to explain what had taken place during the last two times I had been there.

"As you know," he said, "the crux of sorcery is the internal dialogue; that is the key to everything. When a warrior learns to stop it, everything becomes possible; the most farfetched schemes become attainable. The passageway to all the weird and eerie experiences that you have had recently was the fact that you could stop talking to yourself. You have, in complete sobriety, witnessed the ally, Genaro's double, the dreamer and the dreamed, and today you almost learned about the totality of yourself; that was the warrior's feat that Genaro expected you to perform. All this has been possible because of the amount of personal power that you have stored. It started the last time you were here when I caught sight of a very auspicious omen. As you arrived I heard the ally prowling around; first, I heard its soft steps and then I *saw* the moth looking at you as you got out of your car. The ally was motionless, watching you. That to me was the best omen. Had the ally been agitated, moving around as if it was displeased with your presence, the way it always has been, the course of the events would have been different. Many times I have caught sight of the ally in an unfriendly state towards you, but this time the omen was right and I knew that the ally had a piece of knowledge for you. That was the reason why I said that you had an appointment with knowledge, an appointment with a moth that had been pending for a long time. For reasons inconceivable to us the ally selected the form of a moth to manifest itself to you."

"But you said that the ally was formless, and that one could only judge its effects," I said.

"That is right," he said. "But the ally is a moth for the onlookers who are associated with you — Genaro and myself. For you, the ally is only an effect, a sensation in your body, or a sound, or the golden specks of knowledge. It remains as a fact, nonetheless, that by choosing the form of a moth, the ally is telling Genaro and me something of great importance. Moths are the givers of knowledge and the friends and helpers of sorcerers. It is because the ally chose to be a moth around you that Genaro places such a great emphasis on you.

"That night that you met the moth, as I had anticipated, was a true appointment with knowledge for you. You learned the moth's call, felt the gold dust of its wings, but above all, that night for the first time, you were aware that you *saw* and your body learned that we are luminous beings. You have not yet assessed correctly that monumental event in your life. Genaro demonstrated for you with tremendous force and clarity that we are a feeling and that what we call our body is a cluster of luminous fibers that have awareness.

"Last night you were back again under the good auspices of the ally. I came to look at you as you arrived and I knew that I had to call Genaro so he could explain to you the mystery of the dreamer and the dreamed. You believed then, just as you always have, that I was tricking you; but Genaro was not hiding in the bushes as you thought. He came over for you, even if your reason refuses to believe it."

That part of don Juan's elucidation was indeed the hardest to take at its face value. I could not admit it. I said that don Genaro had been real and of this world.

"Everything that you've witnessed so far has been real and of this world," he said. "There is no other world. Your stumbling block is a peculiar insistence on your part and that peculiarity of yours is not going to be cured by explanations. So today Genaro addressed himself directly to your body. A careful examination of what you did today will reveal to you that your body put things together in a most praiseworthy manner. Somehow, you refrained from indulging in your visions at the irrigation ditch. You kept a rare control and aloofness as warriors should; you didn't believe anything, but you still acted efficiently and thus you were capable of following Genaro's call. You actually found him without any aid from me.

"When we arrived at the rock ledge, you were imbued with power and you saw Genaro standing where other sorcerers have stood, for similar reasons. He walked over to you after jumping from the ledge. He himself was all power. Had you proceeded as you did earlier by the irrigation ditch, you would've *seen* him as he really is, a luminous being. Instead, you got frightened, especially when Genaro made you leap. That leap in itself should have been sufficient to transport you beyond your boundaries. But you didn't have the strength and fell back into the world of your reason. Then, of course, you entered into mortal combat with yourself. Something in you, your *will*, wanted to go with Genaro, while your reason opposed him. Had I not helped you, you now would be lying dead and buried in that power place. But even with my help the outcome was dubious for a moment."

We were silent for a few minutes. I waited for him to speak. Finally I asked, "Did don Genaro make me leap up to the rock ledge?"

"Don't take that leap in the sense that you understand a leap," he said. "Once again, this is only a way of speaking. As long as you think that you are a solid body you cannot conceive what I am talking about."

He then spilled some ashes on the ground by the lantern, covering an area about two feet square, and drew a diagram with his fingers, a diagram that had eight points interconnected with lines. It was a geometrical figure.

He had drawn a similar one years before when he tried to explain to me that it was not an illusion that I had observed the same leaf falling four times from the same tree.

The diagram in the ashes had two epicenters; one he called "reason," the other, "will." "Reason" was interconnected directly with a point he called "talking." Through "talking," "reason" was indirectly connected to three other points, "feeling," "dreaming" and "seeing." The other epicenter, "will," was directly connected to "feeling," "dreaming" and "seeing"; but only indirectly to "reason" and "talking."

I remarked that the diagram was different from the one I had recorded years before.

"The outer form is of no importance," he said. "These points represent a human being and can be drawn in any way you want."

"Do they represent the body of a human being?" I asked.

"Don't call it the body," he said. "These are eight points on the fibers of a luminous being. A sorcerer says, as you can see in the diagram, that a human being is, first of all, *will*, because *will* is directly connected to three points, *feeling*, *dreaming* and *seeing*; then next, a human being is *reason*. This is properly a center that is smaller than *will*; it is connected only with *talking*."

"What are the other two points, don Juan?"

He looked at me and smiled.

"You're a lot stronger now than you were the first time we talked about this diagram," he said. "But you're not yet strong enough to know all the eight points. Genaro will someday show you the other two."

"Does everybody have those eight points or only sorcerers?"

"We may say that every one of us brings to the world eight points. Two of them, *reason* and *talking*, are known by everyone. *Feeling* is always vague but somehow familiar. But only in the world of sorcerers does one get fully acquainted with *dreaming*, *seeing* and *will*. And finally, at the outer edge of that world one encounters the other two. The eight points make the totality of oneself."

He showed me in the diagram that in essence all the points could be made to connect with one another indirectly.

I asked him again about the two mysterious remaining points. He showed me that they were connected only to "will" and that they were removed from "feeling," "dreaming" and "seeing," and much more distant from "talking" and "reason." He pointed with his finger to show that they were isolated from the rest and from each other.

"Those two points will never yield to *talking* or to *reason*," he said. "Only *will* can handle them. *Reason* is so removed from them that it is utterly useless to try figuring them out. This is one of the hardest things to realize; after all, the forte of *reason* is to reason out everything."

I asked him if the eight points corresponded to areas or to certain organs in a human being.

"They do," he replied dryly and erased the diagram.

He touched my head and said that that was the center of "reason" and "talking." The tip of my sternum was the center of "feeling." The area below the navel was "will." "Dreaming" was on the right side against the ribs. "Seeing" on the left. He said that sometimes in some warriors "seeing" and "dreaming" were on the right side.

"Where are the other two points?" I asked.

He gave me a most obscene answer and broke into a belly laugh.

"You're so sneaky," he said. "You think I'm a sleepy old goat, don't you?"

I explained to him that my questions created their own momentum.

"Don't try to hurry," he said. "You'll know in due time and then you will be on your own, by yourself."

"Do you mean that I won't see you any more, don Juan?"

"Not ever again," he said. "Genaro and I will be then what we always have been, dust on the road."

I had a jolt in the pit of my stomach.

"What are you saying, don Juan?"

"I'm saying that we all are unfathomable beings, luminous and boundless. You, Genaro and I are stuck together by a purpose that is not our decision."

"What purpose are you talking about?"

"Learning the warrior's way. You can't get out of it, but neither can we. As long as our achievement is pending you will find me or Genaro, but once it is accomplished, you will fly freely and no one knows where the force of your life will take you."

"What is don Genaro doing in this?"

"That subject is not in your realm yet," he said. "Today I have to pound the nail that Genaro put in, the fact that we are luminous beings. We are perceivers. We are an awareness; we are not objects; we have no solidity. We are boundless. The world of objects and solidity is a way of making our passage on earth convenient. It is only a description that was created to help us. We, or rather our *reason*, forget that the description is only a description and thus we entrap the totality of ourselves in a vicious circle from which we rarely emerge in our lifetime.

"At this moment, for instance, you are involved in extricating yourself from the snarls of *reason*. It is preposterous and unthinkable for you that Genaro just appeared at the edge of the chaparral, and yet you cannot deny that you witnessed it. You perceived it as such."

Don Juan chuckled. He carefully drew another diagram in the ashes and covered it with his hat before I could copy it.

"We are perceivers," he proceeded. "The world that we perceive, though, is an illusion. It was created by a description that was told to us since the moment we were born.

"We, the luminous beings, are born with two rings of power, but we use only one to create the world. That ring, which is hooked very soon after we are born, is *reason*, and its companion is *talking*. Between the two they concoct and maintain the world.

"So, in essence, the world that your *reason* wants to sustain is the world created by a description and its dogmatic and inviolable rules, which the *reason* learns to accept and defend.

"The secret of the luminous beings is that they have another ring of power which is never used, the *will*. The trick of the sorcerer is the same trick of the average man. Both have a description; one, the average man, upholds it with his *reason*; the other, the sorcerer, upholds it with his *will*. Both descriptions have their rules and the rules are perceivable, but the advantage of the sorcerer is that *will* is more engulfing than *reason*.

"The suggestion that I want to make at this point is that from now on you should let yourself perceive whether the description is upheld by your *reason* or by your *will*. I feel that is the only way for you to use your daily world as a challenge and a vehicle to accumulate enough personal power in order to get to the totality of yourself.

"Perhaps the next time that you come you'll have enough of it. At any rate, wait until you feel, like you felt today at the irrigation ditch, that an inner voice is telling you to do so. If you come in any other spirit it'll be a waste of time and a danger to you."

I remarked that if I had to wait for that inner voice I would never see them again.

"You'd be surprised how well one can perform if one is against the wall," he said.

He stood up and picked up a bundle of firewood. He placed some dry sticks on the earth stove. The flames cast a yellowish glow on the ground. He then turned off the lantern and squatted in front of his hat, which was covering the drawing he had made in the ashes.

He commanded me to sit calmly, shut off my internal dialogue, and keep my eyes on his hat. I struggled for a few moments and then I felt a sensation of floating, of falling off a cliff. It was as if nothing were supporting me, as if I were not sitting or did not have a body.

Don Juan lifted his hat. Underneath there were spirals of ashes. I watched them without thinking. I felt the spirals moving. I felt them in my stomach. The ashes seemed to pile up. Then they were stirred and fluffed and suddenly don Genaro was sitting in front of me.

The sight forced me instantly into my internal dialogue. I thought that I must have fallen asleep. I began to breathe in short gasps and tried to open my eyes, but my eyes were open.

I heard don Juan telling me to get up and move around. I jumped up and ran to the ramada. Don Juan and don Genaro ran after me. Don Juan brought his lantern. I could not catch my breath. I tried to calm myself as I had done before, by jogging in place while I faced the west. I lifted my arms and began breathing. Don Juan came to my side and said that those movements were done only in the twilight.

Don Genaro yelled that it was twilight for me and both of them began to laugh. Don Genaro ran to the edge of the bushes and then bounced back to the ramada, as if he had been attached to a giant rubber band that made him snap back. He repeated the same movement three or four times and then came to my side. Don Juan had been looking at me fixedly, giggling like a child.

They exchanged a furtive glance. Don Juan said to don Genaro in a loud voice that my reason was dangerous, and that it could kill me if it was not placated.

"For heaven's sake!" don Genaro exclaimed in a roaring voice. "Placate his reason!"

They jumped up and down and laughed like two children.

Don Juan made me sit down underneath the lantern and handed me my notebook.

"Tonight we're really pulling your leg," he said in a conciliatory tone. "Don't be afraid. Genaro was hiding under my hat."

PART TWO

The Tonal and the Nagual

HAVING TO BELIEVE

I walked towards downtown on the Paseo de la Reforma. I was tired; the altitude of Mexico City no doubt had something to do with it. I could have taken a bus or a taxi, but somehow in spite of my fatigue I wanted to walk. It was Sunday afternoon. The traffic was minimal and yet the exhaust fumes of the buses and trucks with diesel engines made the narrow streets of downtown seem like canyons of smog.

I arrived at the Zocalo and noticed that the cathedral of Mexico City seemed to be more slanted than the last time I had seen it. I stepped a few feet inside the enormous halls. A cynical thought crossed my mind.

From there I headed for the Lagunilla market. I had no definite purpose in mind. I walked aimlessly but at a good pace, without looking at anything in particular. I ended up at the stands of old coins and secondhand books.

"Hello, hello! Look who's here!" someone said, tapping me lightly on the shoulder.

The voice and the touch made me jump. I quickly turned to my right. My mouth opened in surprise. The person who had spoken to me was don Juan.

"My God, don Juan!" I exclaimed and a shiver shook my body from head to toe. "What are you doing here?"

"What are you doing here?" he retorted as an echo.

I told him that I had stopped in the city for a couple of days before venturing into the mountains of central Mexico to search for him.

"Well, let's say then that I came down from the mountains to find you," he said, smiling.

He patted me on the shoulder several times. He seemed to be glad to see me. He put his hands on his hips and swelled his chest and asked me whether or not I liked his appearance. It was only then that I noticed he was wearing a suit. The full impact of such an incongruity hit me. I was dumfounded.

"How do you like my *tacuche?*" he asked, beaming.

He used the slang word "tacuche" instead of the standard Spanish word "traje" for suit.

"Today I'm in a suit," he said as if he had to explain; and then, pointing to my open mouth, he added, "Close it! Close it!"

I laughed absent-mindedly. He noticed my confusion. His body shook with laughter as he turned around so I could see him from every angle. His attire was incredible. He was wearing a light brown suit with pin stripes, brown shoes, a white shirt. And a necktie! And that made me wonder if he had any socks on, or was he wearing his shoes without them?

What added to my bewilderment was the maddening sensation I had had that when don Juan tapped me on the shoulder and I turned around I thought I had seen him in his khaki pants and shirt, his sandals and his straw hat, and then as he made me aware of his attire, and as I focused my attention on every detail of it, the complete unit of his dress became fixed, as if I had created it with my thoughts. My mouth seemed to be the area of my body which was most taxed by the surprise. It opened involuntarily. Don Juan touched me gently on my chin, as if he were helping me to close it.

"You certainly are developing a double chin," he said and laughed in short spurts.

I became aware then that he did not have a hat on, and that his short white hair was parted on the right side. He looked like an old Mexican gentleman, an impeccably tailored urban dweller.

I told him that to have found him there was so unnerving to me that I had to sit down. He was very understanding and suggested that we go to a nearby park.

We walked a few blocks in complete silence and then we arrived at the Plaza Garibaldi, a place where musicians offered their services, a sort of musicians' employment center.

Don Juan and I merged with scores of spectators and tourists and walked around the park. After a while he stopped, leaned against a wall and pulled his pants up slightly at the knees; he was wearing light brown socks. I asked him to tell me the meaning of his mysterious apparel. His vague reply was that he simply had to be in a suit that day for reasons that would be clear to me later.

Finding Don Juan in a suit had been so unearthly that my agitation was almost uncontrollable. I had not seen him for several months and I wanted more than anything else in the world to talk with him, but somehow the setting was wrong and my attention meandered around. Don Juan must have noticed my anxiety and suggested that we walk to La Alameda, a more quiet park a few blocks away.

There were not too many people in the park and we had no trouble finding an empty bench. We sat down. My nervousness had given way to a feeling of uneasiness. I did not dare to look at don Juan.

There was a long unnerving pause; still without looking at him, I said that the inner voice had finally driven me to search for him, that the staggering events I had witnessed at his house had affected my life very deeply, and that I just had to talk about them.

He made a gesture of impatience with his hand and said that his policy was never to dwell on past events.

"What's important now is that you've fulfilled my suggestion," he said. "You have taken your daily world as a challenge, and the proof that you have stored sufficient personal power is the indisputable fact that you have found me with no difficulty whatever, at the precise spot where you were supposed to."

"I doubt very much that I could take credit for that," I said.

"I was waiting for you and then you showed up," he said. "That's all I know; that's all any warrior would care to know."

"What's going to happen now that I've found you?" I asked.

"For one thing," he said, "we won't discuss the dilemmas of your *reason;* those experiences belong to another time and to another mood. They are, properly speaking, only steps of an endless ladder;

to emphasize them would mean to take away from the importance of what's taking place now. A warrior cannot possibly afford to do that."

I had an almost invincible desire to complain. It was not that I resented anything that had happened to me but I craved solace and sympathy. Don Juan appeared to know my mood and spoke as if I had actually voiced my thoughts.

"Only as a warrior can one withstand the path of knowledge," he said. "A warrior cannot complain or regret anything. His life is an endless challenge, and challenges cannot possibly be good or bad. Challenges are simply challenges."

His tone was dry and severe, but his smile was warm and disarming.

"Now that you are here, what we'll do is wait for an omen," he said.

"What kind of omen?" I asked.

"We need to find out whether your power can stand on its own," he said. "The last time it petered out miserably; this time the circumstances of your personal life appear to have given you, at least on the surface, all the necessaries to deal with the sorcerers' explanation."

"Is there a chance that you might tell me about it?" I asked.

"It depends on your personal power," he said. "As is always the case in the doings and not-doings of warriors, personal power is the only thing that matters. So far, I should say that you're doing fine."

After a moment's silence, as if wanting to change the subject, he stood up and pointed to his suit.

"I have put on my suit for you," he said in a mysterious tone. "This suit is my challenge. Look how good I look in it! How easy! Eh? Nothing to it!"

Don Juan did look extraordinarily well in a suit. All I could think of as a gauge for comparison was the way my grandfather used to look in his heavy English flannel suit. He always gave me the impression that he felt unnatural, out of place in a suit. Don Juan, on the contrary, was so at ease.

"Do you think it is easy for me to look natural in a suit?" don Juan asked.

I did not know what to say. I concluded to myself, however, that judging by his appearance and by the way he conducted himself, it was the easiest thing in the world for him.

"To wear a suit is a challenge for me," he said. "A challenge as difficult as wearing sandals and a poncho would be for you. You have never had the necessity to take that as a challenge, though. My case is different; I'm an Indian."

We looked at each other. He raised his brows in a silent question, as if asking for my comments.

"The basic difference between an ordinary man and a warrior is that a warrior takes everything as a challenge," he went on, "while an ordinary man takes everything either as a blessing or as a curse. The fact that you're here today indicates that you have tipped the scales in favor of the warrior's way."

His stare made me feel nervous. I tried to get up and walk, but he made me sit down.

"You are going to sit here without fretting until we're through," he said imperatively. "We are waiting for an omen; we can't proceed without it, because it isn't enough that you found me, as it wasn't enough that you found Genaro that day in the desert. Your power must round itself up and give an indication."

"I can't figure out what you want," I said.

"I *saw* something prowling around this park," he said.

"Was it the ally?" I asked.

"No. It wasn't. So, we must sit here and find out what kind of omen your power is rounding up."

He then asked me to give him a detailed account of how I had carried out the recommendations made by don Genaro and himself about my daily world and my relations with people. I felt a bit embarrassed. He put me at ease with the argument that my personal affairs were not private, because they included a task of sorcery that he and don Genaro were fostering in me. I jokingly remarked that my life had been ruined because of that task of sorcery and recounted the difficulties in maintaining my day-to-day world.

I talked for a long time. Don Juan laughed at my account until tears were rolling down his cheeks. He slapped his thighs repeatedly;

that gesture, which I had seen him do hundreds of times, was definitely out of place when it was done on the pants of a suit. I was filled with apprehension, which I was compelled to voice.

"Your suit scares me more than anything you've done to me," I said.

"You'll get used to it," he said. "A warrior must be fluid and must shift harmoniously with the world around him, whether it is the world of *reason*, or the world of *will*.

"The most dangerous aspect of that shifting comes forth every time the warrior finds that the world is neither one nor the other. I was told that the only way to succeed in that crucial shifting was by proceeding in one's actions as if one believed. In other words, the secret of a warrior is that he believes without believing. But obviously a warrior cannot just say he believes and let it go at that. That would be too easy. To just believe would exonerate him from examining his situation. A warrior, whenever he has to involve himself with believing, does it as a choice, as an expression of his innermost predilection. A warrior doesn't believe, a warrior *has* to believe."

He stared at me for a few seconds as I wrote in my notebook. I remained silent. I could not say that I understood the difference, but I did not want to argue or ask questions. I wanted to think about what he had said, but my mind meandered as I looked around. On the street behind us there was a long line of automobiles and buses, blowing their horns. At the edge of the park, perhaps twenty yards away, directly in line with the bench where we were sitting, a group of about seven people, including three policemen in light gray uniforms, stood over a man lying motionless on the grass. He seemed to be drunk or perhaps seriously ill.

I glanced at don Juan. He had also been looking at the man.

I told him that for some reason I was incapable of clarifying by myself what he had just said to me.

"I don't want to ask questions any more," I said. "But if I don't ask you to explain I don't understand. Not to ask questions is very abnormal for me."

"Please, be normal, by all means," he said with feigned seriousness.

I said that I did not understand the difference between believing and having to believe. To me both were the same. To conceive that the statements were different was splitting hairs.

"Remember the story you once told me about your friend and her cats?" he asked casually.

He looked up at the sky and leaned back against the bench, stretching his legs. He put his hands behind his head and contracted the muscles of his whole body. As it always happens, his bones made a loud cracking sound.

He was referring to a story I had once told him about a friend of mine who found two kittens, almost dead, inside a dryer in a laundromat. She revived them and through excellent nourishment and care groomed them into two gigantic cats, a black one and a reddish one.

Two years later she sold her house. Since she could not take the cats with her and was unable to find another home for them, all she could do under the circumstances was to take them to an animal hospital and have them put to sleep.

I helped her take them. The cats had never been inside a car; she tried to calm them down. They scratched and bit her, especially the reddish cat, the one she called Max. When we finally arrived at the animal hospital, she took the black cat first; holding it in her arms, and without saying a word she got out of the car. The cat played with her; pawing her gently as she pushed open the glass door to enter the hospital.

I glanced at Max; he was sitting in the back. The movement of my head must have scared him, for he dove under the driver's seat. I made the seat slide backwards. I did not want to reach under it for fear that he would bite or scratch my hand. The cat was lying inside a depression on the floor of the car. He seemed very agitated; his breathing was accelerated. He looked at me; our eyes met and an overwhelming sensation possessed me. Something took hold of my body, a form of apprehension, despair, or perhaps embarrassment for being part of what was taking place.

I felt a need to explain to Max that it was my friend's decision, and that I was only helping her. The cat kept on looking at me as if he understood my words.

I looked to see if she was coming. I could see her through the glass door. She was talking to the receptionist. My body felt a strange jolt and automatically I opened the door of my car.

"Run, Max, run!" I said to the cat.

He jumped out of the car, dashed across the street with his body close to the ground, like a true feline. The opposite side of the street was empty; there were no cars parked and I could see Max running down the street along the gutter. He reached the corner of a big boulevard and then dove through the storm drain into the sewer.

My friend came back. I told her that Max had left. She got into the car and we drove away without saying a single word.

In the months that followed, the incident became a symbol to me. I fancied or perhaps I saw a weird flicker in Max's eyes when he looked at me before jumping out of the car. And I believed that for an instant that castrated, overweight, and useless pet became a cat.

I told don Juan that I was convinced that when Max had run across the street and plunged into the sewer his "cat spirit" was impeccable, and that perhaps at no other time in his life was his "catness" so evident. The impression that the incident left on me was unforgettable.

I told the story to all of my friends; after telling it and retelling it, my identification with the cat became quite pleasurable.

I thought myself to be like Max, overindulgent, domesticated in many ways, and yet I could not help thinking that there was always the possibility of one moment in which the spirit of man might take over my whole being, just like the spirit of "catness" took over Max's bloated and useless body.

Don Juan had liked the story and had made some casual comments about it. He had said that it was not so difficult to let the spirit of man flow and take over; to sustain it, however, was something that only a warrior could do.

*　　*　　*

"What about the story of the cats?" I asked.

"You told me you believed that you're taking your chances, like Max," he said.

"I do believe that."

"What I've been trying to tell you is that as a warrior you cannot just believe this and let it go at that. With Max, *having* to believe means that you accept the fact that his escape might have been a useless outburst. He might have jumped into the sewer and died instantly. He might have drowned or starved to death, or he might have been eaten by rats. A warrior considers all those possibilities and then chooses to believe in accordance with his innermost predilection.

"As a warrior you *have* to believe that Max made it, that he not only escaped but that he sustained his power. You *have* to believe it. Let's say that without that belief you have nothing."

The distinction became very clear. I thought I really had chosen to believe that Max had survived, knowing that he was handicapped by a lifetime of soft and pampered living.

"Believing is a cinch," don Juan went on. "*Having* to believe is something else. In this case, for instance, power gave you a splendid lesson, but you chose to use only part of it. If you *have* to believe, however, you must use all the event."

"I see what you mean," I said.

My mind was in a state of clarity and I thought I was grasping his concepts with no effort at all.

"I'm afraid you still don't understand," he said, almost whispering.

He stared at me. I held his look for a moment.

"What about the other cat?" he asked.

"Uh? The other cat?" I repeated involuntarily.

I had forgotten about it. My symbol had rotated around Max. The other cat was of no consequence to me.

"But he is!" don Juan exclaimed when I voiced my thoughts. "*Having* to believe means that you have to also account for the other cat. The one that went playfully licking the hands that were carrying him to his doom. That was the cat that went to his death trustingly, filled with his cat's judgments.

"You think you're like Max, therefore you have forgotten about the other cat. You don't even know his name. *Having* to believe means that you must consider everything, and before deciding that you are like Max you must consider that you may be like the other cat; instead of running for your life and taking your chances, you may be going to your doom happily, filled with your judgments."

There was an intriguing sadness in his words, or perhaps the sadness was mine. We remained quiet for a long time. Never had it crossed my mind that I might be like the other cat. The thought was very distressing to me.

A mild commotion and the muffled sound of voices suddenly forced me out of my mental deliberations. Policemen were dispersing some people gathered around the man lying on the grass. Someone had propped the man's head on a rolled up jacket. The man was lying parallel to the street. He was facing east. From where I sat I could almost tell that his eyes were open.

Don Juan sighed.

"What a magnificent afternoon," he said, looking at the sky.

"I don't like Mexico City," I said.

"Why not?"

"I hate the smog."

He shook his head rhythmically is if he were agreeing with me.

"I would rather be with you in the desert, or in the mountains," I said.

"If I were you I would never say that," he said.

"I didn't mean anything wrong, don Juan."

"We both know that. It is not what you mean that matters, though. A warrior, or any man for that matter, cannot possibly wish he were somewhere else; a warrior because he lives by challenge, an ordinary man because he doesn't know where his death is going to find him.

"Look at that man over there lying on the grass. What do you think is wrong with him?"

"He's either drunk or ill," I said.

"He's dying!" don Juan said with ultimate conviction. "When we sat down here I caught a glimpse of his death as it circled around him. That's why I told you not to get up; rain or shine, you can't get up from this bench until the end. This is the omen we have been waiting for. It is late afternoon. Right now the sun is about to set. It is your hour of power. Look! The view of that man is only for us."

He pointed out that from where we sat we had an unobstructed view of the man. A group of curious bystanders were gathered in a half circle on the other side of him, opposite us.

The sight of the man lying on the grass became very disturbing to me. He was lean and dark, still young. His black hair was short and curly. His shirt was unbuttoned and his chest was uncovered. He was wearing an orange cardigan sweater with holes in the elbows, and some old beat up gray slacks. His shoes, of some undefined faded color, were untied. He was rigid. I could not tell whether or not he was breathing. I wondered if he were dying, as don Juan had said. Or was don Juan simply using the event to make a point? My past experiences with him gave me the certainty that somehow he was making everything fit into some mysterious scheme of his.

After a long silence I turned to him. His eyes were closed. He began to talk without opening them.

"That man is about to die now," he said. "You don't believe it, though, do you?"

He opened his eyes and stared at me for a second. His look was so penetrating that it stunned me.

"No. I don't believe it," I said.

I really felt that the whole thing was too easy. We had come to sit in the park and right there, as if everything were being staged, was a man dying.

"The world adjusts itself to itself," don Juan said after listening to my doubts. "This is not a setup. This is an omen, an act of power.

"The world upheld by *reason* makes all this into an event that we can watch for a moment on our way to more important things. All we can say about it is that a man is lying on the grass in the park, perhaps drunk.

"The world upheld by *will* makes it into an act of power, which we can *see*. We can *see* death whirling around the man, setting its hooks deeper and deeper into his luminous fibers. We can *see* the luminous strings losing their tautness and vanishing one by one.

"Those are the two possibilities opened to us luminous beings. You are somewhere in the middle, still wanting to have everything under the rubric of *reason*. And yet, how can you discard the fact that your personal power rounded up an omen? We came to this park, after you had found me where I had been waiting for you—you found me by just walking into me, without thinking, or planning, or deliberately using your *reason*—and after we sat down here to wait for an omen, we became aware of that man, each of us noticed him in our own way, you with your *reason*, I with my *will*.

"That dying man is one of the cubic centimeters of chance that power always makes available to a warrior. The warrior's art is to be perennially fluid in order to pluck it. I have plucked it, but have you?"

I could not answer. I became aware of an immense chasm within myself and for a moment I was somehow cognizant of the two worlds he was talking about.

"What an exquisite omen this is!" he went on. "And all for you. Power is showing you that death is the indispensable ingredient in *having* to believe. Without the awareness of death everything is ordinary, trivial. It is only because death is stalking us that the world is an unfathomable mystery. Power has shown you that. All I have done myself is to round up the details of the omen, so the direction would be clear to you; but in rounding up the details, I have also shown you that everything I have said to you today is what I *have* to believe myself, because that is the predilection of my spirit."

We looked each other in the eye for a moment.

"I remember a poem that you used to read to me," he said, moving his eyes to the side. "About a man who vowed to die in Paris. How does it go?"

The poem was Cesar Vallejo's "Black Stone on a White Stone." I had read and recited the first two stanzas to don Juan countless times at his request.

I will die in Paris while it rains,
on a day which I already remember.
I will die in Paris — and I do not run away —
perhaps in the Autumn, on a Thursday, as it is today.

It will be a Thursday, because today,
the Thursday that I write these lines,
my bones feel the turn,
and never so much as today, in all my road,
have I seen myself alone.

The poem summed up an indescribable melancholy for me.

Don Juan whispered that he *had* to believe that the dying man had had enough personal power to enable him to choose the streets of Mexico City as the place of his death.

"We're back again to the story of the two cats," he said. "We *have* to believe that Max became aware of what was stalking him and, like that man over there, had enough power at least to choose the place of his end. But then there was the other cat, just like there are other men whose death will encircle them while they are alone, unaware, staring at the walls and ceiling of an ugly barren room.

"That man, on the other hand, is dying where he has always lived, in the streets. Three policemen are his guards of honor. And as he fades away his eyes will catch a last glimpse of the lights in the stores across the street — the cars, the trees, the throngs of people milling around — and his ears will be flooded for the last time with the sounds of traffic and the voices of men and women as they walk by.

"So you see, without an awareness of the presence of our death there is no power, no mystery."

I stared at the man for a long time. He was motionless. Perhaps he was dead. But my disbelief did not matter any longer. Don Juan was right. *Having* to believe that the world is mysterious and unfathomable was the expression of a warrior's innermost predilection. Without it he had nothing.

THE ISLAND OF THE TONAL

Don Juan and I met again the next day at the same park around noon. He was still wearing his brown suit. We sat on a bench; he took off his coat, folded it very carefully, but with an air of supreme casualness, and laid it on the bench. His casualness was very studied and yet it was completely natural. I caught myself staring at him. He seemed to be aware of the paradox he was presenting to me and smiled. He straightened his necktie. He had on a beige long-sleeved shirt. It fitted him very well.

"I still have on my suit because I want to tell you something of great importance," he said, patting me on the shoulder. "You had a good performance yesterday. Now it is time to come to some final agreements."

He paused for a long moment. He seemed to be preparing a statement. I had a strange feeling in my stomach. My immediate assumption was that he was going to tell me the sorcerers' explanation. He stood up a couple of times and paced back and forth in front of me, as if it were difficult to voice what he had in mind.

"Let's go to the restaurant across the street and have a bite to eat," he finally said.

He unfolded his coat, and before he put it on he showed me that it was fully lined.

"It is made to order," he said and smiled as if he were proud of it, as if it mattered.

"I have to call your attention to it, or you wouldn't notice it, and it is very important that you are aware of it. You are aware of everything only when you think you should be; the condition of a warrior, however, is to be aware of everything at all times.

"My suit and all this paraphernalia is important because it represents my condition in life. Or rather, the condition of one of the two parts of my totality. This discussion has been pending. I feel that now is the time to have it. It has to be done properly, though, or it will never make sense. I wanted my suit to give you the first clue. I think it has. Now is the time to talk, for in matters of this topic there is no complete understanding without talking."

"What is the topic, don Juan?"

"The totality of oneself," he said.

He stood up abruptly and led me to a restaurant in a large hotel across the street. A hostess with a rather unfriendly disposition gave us a table inside in a back corner. Obviously the choice places were around the windows.

I told don Juan that the woman reminded me of another hostess in a restaurant in Arizona where don Juan and I had once gone to eat, who had asked us, before she handed out the menu, if we had enough money to pay.

"I don't blame this poor woman either," don Juan said, as if sympathizing with her. "She too, like the other one, is afraid of Mexicans."

He laughed softly. A couple of people at the adjacent tables turned their heads around and looked at us.

Don Juan said that without knowing, or perhaps even in spite of herself, the hostess had given us the best table in the house, a table where we could talk and I could write to my heart's content.

I had just taken my writing pad out of my pocket and put it on the table when the waiter suddenly loomed over us. He also seemed to be in a bad mood. He stood over us with a challenging air.

Don Juan proceeded to order a very elaborate meal for himself. He ordered without looking at the menu, as if he knew it by heart. I was at a loss; the waiter had appeared unexpectedly and I had not had time to read the menu, so I told him that I would have the same.

Don Juan whispered in my ear, "I bet you that they don't have what I've ordered."

He stretched his arms and legs and told me to relax and sit comfortably because the meal was going to take forever to be prepared.

"You are at a very poignant crossroad," he said. "Perhaps the last one, and also perhaps the most difficult one to understand. Some of the things I am going to point out to you today will probably never be clear. They are not supposed to be clear anyway. So don't be embarrassed or discouraged. All of us are dumb creatures when we join the world of sorcery, and to join it doesn't in any sense insure us that we will change. Some of us remain dumb until the very end."

I liked it when he included himself among the idiots. I knew that he did not do it out of kindness, but as a didactic device.

"Don't fret if you don't make sense out of what I'm going to tell you," he continued. "Considering your temperament, I'm afraid that you might knock yourself out trying to understand. Don't! What I'm about to say is meant only to point out a direction."

I had a sudden feeling of apprehension. Don Juan's admonitions forced me into an endless speculation. He had warned me on other occasions, in very much the same fashion, and every time he had done so, what he was warning me about had turned out to be a devastating issue.

"It makes me very nervous when you talk to me this way," I said.

"I know it," he replied calmly. "I'm deliberately trying to get you on your toes. I need your attention, your undivided attention."

He paused and looked at me. I laughed nervously and involuntarily. I knew that he was stretching the dramatic possibilities of the situation as far as he could.

"I'm not telling you all this for effect," he said, as if he had read my thoughts. "I am simply giving you time to make the proper adjustments."

At that moment the waiter stopped at our table to announce that they did not have what we had ordered. Don Juan laughed out loud and ordered tortillas and beans. The waiter chuckled scornfully and said that they did not serve them and suggested steak or chicken. We settled for some soup.

We ate in silence. I did not like the soup and could not finish it, but don Juan ate all of his.

"I have put on my suit," he said all of a sudden, "in order to tell you about something, something you already know but which needs to be clarified if it is going to be effective. I have waited until now, because Genaro feels that you have to be not only willing to undertake the road of knowledge, but your efforts by themselves must be impeccable enough to make you worthy of that knowledge. You have done well. Now I will tell you the sorcerers' explanation."

He paused again, rubbed his cheeks and played with his tongue inside his mouth, as if he were feeling his teeth.

"I'm going to tell you about the *tonal* and the *nagual*," he said and looked at me piercingly.

This was the first time in our association that he had used those two terms. I was vaguely familiar with them through the anthropological literature on the cultures of central Mexico. I knew that the "tonal" (pronounced, toh-na'hl) was thought to be a kind of guardian spirit, usually an animal, that a child obtained at birth and with which he had intimate ties for the rest of his life. "Nagual" (pronounced, nah-wa'hl) was the name given to the animal into which sorcerers could allegedly transform themselves, or to the sorcerer that elicited such a transformation.

"This is my *tonal*," don Juan said, rubbing his hands on his chest.

"Your suit?"

"No. My person."

He pounded his chest and his thighs and the side of his ribs.

"My *tonal* is all this."

He explained that every human being had two sides, two separate entities, two counterparts which became operative at the moment of birth; one was called the "tonal" and the other the "nagual."

I told him what anthropologists knew about the two concepts. He let me speak without interrupting me.

"Well, whatever you may think you know about them is pure nonsense," he said. "I base this statement on the fact that whatever I'm telling you about the *tonal* and the *nagual* could not possibly have been told to you before. Any idiot would know that you know nothing about them, because in order to be acquainted with them, you would have to be a sorcerer and you aren't. Or you would've had to talk about them with a sorcerer and you haven't. So disregard everything you've heard before, because it is inapplicable."

"It was only a comment," I said.

He raised his brows in a comical gesture.

"Your comments are out of order," he said. "This time I need your undivided attention, since I am going to acquaint you with the *tonal* and the *nagual*. Sorcerers have a special and unique interest in that knowledge. I would say that the *tonal* and the *nagual* are in the exclusive realm of men of knowledge. In your case, this is the lid that closes everything I have taught you. Thus, I have waited until now to talk about them.

"The *tonal* is not an animal that guards a person. I would rather say that it is a guardian that could be represented as an animal. But that is not the important point."

He smiled and winked at me.

"I'm using your own words now," he said. "The *tonal* is the social person."

He laughed, I supposed, at the sight of my bewilderment.

"The *tonal* is, rightfully so, a protector, a guardian—a guardian that most of the time turns into a guard."

I fumbled with my notebook. I was trying to pay attention to what he was saying. He laughed and mimicked my nervous movements.

"The *tonal* is the organizer of the world," he proceeded. "Perhaps the best way of describing its monumental work is to say that on its shoulders rests the task of setting the chaos of the world in order. It is not farfetched to maintain, as sorcerers do, that everything we know and do as men is the work of the *tonal*.

"At this moment, for instance, what is engaged in trying to make sense out of our conversation is your *tonal*; without it there would be only weird sounds and grimaces and you wouldn't understand a thing of what I'm saying.

"I would say then that the *tonal* is a guardian that protects something priceless, our very being. Therefore, an inherent quality of the *tonal* is to be cagey and jealous of its doings. And since its doings are by far the most important part of our lives, it is no wonder that it eventually changes, in every one of us, from a guardian into a guard."

He stopped and asked me if I had understood. I automatically nodded my head affirmatively and he smiled with an air of incredulity.

"A guardian is broad-minded and understanding," he explained. "A guard, on the other hand, is a vigilante, narrow-minded and most of the time despotic. I say, then, that the *tonal* in all of us has been made into a petty and despotic guard when it should be a broad-minded guardian."

I definitely was not following the trend of his explanation. I heard and wrote down every word and yet I seemed to be stuck with some internal dialogue of my own.

"It is very hard for me to follow your point," I said.

"If you didn't get hooked on talking to yourself you would have no quarrels," he said cuttingly.

His remark threw me into a long explanatory statement. I finally caught myself and apologized for my insistence on defending myself.

He smiled and made a gesture that seemed to indicate that my attitude had not really annoyed him.

"The *tonal* is everything we are," he proceeded. "Name it! Anything we have a word for is the *tonal*. And since the *tonal* is its own doings, then everything, obviously, has to fall under its domain."

I reminded him that he had said that the "tonal" was the social person, a term which I myself had used with him to mean a human being as the end result of socialization processes. I pointed out that if the "tonal" was that product, it could not be everything, as he had said, because the world around us was not the product of socialization.

Don Juan reminded me that my argument had no basis for him, and that, long before, he had already made the point that there was no world at large but only a description of the world which we had learned to visualize and take for granted.

"The *tonal* is everything we know," he said. "I think this in itself is enough reason for the *tonal* to be such an overpowering affair."

He paused for a moment. He seemed to be definitely waiting for comments or questions, but I had none. Yet I felt obligated to voice a question and struggled to formulate an appropriate one. I failed. I felt that the admonitions with which he had opened our conversation had perhaps served as a deterrent to any inquiry on my part. I felt strangely numb. I could not concentrate and order my thoughts. In fact I felt and knew, without the shadow of a doubt, that I was incapable of thinking and yet I knew this without thinking, if that were at all possible.

I looked at don Juan. He was staring at the middle part of my body. He lifted his eyes and my clarity of mind returned instantly.

"The *tonal* is everything we know," he repeated slowly. "And that includes not only us, as persons, but everything in our world. It can be said that the *tonal* is everything that meets the eye.

"We begin to groom it at the moment of birth. The moment we take the first gasp of air we also breathe in power for the *tonal*. So, it is proper to say that the *tonal* of a human being is intimately tied to his birth.

"You must remember this point. It is of great importance in understanding all this. The *tonal* begins at birth and ends at death."

I wanted to recapitulate all the points that he had made. I went as far as opening my mouth to ask him to repeat the salient points of our conversation, but to my amazement I could not vocalize my words. I was experiencing a most curious incapacity, my words were heavy and I had no control over that sensation.

I looked at don Juan to signal him that I could not talk. He was again staring at the area around my stomach.

He lifted his eyes and asked me how I felt. Words poured out of me as if I had been unplugged. I told him that I had been having the peculiar sensation of not being able to talk or think and yet my thoughts had been crystal clear.

"Your thoughts have been crystal clear?" he asked.

I realized then that the clarity had not pertained to my thoughts, but to my perception of the world.

"Are you doing something to me, don Juan?" I asked.

"I am trying to convince you that your comments are not necessary," he said and laughed.

"You mean you don't want me to ask questions?"

"No, no. Ask anything you want, but don't let your attention waver."

I had to admit that I had been distracted by the immensity of the topic.

"I still cannot understand, don Juan, what you mean by the statement that the *tonal* is everything," I said after a moment's pause.

"The *tonal* is what makes the world."

"Is the *tonal* the creator of the world?"

Don Juan scratched his temples.

"The *tonal* makes the world only in a manner of speaking. It cannot create or change anything, and yet it makes the world because its function is to judge, and assess, and witness. I say that the *tonal* makes the world because it witnesses and assesses it according to *tonal* rules. In a very strange manner the *tonal* is a creator that doesn't create a thing. In other words, the *tonal* makes up the rules by which it apprehends the world. So, in a manner of speaking, it creates the world."

He hummed a popular tune, beating the rhythm with his fingers on the side of his chair. His eyes were shining; they seemed to sparkle. He chuckled, shaking his head.

"You're not following me," he said, smiling.

"I am. I have no problems," I said, but I did not sound very convincing.

"The *tonal* is an island," he explained. "The best way of describing it is to say that the *tonal* is this."

He ran his hand over the table top.

"We can say that the *tonal* is like the top of this table. An island. And on this island we have everything. This island is, in fact, the world.

"There is a personal *tonal* for every one of us, and there is a collective one for all of us at any given time, which we can call the *tonal* of the times."

He pointed to the rows of tables in the restaurant.

"Look! Every table has the same configuration. Certain items are present on all of them. They are, however, individually different from each other; some tables are more crowded than others; they have different food on them, different plates, different atmosphere, yet we have to admit that all the tables in this restaurant are very alike. The same thing happens with the *tonal*. We can say that the *tonal* of the times is what makes us alike, in the same way it makes all the tables in this restaurant alike. Each table separately, nevertheless, is an individual case, just like the personal *tonal* of each of us. But the important factor to keep in mind is that everything we know about ourselves and about our world is on the island of the *tonal*. See what I mean?"

"If the *tonal* is everything we know about ourselves and our world, what, then, is the *nagual*?"

"The *nagual* is the part of us which we do not deal with at all."

"I beg your pardon?"

"The *nagual* is the part of us for which there is no description — no words, no names, no feelings, no knowledge."

"That's a contradiction, don Juan. In my opinion if it can't be felt or described or named, it cannot exist."

"It's a contradiction only in your opinion. I warned you before, don't knock yourself out trying to understand this."

"Would you say that the *nagual* is the mind?"

"No. The mind is an item on the table. The mind is part of the *tonal*. Let's say that the mind is the chili sauce."

He took a bottle of sauce and placed it in front of me.

"Is the *nagual* the soul?"

"No. The soul is also on the table. Let's say that the soul is the ashtray."

"Is it the thoughts of men?"

"No. Thoughts are also on the table. Thoughts are like the silverware."

He picked up a fork and placed it next to the chili sauce and the ashtray.

"Is it a state of grace? Heaven?"

"Not that either. That, whatever it might be, is also part of the *tonal*. It is, let's say, the napkin."

I went on giving possible ways of describing what he was alluding to: pure intellect, psyche, energy, vital force, immortality, life principle. For each thing I named he found an item on the table to serve as a counterpart and shoved it in front of me, until he had all the objects on the table stashed in one pile.

Don Juan seemed to be enjoying himself immensely. He giggled and rubbed his hands every time I named another possibility.

"Is the *nagual* the Supreme Being, the Almighty, God?" I asked.

"No. God is also on the table. Let's say that God is the tablecloth."

He made a joking gesture of pulling the tablecloth in order to stack it up with the rest of the items he had put in front of me.

"But, are you saying that God does not exist?"

"No. I didn't say that. All I said was that the *nagual* was not God, because God is an item of our personal *tonal* and of the *tonal* of the times. The *tonal* is, as I've already said, everything we think the world is composed of, including God, of course. God has no more importance other than being a part of the *tonal* of our time."

"In my understanding, don Juan, God is everything. Aren't we talking about the same thing?"

"No. God is only everything you can think of, therefore, properly speaking, he is only another item on the island. God cannot be witnessed at will, he can only be talked about. The *nagual*, on the other hand, is at the service of the warrior. It can be witnessed, but it cannot be talked about."

"If the *nagual* is not any of the things I have mentioned," I said, "perhaps you can tell me about its location. Where is it?"

Don Juan made a sweeping gesture and pointed to the area beyond the boundaries of the table. He swept his hand, as if with the back of it he were cleaning an imaginary surface that went beyond the edges of the table.

"The *nagual* is there," he said. "There, surrounding the island. The *nagual* is there, where power hovers.

"We sense, from the moment we are born, that there are two parts to us. At the time of birth, and for a while after, we are all *nagual*. We sense, then, that in order to function we need a counterpart to what we have. The *tonal* is missing and that gives us, from the very beginning, a feeling of incompleteness. Then the *tonal* starts to develop and it becomes utterly important to our functioning, so important that it opaques the shine of the *nagual*, it overwhelms it. From the moment we become all *tonal* we do nothing else but to increment that old feeling of incompleteness which accompanies us from the moment of our birth, and which tells us constantly that there is another part to give us completeness.

"From the moment we become all *tonal* we begin making pairs. We sense our two sides, but we always represent them with items of the *tonal*. We say that the two parts of us are the soul and the body. Or mind and matter. Or good and evil. God and Satan. We never realize, however, that we are merely pairing things on the island, very much like pairing coffee and tea, or bread and tortillas, or chili and mustard. I tell you, we are weird animals. We get carried away and in our madness we believe ourselves to be making perfect sense."

Don Juan stood up and addressed me as if he were an orator. He pointed his index finger at me and made his head shiver.

"Man doesn't move between good and evil," he said in a hilariously rhetorical tone, grabbing the salt and pepper shakers in both hands. "His true movement is between negativeness and positiveness."

He dropped the salt and pepper and clutched a knife and fork.

"You're wrong! There is no movement," he continued as if he were answering himself. "Man is only mind!"

He took the bottle of sauce and held it up. Then he put it down.

"As you can see," he said softly, "we can easily replace chili sauce for mind and end up saying, 'Man is only chili sauce!' Doing that won't make us more demented than we already are."

"I'm afraid I haven't asked the right question," I said. "Maybe we could arrive at a better understanding if I asked what one can specifically find in that area beyond the island?"

"There is no way of answering that. If I would say, Nothing, I would only make the *nagual* part of the *tonal*. All I can say is that there, beyond the island, one finds the *nagual*."

"But, when you call it the *nagual*, aren't you also placing it on the island?"

"No. I named it only because I wanted to make you aware of it."

"All right! But becoming aware of it is the step that has turned the *nagual* into a new item of my *tonal*."

"I'm afraid you do not understand. I have named the *tonal* and the *nagual* as a true pair. That is all I have done."

He reminded me that once, while trying to explain to him my insistence on meaning, I had discussed the idea that children might not be capable of comprehending the difference between "father" and "mother" until they were quite developed in terms of handling meaning, and that they would perhaps believe that it might be that "father" wears pants and "mother" skirts, or other differences dealing with hairstyle, or size of body, or items of clothing.

"We certainly do the same thing with the two parts of us," he said. "We sense that there is another side to us. But when we try to pin down that other side the *tonal* gets hold of the baton, and as a director it is quite petty and jealous. It dazzles us with its cunningness and forces us to obliterate the slightest inkling of the other part of the true pair, the *nagual*."

THE DAY OF THE TONAL

As we left the restaurant I told don Juan that he had been correct in warning me about the difficulty of the topic, and that my intellectual prowess was inadequate to grasp his concepts and explanations. I suggested that perhaps if I should go to my hotel and read my notes, my comprehension of the subject might improve. He tried to put me at ease; he said that I was worrying about words. While he was speaking I experienced a shiver, and for an instant I sensed that there was indeed another area within me.

I mentioned to don Juan that I was having some inexplicable feelings. My statement apparently aroused his curiosity. I told him that I had had the same feelings before, and that they seemed to be momentary lapses, interruptions in my flow of awareness. They always manifested themselves as a jolt in my body followed by the sensation that I was suspended in something.

We headed for downtown, walking leisurely. Don Juan asked me to relate all the details of my lapses. I had a hard time describing them, beyond the point of calling them moments of forgetfulness, or absent-mindedness, or not watching what I was doing.

He patiently rebuffed me. He pointed out that I was a demanding person, had an excellent memory, and was very careful in my actions. It had occurred to me at first that those peculiar lapses were associated with stopping the internal dialogue, but I also had had them when I had talked to myself extensively. They seemed to stem from an area independent of everything I knew.

Don Juan patted me on the back. He smiled with apparent delight.

"You're finally beginning to make real connections," he said.

I asked him to explain his cryptic statement, but he abruptly stopped our conversation and signaled me to follow him to a small park in front of a church.

"This is the end of our journey to downtown," he said and sat down on a bench. "Right here we have an ideal spot to watch people. There are some who walk by on the street and others who come to church. From here we can see everyone."

He pointed to a wide business street and to the gravel walk leading to the steps of the church. Our bench was located midway between the church and the street.

"This is my very favorite bench," he said, caressing the wood.

He winked at me and added with a grin, "It likes me. That's why no one was sitting on it. It knew I was coming."

"The bench knew that?"

"No! Not the bench. My *nagual*."

"Does the *nagual* have consciousness? Is it aware of things?"

"Of course. It is aware of everything. That's why I'm interested in your account. What you call lapses and feelings is the *nagual*. In order to talk about it we must borrow from the island of the *tonal*, therefore it is more convenient not to explain it but to simply recount its effects."

I wanted to say something else about those peculiar feelings, but he hushed me.

"No more. Today is not the day of the *nagual*, today is the day of the *tonal*," he said. "I put on my suit because today I am all *tonal*."

He stared at me. I was about to tell him that the subject was proving to be more difficult than anything he had ever explained to me; he seemed to have anticipated my words.

"It is difficult," he continued. "I know it. But considering that this is the final lid, the last stage of what I've been teaching you, it is not too farfetched to say that it envelops everything I mentioned since the first day we met."

We remained quiet for a long while. I felt that I had to wait for him to resume his explanation, but I had a sudden attack of appre-hension and hurriedly asked, "Are the *nagual* and the *tonal* within ourselves?"

He looked at me piercingly.

"Very difficult question," he said. "You yourself would say that they are within ourselves. I myself would say that they are not, but neither of us would be right. The *tonal* of your time calls for you to maintain that everything dealing with your feelings and thoughts takes place within yourself. The sorcerers' *tonal* says the opposite, everything is outside. Who's right? No one. Inside, outside, it doesn't really matter."

I raised a point. I said that when he talked about the "tonal" and the "nagual" it sounded as if there was still a third part. He had said that the "tonal" "forces us" to perform acts. I asked him to tell me who he was referring to as being forced.

He did not answer me directly.

"To explain all this is not that simple," he said. "No matter how clever the checkpoints of the *tonal* are the fact of the matter is that the *nagual* surfaces. Its coming to the surface is always inadvertent, though. The *tonal*'s great art is to suppress any manifestation of the *nagual* in such a manner that even if its presence should be the most obvious thing in the world, it is unnoticeable."

"For whom is it unnoticeable?"

He chuckled, shaking his head up and down. I pressed him for an answer.

"For the *tonal*," he said. "I'm speaking about it exclusively. I may go around in circles but that shouldn't surprise or annoy you. I warned you about the difficulty of understanding what I have to tell. I went through all that rigamarole because my *tonal* is aware that it is speaking about itself. In other words, my *tonal* is using itself in order to understand the information I want your *tonal* to be clear about. Let's say that the *tonal*, since it is keenly aware of how taxing it is to speak of itself, has created the terms 'I,' 'myself,' and so forth as a bal-ance and thanks to them it can talk with other *tonals*, or with itself, about itself.

"Now when I say that the *tonal* forces us to do something, I don't mean that there is a third party there. Obviously it forces itself to follow its own judgments.

"On certain occasions, however, or under certain special circumstances, something in the *tonal* itself becomes aware that there is more to us. It is like a voice that comes from the depths, the voice of the *nagual*. You see, the totality of ourselves is a natural condition which the *tonal* cannot obliterate altogether, and there are moments, especially in the life of a warrior, when the totality becomes apparent. At those moments one can surmise and assess what we really are.

"I was concerned with those jolts you have had, because that is the way the *nagual* surfaces. At those moments the *tonal* becomes aware of the totality of oneself. It is always a jolt because that awareness disrupts the lull. I call that awareness the totality of the being that is going to die. The idea is that at the moment of death the other member of the true pair, the *nagual*, becomes fully operative and the awareness and memories and perceptions stored in our calves and thighs, in our back and shoulders and neck, begin to expand and disintegrate. Like the beads of an endless broken necklace, they fall asunder without the binding force of life."

He looked at me. His eyes were peaceful. I felt ill at ease, stupid.

"The totality of ourselves is a very tacky affair," he said. "We need only a very small portion of it to fulfill the most complex tasks of life. Yet when we die, we die with the totality of ourselves. A sorcerer asks the question, 'If we're going to die with the totality of ourselves, why not, then, live with that totality?' "

He signaled me with his head to watch the scores of people that went by.

"They're all *tonal*," he said. "I am going to single some of them out so your *tonal* will assess them, and in assessing them it will assess itself."

He directed my attention to two old ladies that had emerged from the church. They stood at the top of the limestone steps for a moment and then began to walk down with infinite care, resting on every step.

"Watch those two women very carefully," he said. "But don't see them as persons, or as faces that hold things in common with us; see them as *tonals*."

The two women got to the bottom of the steps. They moved as if the rough gravel were marbles and they were about to roll and lose their balance on them. They walked arm in arm, propping each other up with the weight of their bodies.

"Look at them!" don Juan said in a low voice. "Those women are the best example of the most miserable *tonal* one can find."

I noticed that the two women were small-boned but fat. They were perhaps in their early fifties. They had a painful look in their faces, as if walking down the church steps had been beyond their strength.

They were in front of us; they vacillated for a moment and then they came to a halt. There was one more step on the gravel walk.

"Watch your step, ladies," don Juan shouted as he stood up dramatically.

The women looked at him, apparently confused by his sudden outburst.

"My mom broke her hip right there the other day," he added and dashed over to help them.

They thanked him profusely and he advised them that if they ever lost their balance and fell down, they had to remain motionless on the spot until the ambulance came. His tone was sincere and convincing. The women crossed themselves.

Don Juan sat down again. His eyes were beaming. He spoke softly.

"Those women are not that old and their bodies are not that weak, and yet they are decrepit. Everything about them is dreary — their clothes, their smell, their attitude. Why do you think that's so?"

"Maybe they were born that way," I said.

"No one is born that way. We make ourselves that way. The *tonal* of those women is weak and timid.

"I said that today was going to be the day of the *tonal;* I meant that today I want to deal with it exclusively. I also said that I had put on my suit for that specific purpose. With it I wanted to show you that a warrior treats his *tonal* in a very special manner. I've pointed out to you that my suit has been made to order and that everything I have on today fits me to perfection. It is not my vanity that I wanted to show, but my warrior's spirit, my warrior's *tonal*.

"Those two women gave you your first view of the *tonal* today. Life can be as merciless with you as it is with them, if you are careless with your *tonal*. I put myself as the counterpoint. If you understand correctly I should not need to stress this point."

I had a sudden attack of uncertainty and asked him to spell out what I should have understood.

I must have sounded desperate. He laughed out loud.

"Look at that young man in green pants and a pink shirt," don Juan whispered, pointing to a very thin and very dark complexioned, sharp-featured young man who was standing almost in front of us. He seemed to be undecided whether to go towards the church or towards the street. Twice he raised his hand in the direction of the church as though he were talking to himself and were about to start moving towards it. Then he stared at me with a blank expression.

"Look at the way he's dressed," don Juan said in a whisper. "Look at those shoes!"

The young man's clothes were tattered and wrinkled, and his shoes were in absolute pieces.

"He's obviously very poor," I said.

"Is that all you can say about him?" he asked.

I enumerated a series of reasons that might have accounted for the young man's shabbiness: poor health, bad luck, indolence, indifference to his personal appearance, or the chance that he may have just been released from prison.

Don Juan said that I was merely speculating, and that he was not interested in justifying anything by suggesting that the man was a victim of unconquerable forces.

"Maybe he's a secret agent made to look like a bum," I said jokingly.

The young man walked away towards the street with a disjointed gait.

"He's not made to look like a bum; he is a bum," don Juan said. "Look how weak his body is. His arms and legs are thin. He can hardly walk. No one can pretend to look that way. There is something definitely wrong with him, not his circumstances, though. I have to stress again that I want you to see that man as a *tonal*."

"What does it entail to see a man as a *tonal*?"

"It entails to cease judging him in a moral sense, or excusing him on the grounds that he is like a leaf at the mercy of the wind. In other words, it entails seeing a man without thinking that he is hopeless or helpless.

"You know exactly what I am talking about. You can assess that young man without condemning or forgiving him."

"He drinks too much," I said.

My statement was not volitional. I just made it without really knowing why. For an instant I even felt that someone standing behind me had voiced the words. I was moved to explain that my statement was another of my speculations.

"That was not the case," don Juan said. "Your tone of voice had a certainty that you lacked before. You didn't say, 'Maybe he's a drunkard.' "

I felt embarrassed although I could not exactly determine why. Don Juan laughed.

"You *saw* through the man," he said. "That was *seeing*. *Seeing* is like that. Statements are made with great certainty, and one doesn't know how it happened.

"You know that young man's *tonal* was shot, but you don't know how you know it."

I had to admit that somehow I had had that impression.

"You're right," don Juan said. "It doesn't really matter that he's young, he's as decrepit as the two women. Youth is in no way a barrier against the deterioration of the *tonal*.

"You thought that there might be a great many reasons for that man's condition. I find that there is only one, his *tonal*. It is not that his *tonal* is weak because he drinks; it is the other way around, he drinks because his *tonal* is weak. That weakness forces him to be what he is. But the same thing happens to all of us, in one form or another."

"But aren't you also justifying his behavior by saying that it's his *tonal?*"

"I'm giving you an explanation that you have never encountered before. It is not a justification or a condemnation, though. That young man's *tonal* is weak and timid. And yet he's not unique. All of us are more or less in the same boat."

At that moment a very large man passed in front of us heading towards the church. He was wearing an expensive dark gray business suit and was carrying a briefcase. The collar of his shirt was unbuttoned and his necktie loose. He was sweating profusely. He had a very light complexion which made the perspiration all the more obvious.

"Watch him!" don Juan ordered me.

The man's steps were small but heavy. There was a wobbling quality to his walking. He did not go up to the church; he circumvented it and disappeared behind it.

"There is no need to treat the body in such an awful manner," don Juan said with a note of scorn. "But the sad fact is that all of us have learned to perfection how to make our *tonal* weak. I have called that indulging."

He put his hand on my notebook and did not let me write any more. His rationale was that as long as I kept on taking notes I was incapable of concentrating. He suggested I should relax, shut off the internal dialogue and let go, merging with the person being observed.

I asked him to explain what he meant by "merging." He said there was no way to explain it, that it was something that the body felt or did when put in observational contact with other bodies. He then clarified the issue by saying that in the past he had called that process "seeing," and that it consisted of a lull of true silence within, followed by an outward elongation of something in the self, an elongation that met and merged with the other body, or with anything within one's field of awareness.

At that point I wanted to get back to my writing pad, but he stopped me and began to single out different people from the crowd that passed by.

He pointed out dozens of persons covering a wide range of types among men, women and children of various ages. Don Juan said that he had selected persons whose weak "tonal" could fit into a categorization scheme, and thus he had acquainted me with a preconceived variety of indulging.

I did not remember all the people he had pointed out and discussed. I complained that if I had taken notes I could have at least sketched out the intricacies of his schemata on indulging. As it was he did not want to repeat it or perhaps he did not remember it either.

He laughed and said that he did not remember it, because in the life of a sorcerer it was the "nagual" that was accountable for creativity.

He looked at the sky and said that it was getting late, and that from that moment on we were going to change direction. Instead of weak "tonals" we were going to wait for the appearance of a "proper tonal." He added that only a warrior had a "proper tonal," and that the average man, at best, could have a "right tonal."

After a few minutes' wait he slapped his thigh and chuckled.

"Look who's coming now," he said, pointing to the street with a movement of his chin. "It is as if they were made to order."

I saw three male Indians approaching. They had on some short brown woolen ponchos, white pants that came to their mid calf, long-sleeved white tops, dirty worn-out sandals and old straw hats. Each of them carried a bundle tied to his back.

Don Juan stood up and went to meet them. He spoke to them. They seemed surprised and surrounded him. They smiled at him. He was apparently telling them something about me; the three of them turned around and smiled at me. They were about ten or twelve feet away; I listened carefully but I could not hear what they were saying.

Don Juan reached in his pocket and handed them some bills. They appeared to be pleased; they moved their feet nervously. I liked them very much. They looked like children. All of them had small white teeth and very pleasing mild features. One, by all appearances the oldest, had whiskers. His eyes were tired but very kind. He took off his hat and came closer to the bench. The others followed him. The three of them greeted me in unison. We shook hands. Don Juan told me to give them some money. They thanked me and after a polite silence they said good-by. Don Juan sat back down on the bench and we watched them disappear in the crowd.

I told don Juan that for some strange reason I had liked them very much.

"It isn't so strange," he said. "You must've felt that their *tonal* is just right. It is right, but not for our time.

"You probably felt they were like children. They are. And that is very tough. I understand them better than you, thus I couldn't help but feel a tinge of sadness. Indians are like dogs, they have nothing. But that is the nature of their fortune and I shouldn't feel sad. My sadness, of course, is my own way of indulging."

"Where are they from, don Juan?"

"From the Sierras. They've come here to seek their fortune. They want to become merchants. They're brothers. I told them that I also came from the Sierras and I'm a merchant myself. I said that you were my partner. The money we gave them was a token; a warrior should give tokens like that all the time. They no doubt need the money, but need should not be an essential consideration for a token. The thing to look for is feeling. I personally was moved by those three.

"Indians are the losers of our time. Their downfall began with the Spaniards and now under the reign of their descendants the Indians have lost everything. It is not an exaggeration to say that the Indians have lost their *tonal*."

"Is that a metaphor, don Juan?"

"No. It is a fact. The *tonal* is very vulnerable. It cannot withstand maltreatment. The white man, from the day he set foot on this land, has systematically destroyed not only the Indian *tonal* of the time, but also the personal *tonal* of every Indian. One can easily surmise that for the poor average Indian the reign of the white man has been sheer hell. And yet the irony is that for another kind of Indian it has been sheer bliss."

"Who are you talking about? What kind of Indian is that?"

"The sorcerer. For the sorcerer the Conquest was the challenge of a lifetime. They were the only ones who were not destroyed by it but adapted to it and used it to their ultimate advantage."

"How was that possible, don Juan? I was under the impression that the Spaniards left no stone unturned."

"Let's say that they turned over all the stones that were within the limits of their own *tonal*. In the Indian life, however, there were things that were incomprehensible to the white man; those things he did not even notice. Perhaps it was the sheer luck of the sorcerers, or perhaps it was their knowledge that saved them. After the *tonal* of the time and the personal *tonal* of every Indian was obliterated, the sorcerers found themselves holding on to the only thing left uncontested, the *nagual*. In other words, their *tonal* took refuge in their *nagual*. This couldn't have happened had it not been for the excruciating conditions of a vanquished people. The men of knowledge of today are the product of those conditions and are the ultimate connoisseurs of the *nagual* since they were left there thoroughly alone. There, the white man has never ventured. In fact, he doesn't even have the idea it exists."

I felt compelled at that point to present an argument. I sincerely contended that in European thought we had accounted for what he called the "nagual." I brought in the concept of the Transcendental Ego, or the unobserved observer present in all our thoughts, perceptions and feelings. I explained to don Juan that the individual could perceive or intuit himself, as a self, through the Transcendental Ego, because this was the only thing capable of judgment, capable of disclosing reality within the realm of its consciousness.

Don Juan was unruffled. He laughed.

"Disclosing reality," he said, mimicking me. "That's the *tonal*."

I argued that the "tonal" may be called the Empirical Ego found in one's passing stream of consciousness or experience, while the Transcendental Ego was found behind that stream.

"Watching, I suppose," he said mockingly.

"That's right. Watching itself," I said.

"I hear you talking," he said. "But you're saying nothing. The *nagual* is not experience or intuition or consciousness. Those terms and everything else you may care to say are only items on the island of the *tonal*. The *nagual*, on the other hand, is only effect. The *tonal* begins at birth and ends at death, but the *nagual* never ends. The *nagual* has no limit. I've said that the *nagual* is where power hovers; that was only a way of alluding to it. By reasons of its effect, perhaps the *nagual* can be best understood in terms of power. For instance, when you felt numb and couldn't talk earlier today, I was actually soothing you; that is, my *nagual* was acting upon you."

"How was that possible, don Juan?"

"You won't believe this, but no one knows how. All I know is that I wanted your undivided attention and then my *nagual* went to work on you. I know that much because I can witness its effect, but I don't know how it works."

He was quiet for a while. I wanted to keep on the same topic. I attempted to ask a question; he silenced me.

"One can say that the *nagual* accounts for creativity," he finally said and looked at me piercingly. "The *nagual* is the only part of us that can create."

He remained quiet, looking at me. I felt he was definitely leading me into an area I had wished he would elucidate further. He had said that the "tonal" did not create anything, but only witnessed and assessed. I asked how he explained the fact that we construct superb structures and machines.

"That's not creativity," he said. "That's only molding. We can mold anything with our hands, personally or in conjunction with the hands of other *tonals*. A group of *tonals* can mold anything, superb structures as you said."

"But what's creativity then, don Juan?"

He stared at me, squinting his eyes. He chuckled softly, lifted his right hand over his head and twisted his wrist with a sharp jerk, as if he were turning a door knob.

"Creativity is this," he said and brought his hand with a cupped palm to the level of my eyes.

It took me an incredibly long time to focus my eyes on his hand. I felt that a transparent membrane was holding my whole body in a fixed position and that I had to break it in order to place my sight on his hand.

I struggled until beads of perspiration ran into my eyes. Finally I heard or felt a pop and my eyes and head jerked free.

On his right palm there was the most curious rodent I had ever seen. It looked like a bushy-tailed squirrel. The tail, however, was more like a porcupine's. It had stiff quills.

"Touch it!" don Juan said softly.

I automatically obeyed him and ran my finger on its soft back. Don Juan brought his hand closer to my eyes and then I noticed something that threw me into nervous spasms. The squirrel had eyeglasses and big teeth.

"It looks like a Japanese," I said and began to laugh hysterically.

The rodent then started to grow in don Juan's palm. And while my eyes were still filled with tears of laughter, the rodent became so enormous that it disappeared. It literally went out of the frame of my vision. It happened so rapidly that I was caught in the middle of a spasm of laughter. When I looked again, or when I wiped my eyes and focused them properly, I was looking at don Juan. He was sitting on the bench and I was standing in front of him, although I did not remember having stood up.

For a moment my nervousness was uncontainable. Don Juan calmly got up, forced me to sit, propped my chin between the bicep and forearm of his left arm and hit me on the very top of my head with the knuckles of his right hand. The effect was like the jolt of an electric current. It calmed me down immediately.

There were so many things that I wanted to ask. But my words could not wade through all those thoughts. I then became keenly aware that I had lost control over my vocal cords. I did not want to struggle to speak, however, and leaned against the back of the bench. Don Juan said forcefully that I had to pull myself together and stop indulging. I felt a bit dizzy. He imperatively ordered me to write my notes and handed me my pad and pencil after picking them up from underneath the bench.

I made a supreme effort to say something and again I had the clear sensation that a membrane was enveloping me. I puffed and groaned for a moment, while don Juan laughed, until I heard or felt another pop.

I began to write immediately. Don Juan spoke as if he were dictating to me.

"One of the acts of a warrior is never to let anything affect him," he said. "Thus, a warrior may be seeing the devil himself, but he won't let anyone know that. The control of a warrior has to be impeccable."

He waited until I had finished writing and then asked me laughingly, "Did you get all that?"

I suggested that we should go to a restaurant and have dinner. I was famished. He said that we had to stay until the "proper tonal" appeared. He added in a serious tone that if the "proper tonal" did not come that day we had to remain on the bench until it cared to show up.

"What is a *proper tonal?*" I asked.

"A *tonal* that is just right, balanced and harmonious. You are supposed to find one today, or rather your power is supposed to bring one to us."

"But how can I tell it apart from other *tonals?*"

"Never mind that. I will point it out to you."

"What is it like, don Juan?"

"Hard to tell. It depends on you. This is a show for you, therefore you will set up those conditions yourself."

"How?"

"I don't know that. Your power, your *nagual*, will do that.

"There are, roughly speaking, two sides to every *tonal*. One is the outer part, the fringe, the surface of the island. That's the part related to action and acting, the rugged side. The other part is the decision and judgment, the inner *tonal*, softer, more delicate and more complex.

"The *proper tonal* is a *tonal* where the two levels are in perfect harmony and balance."

Don Juan stopped talking. It was fairly dark by then and I had a hard time taking notes. He told me to stretch and relax. He said that it had been quite an exhausting day but very prolific and that he was sure the "proper tonal" would show up.

Dozens of people went by. We sat in a relaxed silence for ten or fifteen minutes. Then don Juan stood up abruptly.

"By golly you've done it! Look what's coming there. A girl!"

He pointed with a nod of his head to a young woman who was crossing the park and was approaching the vicinity of our bench. Don Juan said that that young woman was the "proper tonal" and that if she would stop to talk to either one of us it would be an extraordinary omen and we would have to do whatever she wanted.

I could not clearly distinguish the young woman's features, although there was still enough light. She came within a couple of feet but went by without looking at us. Don Juan ordered me in a whisper to get up and go talk to her.

I ran after her and asked for directions. I got very close to her. She was young, perhaps in her mid-twenties, of medium height, very attractive and well-groomed. Her eyes were clear and peaceful. She smiled at me as I spoke. There was something winning about her. I liked her as much as I had liked the three Indians.

I went back to the bench and sat down.

"Is she a warrior?" I asked.

"Not quite," don Juan said. "Your power is not that keen yet to bring a warrior. But she's a just right *tonal*. One that could turn into a *proper tonal*. Warriors come from that stock."

His statements aroused my curiosity. I asked him if women could be warriors. He looked at me, apparently baffled by my question.

"Of course they can," he said, "and they are even better equipped for the path of knowledge than men. But then men are a bit more resilient. I would say, however, that, all in all, women have a slight advantage."

I said that it puzzled me that we had never talked about women in relation to his knowledge.

"You're a man," he said, "therefore I use the masculine gender when I talk to you. That's all. The rest is the same."

I wanted to question him further but he made a gesture to close the topic. He looked up. The sky was almost black. The banks of clouds looked extremely dark. There were still, however, some areas where the clouds were slightly orange.

"The end of the day is your best time," don Juan said. "The appearance of that young woman at the very edge of the day is an omen. We were talking about the *tonal*, therefore it is an omen about your *tonal*."

"What does the omen mean, don Juan?"

"It means that you have very little time left to organize your arrangements. Any arrangements that you might have constructed have to be viable arrangements because you don't have time to make new ones. Your arrangements must work now, or they are not arrangements at all.

"I suggest that when you go back home you check your lines and make sure they are strong. You will need them."

"What's going to happen to me, don Juan?"

"Years ago you bid for power. You have followed the hardships of learning faithfully, without fretting or rushing. You are now at the edge of the day."

"What does that mean?"

"For a *proper tonal* everything on the island of the *tonal* is a challenge. Another way of saying it is that for a warrior everything in this world is a challenge. The greatest challenge of all, of course, is his bid for power. But power comes from the *nagual*, and when a warrior finds himself at the edge of the day it means that the hour of the *nagual* is approaching, the warrior's hour of power."

"I still don't understand the meaning of all this, don Juan. Does it mean that I am going to die soon?"

"If you're stupid, you will," he retorted cuttingly. "But putting it in milder terms, it means that you're about to shiver in your pants. You bid for power once and that bidding is irreversible. I won't say that you're about to fulfill your destiny, because there is no destiny. The only thing that one can say then is that you're about to fulfill your power. The omen was clear. That young woman came to you at the edge of the day. You have little time left, and none of it for crap. A fine state. I would say that the best of us always comes out when we are against the wall, when we feel the sword dangling overhead. Personally, I wouldn't have it any other way."

SHRINKING THE TONAL

On Wednesday morning I left my hotel around nine forty-five. I walked slowly, allowing myself fifteen minutes to reach the place where don Juan and I had agreed to meet. He had picked a corner on the Paseo de la Reforma, five or six blocks away, in front of the ticket office of an airline.

I had just finished eating breakfast with a friend of mine. He had wanted to walk with me but I had insinuated that I was going to meet a girl. I deliberately walked on the opposite side of the street from where the airline office was. I had the nagging suspicion that my friend, who had always wanted me to introduce him to don Juan, knew that I was going to meet him and might be following me. I was afraid that if I turned around I would find him behind me.

I saw don Juan at a magazine stand, on the other side of the street. I started to cross over but had to stop on the divider and wait there until it was safe to walk all the way across the wide boulevard. I turned around casually to see if my friend was following me. He was standing on the corner behind me. He smiled sheepishly and waved his hand, as if telling me that he had been incapable of controlling himself. I dashed across the street without giving him time to catch up with me.

Don Juan seemed to be aware of my predicament. When I reached him, he gave a furtive glance over my shoulder.

"He's coming," he said. "We'd better go down the side street."

He pointed to a street which cut diagonally into the Paseo de la

Reforma at the point where we were standing. I quickly oriented myself. I had never been on that street, but two days before I had been in the airline ticket office. I knew its peculiar layout. The office was on the pointed corner made by the two streets. It had a door opening onto each street, and the distance between the two doors must have been about ten to twelve feet. There was an aisle through the office from door to door, and one could easily go from one street to the other. There were desks on one side of that pathway and a large round counter with clerks and cashiers on the other side. The day I had been there, the place had been filled with people.

I wanted to hurry up, perhaps even run, but don Juan's pace was relaxed. As we reached the office door, on the diagonal street, I knew, without having to turn around, that my friend had also run across the boulevard and was about to turn into the street where we were walking. I looked at don Juan, hoping that he had a solution. He shrugged his shoulders. I felt annoyed and could not think of anything myself, short of punching my friend in the nose. I must have sighed or exhaled at that very moment, because the next thing I felt was sudden loss of air due to a formidable shove that don Juan had given me, which sent me whirling through the door of the airline office. Propelled by his tremendous push, I practically flew into the room. Don Juan had caught me so unprepared that my body had not offered any resistance; my fright merged with the actual jolt of his thrust. I automatically put my arms in front of me to protect my face. The force of don Juan's shove had been so great that saliva flew out of my mouth and I experienced a mild vertigo as I stumbled inside the room. I nearly lost my balance and had to make a supreme effort not to fall down. I twirled around a couple of times; it seemed that the speed of my movements made the scene blurry. I vaguely noticed a crowd of customers conducting their business. I felt extremely embarrassed. I knew that everyone was looking at me as I reeled across the room. The idea that I was making a fool out of myself was more than discomforting. A series of thoughts flashed through my mind. I had the certainty that I was going to fall on my face. Or I would bump into a customer, perhaps an old lady, who would be injured by the impact. Or worse yet, the glass door at the other end would be closed and I would smash against it.

In a dazed state I reached the door to the Paseo de la Reforma. It was open and I stepped out. My preoccupation of the moment was that I had to keep cool, turn to my right and walk on the boulevard towards downtown as if nothing had happened. I was sure that don Juan would join me and that perhaps my friend might have kept on walking along the diagonal street.

I opened my eyes, or rather I focused them on the area in front of me. I had a long moment of numbness before I fully realized what had happened. I was not on the Paseo de la Reforma, as I should have been, but in the Lagunilla market one and a half miles away.

What I experienced at the moment of that realization was such an intense astonishment that all I could do was stare, stupefied.

I looked around in order to orient myself. I realized that I was actually standing very close to where I had met don Juan on my first day in Mexico City. Perhaps I was even on the same spot. The stands that sold old coins were five feet away. I made a supreme effort to take hold of myself. Obviously I had to be experiencing a hallucination. It could not possibly be any other way. I quickly turned to go back through the door into the office, but behind me there was only a row of stands with secondhand books and magazines. Don Juan was standing next to me, to my right. He had an enormous smile on his face.

There was a pressure in my head, a tickling feeling, as if carbonated soda were going through my nose. I was speechless. I tried to say something without success.

I clearly heard don Juan say that I should not try to talk or think, but I wanted to say something, anything. An awful nervousness was building up inside my chest. I felt tears rolling down my cheeks.

Don Juan did not shake me, as he usually does when I fall prey to an uncontrollable fear. Instead he patted me gently on the head.

"Now, now, little Carlos," he said. "Don't lose your marbles."

He held my face in his hands for an instant.

"Don't try to talk," he said.

He let my face go and pointed to what was taking place all around us.

"This is not for talking," he said. "This is only for watching. Watch! Watch everything!"

I was really crying. My reaction to my crying was very strange, however; I kept on weeping without any concern. It did not matter to me, at that moment, whether or not I was making a fool out of myself.

I looked around. Right in front of me there was a middle-aged man wearing a pink short-sleeved shirt and dark gray pants. He seemed to be an American. A chubby woman, apparently his wife, was holding on to his arm. The man was handling some coins, while a thirteen- or fourteen-year-old boy, perhaps the son of the proprietor, watched him. The boy followed every movement the older man made. Finally, the man put the coins back on the table and the boy immediately relaxed.

"Watch everything!" don Juan demanded again.

There was nothing unusual to watch. People were passing by, going in every direction. I turned around. A man, who appeared to run the magazine stand, was staring at me. He blinked repeatedly as if he were about to fall asleep. He seemed tired or sick and looked seedy.

I felt that there was nothing to watch, at least nothing of real consequence. I stared at the scene. I found that it was impossible to concentrate my attention on anything. Don Juan walked in a circle around me. He acted as if he were assessing something in me. He shook his head and puckered his lips.

"Come, come," he said, grabbing me gently by the arm. "It's time to walk."

As soon as we began to move I noticed that my body was very light. In fact, I felt that the soles of my feet were spongy. They had a peculiar rubbery, springing quality.

Don Juan must have been aware of my sensations; he held me tightly, as if not to let me escape; he pressed down on me, as though he were afraid I would move upwards beyond his reach, like a balloon.

Walking made me feel better. My nervousness gave way to a comfortable easiness.

Don Juan insisted again that I should observe everything. I told him that there was nothing I wanted to watch, that it made no difference to me what people were doing in the market, and that I did not want to feel like an idiot dutifully observing some moronic activity of someone buying coins and old books, while the real thing was escaping through my fingers.

"What is the real thing?" he asked.

I stopped walking and vehemently told him that the important thing was whatever he had done to make me perceive that I had covered the distance between the ticket office and the market in seconds.

At that point I began to shiver and felt I was going to get ill. Don Juan made me put my hands against my stomach.

He pointed all around him and stated again, in a matter-of-fact tone, that the mundane activity around us was the only thing of importance.

I felt annoyed with him. I had the physical feeling of spinning. I took a deep breath.

"What did you do, don Juan?" I asked with forced casualness.

With a reassuring tone he said that he could tell me about that any time, but that whatever was happening all around me was not ever going to be repeated. I had no quarrel with that. The activity I was witnessing obviously could not be repeated again in all its complexity. My point was that I could observe a very similar activity any time. On the other hand, the implication of having been transported over the distance, in whatever form, was of immeasurable significance.

When I voiced these opinions don Juan made his head shiver as if what he had heard me say was actually painful to him.

We walked in silence for a moment. My body was feverish. I noticed that the palms of my hands and the soles of my feet were burning hot. The same unusual heat also seemed to be localized in my nostrils and eyelids.

"What did you do, don Juan?" I asked him pleadingly.

He did not answer me but patted me on the chest and laughed. He said that men were very frail creatures, who made themselves even more frail with their indulging. In a very serious tone he exhorted me not to feel that I was about to perish but to push myself beyond my limits and to simply engage my attention on the world around me.

We continued walking at a very slow pace. My preoccupation was paramount. I could not pay attention to anything. Don Juan stopped and seemed to deliberate whether or not to speak. He opened his mouth to say something, but then he appeared to change his mind and we began to walk again.

"What happened is that you came here," he said abruptly as he turned and stared at me.

"How did that happen?"

He said that he did not know, and that the only thing he did know was that I had selected that place myself.

Our impasse became even more hopeless as we kept on talking. I wanted to know the steps and he insisted that the selection of the place was the only thing we could discuss, and since I did not know why I had chosen it, there was essentially nothing to talk about. He criticized, without getting angry, my obsession to reason out everything as an unnecessary indulging. He said that it was simpler and more effective just to act, without seeking explanations, and that by talking about my experience and by thinking about it I was dissipating it.

After a few moments he said that we had to leave that place because I had spoiled it and it would become increasingly injurious to me.

We left the market and walked to the Alameda Park. I was exhausted. I plunked down on a bench. It was only then that it occurred to me to look at my watch. It was 10:20 A.M. I had to make quite an effort in order to focus my attention. I did not remember the exact time when I had met don Juan. I calculated that it must have been around ten. And it could not have taken us more than ten minutes to walk from the market to the park, which left only ten minutes unaccounted for.

I told don Juan about my calculations. He smiled. I had the certainty that his smile hid his contempt for me, yet there was nothing in his face to betray that feeling.

"You think I'm a hopeless idiot, don't you, don Juan?"

"Ah ha!" he said and jumped to his feet.

His reaction was so unexpected that I also jumped up at the same time.

"Tell me exactly what you think my feelings are," he said emphatically.

I felt I knew his feelings. It was as if I were feeling them myself. But when I tried to say what I felt, I realized I could not talk about it. To speak required a tremendous effort.

Don Juan said that I did not have enough power yet to "see" him. But I could certainly "see" enough to find myself suitable explanations for what was happening.

"Don't be bashful," he said. "Tell me exactly what you *see*."

I had a sudden and strange thought, very similar to thoughts that usually come to my mind just before falling asleep. It was more than a thought; a complete image would be a better description of it. I saw a tableau containing various personages. The one which was directly in front of me was a man sitting behind a window frame. The area beyond the frame was diffuse, but the frame and the man were crystal clear. He was looking at me; his head was turned slightly to his left, so he was actually looking askance at me. I could see his eyes moving to keep me within focus. He was leaning on the windowsill with his right elbow. His hand was clenched into a fist and his muscles were contracted.

To the left of the man there was another image in the tableau. It was a flying lion. That is, the head and the mane were those of a lion but the lower part of its body belonged to a curly white French poodle.

I was about to focus my attention on it, when the man made a smacking sound with his lips and stuck his head and trunk out of the window. His whole body emerged as if something were pushing him. He hung for a moment, grabbing the windowsill with the tips of his fingers as he swung like a pendulum. Then he let go.

I experienced in my own body the sensation of falling. It was not a plummeting down, but a soft descent, and then a cushioned floating. The man was weightless. He remained stationary for a moment and then he went out of sight as if an uncontrollable force had sipped him away through a crack in the tableau. An instant later he was back at the window looking askance at me. His right forearm was resting on the windowsill, only this time his hand was waving good-by to me.

Don Juan's comment was that my "seeing" was too elaborate.

"You can do better than that," he said. "You want me to explain what happened. Well, I want you to use your *seeing* to do that. You *saw*, but you *saw* crap. That kind of information is useless to a warrior. It would take too long to figure out what's what. *Seeing* must be direct, for a warrior can't use his time to unravel what he himself is *seeing*. *Seeing* is *seeing* because it cuts through all that nonsense."

I asked him if he thought that my vision had only been a hallucination and not really "seeing." He was convinced it had been "seeing" because of the intricacy of detail, but that it was inappropriate for the occasion.

"Do you think that my visions explain anything?" I asked.

"Sure they do. But I wouldn't try to unravel them if I were you. In the beginning *seeing* is confusing and it's easy to get lost in it. As the warrior gets tighter, however, his *seeing* becomes what it should be, a direct knowing."

As don Juan spoke I had one of those peculiar lapses of feelings and I clearly sensed that I was about to unveil something which I already knew, a thing which eluded me by turning into something very blurry. I became aware that I was involved in a struggle. The more I tried to define or reach that elusive piece of knowledge the deeper it sank.

"That *seeing* was too . . . too visionary," don Juan said.

The sound of his voice shook me.

"A warrior asks a question, and through his *seeing* he gets an answer, but the answer is simple, never embellished to the point of flying French poodles."

We laughed at the image. And half jokingly I told him that he was too strict, that anyone going through what I had gone through that morning deserved a bit of leniency.

"That is the easy way out," he said. "That is the indulging way. You hinge the world on the feeling that everything is too much for you. You're not living like a warrior."

I told him that there were so many facets of what he called a warrior's way that it was impossible to fulfill all of them, and that the meaning of it became clear only as I encountered new instances where I had to apply it.

"A rule of thumb for a warrior," he said, "is that he makes his decisions so carefully that nothing that may happen as a result of them can surprise him, much less drain his power.

"To be a warrior means to be humble and alert. Today you were supposed to watch the scene which was unfolding in front of your eyes, not to ponder how all that was possible. You focused your attention on the wrong place. If I wanted to be lenient with you I could easily say that since this was the first time it had happened to you, you were not prepared. But that's not permissible, because you came here as a warrior, ready to die; therefore, what happened to you today shouldn't have caught you with your pants down."

I conceded that my tendency was to indulge in fear and bewilderment.

"Let's say that a rule of thumb for you should be that when you come to see me you should come prepared to die," he said. "If you come here ready to die, there shouldn't be any pitfalls, or any unwelcome surprises, or any unnecessary acts. Everything should gently fall into place because you're expecting nothing."

"That's easy to say, don Juan. I am on the receiving end, though. I am the one who has to live with all this."

"It is not that you have to live with all this. You are all this. You're not just tolerating it for the time being. Your decision to join forces with this evil world of sorcery should have burned all the lingering feelings of confusion and should give you the spunk to claim all this as your world."

I felt embarrassed and sad. Don Juan's actions, no matter how prepared I was, taxed me in such a way that every time I came in contact with him I was left with no other recourse but to act and feel like a half-rational, nagging person. I had a surge of wrath and did not want to write any more. At that moment I wanted to rip my notes and throw everything in the trash can. And I would have done that had it not been for don Juan, who laughed and held my arm, restraining me.

In a mocking tone he said that my "tonal" was about to fool itself again. He recommended that I should go to the fountain and splash water on my neck and ears.

The water soothed me. We were quiet for a long time.

"Write, write," don Juan coaxed me in a friendly tone. "Let's say that your notebook is the only sorcery you have. To rip it up is another way of opening yourself to your death. It will be another of your tantrums, a flashy tantrum at best, not a change. A warrior doesn't ever leave the island of the *tonal*. He uses it."

He pointed all around me with a quick movement of his hand and then touched my notebook.

"This is your world. You can't renounce it. It is useless to get angry and feel disappointed with oneself. All that that proves is that one's *tonal* is involved in an internal battle; a battle within one's *tonal* is one of the most inane contests I can think of. The tight life of a warrior is designed to end that struggle. From the beginning I have taught you to avoid wear and tear. Now there is no longer a war within you, not as it used to be, because the warrior's way is harmony—the harmony between actions and decisions, at first, and then the harmony between *tonal* and *nagual*.

"Throughout the time I have known you, I have talked to both your *tonal* and your *nagual*. That is the way the instruction should be conducted.

"In the beginning, one has to talk to the *tonal*. It is the *tonal* that has to relinquish control. But it should be made to do so gladly. For example, your *tonal* has relinquished some controls without much struggle, because it became clear to it that, had it remained the way it was, the totality of you would be dead by now. In other words, the *tonal* is made to give up unnecessary things like self-importance and indulging, which only plunge it into boredom. The whole trouble is that the *tonal* clings to those things when it should be glad to rid itself of that crap. The task then is to convince the *tonal* to become free and fluid. That's what a sorcerer needs before anything else, a strong, free *tonal*. The stronger it gets the less it clings to its doings, and the easier it is to shrink it. So what happened this morning was that I saw the opportunity to shrink your *tonal*. For an instant, you were absent-minded, hurrying, not thinking, and I grabbed that moment to shove you.

"The *tonal* shrinks at given times, especially when it is embarrassed. In fact, one of the features of the *tonal* is its shyness. Its shyness is not really an issue. But there are certain instances when the *tonal* is taken by surprise, and its shyness unavoidably makes it shrink.

"This morning I plucked my cubic centimeter of chance. I noticed the open door of that office and gave you a shove. A shove is then the technique for shrinking the *tonal*. One must shove at the precise instant; for that, of course, one must know how to *see*.

"Once the man has been shoved and his *tonal* has shrunk, his *nagual*, if it is already in motion, no matter how small this motion is, will take over and achieve extraordinary deeds. Your *nagual* took over this morning and you ended up in the market."

He remained silent for a moment. He seemed to be waiting for questions. We looked at each other.

"I really don't know how," he said as if reading my mind. "All I know is that the *nagual* is capable of inconceivable feats.

"This morning I asked you to watch. That scene in front of you, whatever it may have been, had an incalculable value for you. But instead of following my advice, you indulged in self-pity and confusion and did not watch.

"For a while you were all *nagual* and could not talk. That was the time to watch. Then, little by little, your *tonal* took over again; and rather than plunging you into a deadly battle between your *tonal* and *nagual*, I walked you here."

"What was there in that scene, don Juan? What was so important?"

"I don't know. It wasn't happening to me."

"What do you mean?"

"It was your experience, not mine."

"But you were with me. Weren't you?"

"No. I wasn't. You were alone. I repeatedly told you to watch everything, because that scene was only for you."

"But you were next to me, don Juan."

"No. I wasn't. But it's useless to talk about it. Whatever I may say doesn't make sense, because during those moments we were in *nagual*'s time. The affairs of the *nagual* can be witnessed only with the body, not the reason."

"If you were not with me, don Juan, who or what was the person I witnessed as you?"

"It was me and yet I wasn't there."

"Where were you then?"

"I was with you, but not there. Let's say that I was around you but not in the particular place where your *nagual* had taken you."

"You mean you didn't know that we were at the market?"

"No, I didn't. I just tagged along in order not to lose you."

"This is truly awesome, don Juan."

"We were in *nagual*'s time, and there is nothing awesome about it. We are capable of much more than that. That is the nature of us as luminous beings. Our flaw is to insist on remaining on our monotonous, tiring, but convenient island. The *tonal* is the villain and it shouldn't be."

I described the little bit I remembered. He wanted to know if I had witnessed any features of the sky, such as daylight, clouds, the sun. Or if I had heard noises of any sort. Or if I had caught sight of unusual people or events. He wanted to know if there had been any fights. Or if people were yelling, and if they were, what they had said.

I could not answer any of his questions. The plain truth was that I had accepted the event at its apparent face value, admitting as a truism that I had "flown" over a considerable distance in one or two seconds, and that thanks to don Juan's knowledge, whatever it may have been, I had landed in all my material corporeality inside the market.

My reactions were a direct corollary of such an interpretation. I wanted to know the procedures, the member's knowledge, the "how to do it." Therefore, I did not care to observe what I was convinced were the ordinary happenings of a mundane event.

"Do you think that people saw me in the market?" I asked.

Don Juan did not answer. He laughed and tapped me lightly with his fist.

I tried to remember if I had actually had any physical contact with people. My memory failed me.

"What did the people in the airline office see when I stumbled in?" I asked.

"They probably saw a man staggering from one door to the other."

"But did they see me disappear into thin air?"

"That is taken care of by the *nagual*. I don't know how. All I can tell you is that we are fluid, luminous beings made out of fibers. The agreement that we are solid objects is the *tonal*'s doing. When the *nagual* shrinks, extraordinary things are possible. But they are only extraordinary for the *tonal*.

"For the *nagual*, it's nothing to move the way you did this morning. Especially for your *nagual*, which is already capable of difficult ploys. As a matter of fact, it has plunged into something terribly weird. Can you feel what it is?"

A million questions and feelings came to me all at once. It was as if a gust of wind had blown off my veneer of composure. I shivered. My body felt it was at the edge of an abyss. I struggled with some mysterious but concrete piece of knowledge. It was as if I were on the verge of being shown something, and yet some stubborn part of me insisted on blowing a cloud over it. The struggle made me numb by degrees, until I could not feel my body. My mouth was open and my eyes were half closed. I had the feeling I could see my face getting harder and harder until it was the face of a dried corpse with the yellowish skin stuck tight to the skull.

The next thing I felt was a jolt. Don Juan was standing by me holding an empty bucket of water. He had soaked me. I coughed and wiped the water from my face and felt another cold seizure in my back. I jumped up from the bench. Don Juan had poured some water down my neck.

There was a group of children looking at me and laughing. Don Juan smiled at me. He held my notebook and said that we had better go to my hotel so I could change my clothes. He led me out of the park. We stood on the curb for a moment before a cab came along.

Hours later, after eating lunch and resting, don Juan and I sat on his favorite bench in the park by the church. In an oblique manner we got to the topic of my strange reaction. He seemed to be very cautious. He did not confront me directly with it.

"Things like that are known to happen," he said. "The *nagual*, once it learns to surface, may cause a great damage to the *tonal* by coming out without any control. Your case is special, though. You are given to indulging in such an exaggerated manner that you would die and not even mind it, or worse yet, not even be aware that you're dying."

I told him that my reaction began when he had asked me if I could feel what my "nagual" had done I thought I knew exactly what he was alluding to, but when I tried to describe what it was, I found I could not think clearly. I experienced a sensation of lightheadedness, almost an indifference, as if I did not really care about anything. Then that sensation grew into a mesmerizing concentration. It was as though all of me was slowly being sucked out. What attracted and trapped my attention was the clear sensation that a portentous secret was about to be revealed to me and I did not want anything to interfere with such a revelation.

"What was going to be revealed to you was your death," don Juan said. "That's the danger of indulging. Especially for you, since you are naturally so exaggerated. Your *tonal* is so given to indulging that it threatens the totality of you. This is a terrible way of being."

"What can I do?"

"Your *tonal* has to be convinced with reasons, your *nagual* with actions, until one props the other. As I have told you, the *tonal* rules, and yet it is very vulnerable. The *nagual*, on the other hand, never, or almost never, acts out; but when it does, it terrifies the *tonal*.

"This morning your *tonal* got frightened and began to shrink by itself, and then your *nagual* began to take over.

"I had to borrow a bucket from one of the photographers in the park in order to whip your *nagual* like a bad dog back to its place. The *tonal* must be protected at any cost. The crown has to be taken away from it, but it must remain as the protected overseer.

"Any threat to the *tonal* always results in its death. And if the *tonal* dies, so does the whole man. Because of its inherent weakness the *tonal* is easily destroyed, and thus one of the balancing arts of the warrior is to make the *nagual* emerge in order to prop up the *tonal*. I say it is an art, because sorcerers know that only by boosting the *tonal* can the *nagual* emerge. See what I mean? That boosting is called personal power."

Don Juan stood up, stretched his arms and arched his back. I started to stand up myself, but he gently pushed me down.

"You must stay on this bench until twilight," he said. "I have to leave right away. Genaro is waiting for me in the mountains. So come to his house in three days and we will meet there."

"What are we going to do at don Genaro's house?" I asked.

"Depending on whether you have enough power," he said, "Genaro may show you the *nagual*."

There was one more thing that I had to voice at that point. I had to know whether his suit was a shocking device for me alone or was it actually part of his life. Never had any of his acts caused so much havoc in me as his wearing a suit. It was not only the act in itself that was so awesome to me, but the fact that don Juan was elegant. His legs had a youthful agility. It was as if wearing shoes had shifted his point of balance and his steps were longer and more firm than usual.

"Do you wear a suit all the time?" I asked.

"Yes," he replied with a charming smile. "I have others, but I didn't want to wear a different suit today, because it would've scared you even more."

I did not know what to think. I felt that I had arrived at the end of my path. If don Juan could wear a suit and be elegant in it, anything was possible.

He seemed to enjoy my confusion and laughed.

"I'm a stockholder," he said in a mysterious but unaffected tone and walked away.

The next morning, on Thursday, I asked a friend of mine to walk with me from the door of the office where don Juan had pushed me to the Lagunilla market. We took the most direct route. It took us thirty-five minutes. Once we arrived there, I tried to orient myself. I failed. I walked into a clothing store at the very corner of the wide avenue where we were standing.

"Pardon me," I said to a young woman who was gently cleaning a hat with a duster. "Where are the stands of coins and secondhand books?"

"We don't have any," she said in a nasty tone.

"But I saw them, somewhere in this market, yesterday."

"No kidding," she said and walked behind the counter.

I ran after her and pleaded with her to tell me where they were. She looked me up and down.

"You couldn't have seen them yesterday," she said. "Those stands are assembled only on Sunday, right here along this wall. We don't have them the rest of the week."

"Only on Sunday?" I repeated mechanically.

"Yes. Only on Sunday. That's the way. The rest of the week they would interfere with the traffic."

She pointed to the wide avenue filled with cars.

IN NAGUAL'S TIME

I ran up a slope in front of don Genaro's house and saw don Juan and don Genaro sitting on a cleared area by the door. They smiled at me. There was such warmth and innocence in their smiles that my body experienced a state of immediate alarm. I automatically slowed down to a walk. I greeted them.

"How are you?" don Genaro asked me in such an affected tone that we all laughed.

"He's in very good shape," don Juan interjected before I could answer.

"I can see that," don Genaro retorted. "Look at that double chin! And look at those chunks of bacon fat on the jowls!"

Don Juan held his stomach as he laughed.

"Your face is round," don Genaro went on. "What have you been doing? Eating?"

Don Juan jokingly assured him that my life style required that I eat a great deal. In a most friendly way they teased me about my life, and then don Juan asked me to sit down between them. The sun had already set behind the huge range of mountains to the west.

"Where's your famous notebook?" don Genaro asked me, and when I got it out of my pocket he yelled, "Yippee!" and took it from my hands.

Obviously he had observed me with great care and knew my mannerisms to perfection. He held the notebook with both hands and played with it nervously, as if he did not know what to do with it.

Twice he seemed to be on the verge of throwing it away but appeared to contain himself. Then he held it against his knees and pretended to write feverishly in it, the way I do.

Don Juan laughed so hard that he was about to choke.

"What did you do after I left you?" don Juan asked after they had quieted down.

"I went to the market on Thursday," I said.

"What were you doing there? Retracing your steps?" he retorted.

Don Genaro fell backwards and with his lips made the dry sound of a head hitting the ground. He looked at me askance and winked.

"I had to do it," I said. "And I found out that on weekdays there are no stands that sell coins and secondhand books."

Both of them laughed. Then don Juan said that asking questions was not going to reveal anything new.

"What really took place, don Juan?" I asked.

"Believe me, there is no way of knowing that," he said dryly. "In those matters you and I are on equal ground. My advantage over you at this moment is that I know how to get to the *nagual*, and you don't. But once I have gotten there I have no more advantage and no more knowledge than you."

"Did I really land in the market, don Juan?" I asked.

"Of course. I've told you, the *nagual* is at the warrior's command. Isn't it so, Genaro?"

"Right!" don Genaro exclaimed in a booming voice and stood up in one single motion. It was as though his voice had pulled him from a lying position to a perfectly vertical one.

Don Juan was practically rolling on the ground laughing. Don Genaro, with a nonchalant air, took a comical bow and said good-by.

"Genaro will see you tomorrow morning," don Juan said. "Now you must sit here in total silence."

We did not say another word. After hours of silence I fell asleep.

I looked at my watch. It was almost six in the morning. Don Juan examined the solid mass of heavy white clouds over the eastern horizon and concluded that it was going to be an overcast day. Don

Genaro sniffed the air and added that it was also going to be hot and windless.

"How far are we going?" I asked.

"To those eucalyptus trees over there," don Genaro replied, pointing to what seemed to be a grove of trees about a mile away.

When we reached the trees I realized that it was not a grove; the eucalyptus had been planted in straight lines in order to mark the boundaries of fields cultivated with different crops. We walked along the edge of a corn field, along a line of enormous trees, thin and straight, over a hundred feet high, and arrived at an empty field. I figured that the crop must have just been harvested. There were only the dried stalks and leaves of some plants I did not recognize. I bent over to pick up a leaf but don Genaro stopped me. He held my arm with great force. I recoiled in pain and then I noticed that he had only placed his fingers gently on my arm.

He was definitely aware of what he had done and of what I was experiencing. He swiftly lifted his fingers off my arm and then again placed them gently on it. He repeated it once more and laughed like a delighted child when I winced. Then he turned his profile to me. His aquiline nose made him look like a bird, a bird with strange long white teeth.

In a soft voice don Juan told me not to touch anything. I asked him if he knew what kind of crop had been cultivated there. He seemed to be about to tell me, but don Genaro interceded and said that it was a field of worms.

Don Juan looked at me fixedly, without cracking a smile. Don Genaro's meaningless answer appeared to be a joke. I waited for a cue to start laughing, but they just stared at me.

"A field of gorgeous worms," don Genaro said. "Yes, what was grown here was the most delightful worms you've ever seen."

He turned to don Juan. They looked at each other for an instant.

"Isn't it so?" he asked.

"Absolutely true," don Juan said, and turning to me he added in a soft voice, "Genaro holds the baton today; only he can tell what's what, so do exactly as he says."

The idea that don Genaro had the control filled me with terror. I turned to don Juan to tell him about it; but before I had time to voice my words, don Genaro let out a long formidable scream; a yell so loud and frightening that I felt the back of my neck swell and my hair flowing out as if a wind were blowing it. I had an instant of complete disassociation and would have remained glued to the spot had it not been for don Juan, who with incredible speed and control turned my body around so my eyes could witness an inconceivable feat. Don Genaro was standing horizontally, about one hundred feet above the ground, on the trunk of a eucalyptus tree which was perhaps fifty yards away. That is, he was standing with his legs three feet apart, perpendicular to the tree. It was as if he had hooks on his shoes, and with them was capable of defying gravity. His arms were crossed over his chest and his back was turned to me.

I stared at him. I did not want to blink for fear of losing sight of him. I made a quick judgment and concluded that if I could maintain him within my field of vision I might detect a clue, a movement, a gesture, or anything that would help me understand what was taking place.

I felt don Juan's head next to my right ear and I heard him whisper that any attempt to explain was useless and idiotic. I heard him repeat, "Push your belly down, down."

It was a technique he had taught me, years before, to use in moments of great danger, fear, or stress. It consisted of pushing the diaphragm down while taking four sharp gasps of air through the mouth, followed by four deep inhalations and exhalations through the nose. He had explained that the gasps of air had to be felt as jolts in the middle part of the body, and that keeping the hands tightly clasped, covering the navel, gave strength to the midsection and helped to control the gasps and the deep inhalations, which had to be held for a count of eight as one pressed the diaphragm down. The exhalations were done twice through the nose and twice through the mouth in a slow or accelerated fashion, depending on one's preference.

I automatically obeyed don Juan. I did not dare, however, to take my eyes away from don Genaro. As I kept on breathing, my body relaxed and I was aware that don Juan was twisting my legs. Apparently when he had turned me around my right foot had caught in a clump of dirt and my leg was uncomfortably bent. When he straightened me out I realized that the shock of seeing don Genaro standing on the trunk of a tree had made me oblivious to my discomfort.

Don Juan whispered in my ear that I should not stare at don Genaro. I heard him say, "Blink, blink."

For a moment I felt reluctant. Don Juan commanded me again. I was convinced that the whole affair was somehow linked to me as the onlooker, and if I, as the sole witness of don Genaro's deed, had stopped looking at him he would have fallen to the ground or perhaps the whole scene would have vanished.

After an excruciatingly long period of immobility, don Genaro swiveled on his heels, forty-five degrees to his right, and began to walk up the trunk. His body shivered. I saw him take one small step after another until he had taken eight. He even circumvented a branch. Then, with his arms still crossed over his chest, he sat down on the trunk with his back to me. His legs dangled as if he were sitting on a chair, as if gravity had no effect on him. He then sort of walked on his seat, downwards. He reached a branch that was parallel to his body and leaned on it with his left arm and his head for a few seconds; he seemed to be leaning more for dramatic effect than for support. He then kept on moving on his seat, inching his way from the trunk onto the branch, until he had changed his position and was sitting as one might normally sit on a branch.

Don Juan giggled. I had a horrible taste in my mouth. I wanted to turn round and face don Juan, who was slightly behind me to my right, but I did not dare miss any of don Genaro's actions.

He dangled his feet for a while, then crossed them and swung them gently, and finally he slipped upwards back onto the trunk.

Don Juan took my head gently in both hands and twisted my neck to the left until my line of vision was parallel to the tree rather than perpendicular to it. Looking at don Genaro from that angle, he did not appear to be defying gravity. He was simply sitting on the trunk of a tree. I noticed then that if I stared and did not blink, the background became vague and diffuse, and the clarity of don Genaro's body became more intense; his shape became dominant, as if nothing else existed.

Don Genaro swiftly slid downward back onto the branch. He sat dangling his feet, like on a trapeze. Looking at him from a twisted perspective made both positions, especially sitting on the tree trunk, seem feasible.

Don Juan shifted my head to the right until it was resting on my shoulder. Don Genaro's position on the branch seemed perfectly normal, but when he moved onto the trunk again, I could not make the necessary perceptual adjustment and I saw him as if he were upside down, with his head towards the ground.

Don Genaro moved back and forth various times, and don Juan shifted my head from side to side every time don Genaro moved. The result of their manipulations was that I completely lost track of my normal perspective, and without it don Genaro's actions were not as awesome.

Don Genaro remained on the branch for a long time. Don Juan straightened my neck and whispered that don Genaro was about to descend. I heard him whisper in an imperative tone, "Press down, down."

I was in the middle of a fast exhalation when don Genaro's body seemed to be transfixed by some sort of tension; it glowed, became lax, swung backwards, and hung by the knees for a moment. His legs seemed to be so flaccid that they could not stay bent and he fell to the ground.

At the moment he began his downward fall, I also had the sensation of falling through endless space. My whole body experienced a painful and at the same time extremely pleasurable anguish; an anguish of such intensity and duration that my legs could no longer support the weight of my body and I fell down on the soft dirt. I could barely move my arms to buffer my fall. I was breathing so heavily that the soft dirt got into my nostrils and made them itch. I tried to get up; my muscles seemed to have lost their strength.

Don Juan and don Genaro came and stood over me. I heard their voices as if they were quite a distance from me, and yet I felt them pulling me. They must have lifted me up, each holding one of my arms and one of my legs, and carried me over a short distance. I was perfectly aware of the uncomfortable position of my neck and head, which hung limp. My eyes were open. I could see the ground and tufts of weeds passing under me. Finally, I had a cold seizure. Water entered into my mouth and nose and made me cough. My arms and legs moved frantically. I began to swim but the water was not deep enough and I found myself standing up in the shallow river where they had dumped me.

Don Juan and don Genaro laughed themselves silly. Don Juan rolled up his pants and came over closer to me; he looked me in the eye and said that I was not complete yet and pushed me gently back into the water. My body did not offer any resistance. I did not want to be dunked again but there was no way of connecting my volition to my muscles and I crumbled backwards. The coldness was even more intense. I quickly jumped up and scurried out on the opposite bank by mistake. Don Juan and don Genaro yelled and whistled and threw rocks into the bushes ahead of me, as though they were corralling a steer that was running astray. I crossed back over the river and sat on a rock next to them. Don Genaro handed me my clothes and then I noticed that I was naked, although I could not remember when or how I got my clothes off. I was dripping wet and did not want to put them on right away. Don Juan turned to don Genaro and in a booming tone said, "For heaven's sake, give the man a towel!" It took me a couple of seconds to realize the absurdity.

I felt very good. In fact, I was so happy that I did not want to talk. I had the certainty, however, that if I showed my euphoria they would have dumped me into the water again.

Don Genaro watched me. His eyes had the glint of a wild animal's. They pierced through me.

"Good for you," don Juan said to me all of a sudden. "You're contained now, but down by the eucalyptus trees you indulged like a son of a bitch."

I wanted to laugh hysterically. Don Juan's words seemed so utterly funny that I had to make a supreme effort to contain myself. And then some part of me flashed a command. An uncontrollable itching in the midsection of my body made me take off my clothes and plunge back into the water. I stayed in the river for about five minutes. The coldness restored my sense of sobriety. When I got out I was myself again.

"Good show," don Juan said, tapping me on the shoulder.

They led me back to the eucalyptus trees. As we walked, don Juan explained that my "tonal" had been dangerously vulnerable, and that the incongruity of don Genaro's acts seemed to be too much for it. He said that they had decided not to tamper with it any more and go back to don Genaro's house, but the fact that I knew I had to plunge myself into the river again had changed everything. He did not say, however, what they intended to do.

We stood in the middle of the field, on the same spot we had been before. Don Juan was to my right and don Genaro to my left. They both stood with their muscles tensed, in a state of alertness. They maintained that tenseness for about ten minutes. I shifted my eyes from one to the other. I thought that don Juan would cue me on what to do. I was right. At one moment he relaxed his body and kicked some hard clumps of dirt. Without looking at me, he said, "I think we'd better go." I automatically reasoned that don Genaro must have had the intention of giving me another demonstration of the "nagual" but had decided not to. I felt relieved. I waited another moment for a final confirmation. Don Genaro also eased off and then both of them took one step forward. I knew then that we were through there. But at the very instant I loosened up, don Genaro again let out his incredible yell.

I began to breathe frantically. I looked around. Don Genaro had disappeared. Don Juan was standing in front of me. His body convulsed with laughter. He turned to me.

"I'm sorry," he said in a whisper. "There's no other way."

I wanted to ask about don Genaro, but I felt that if I did not keep on breathing and pressing down on my diaphragm I would die. Don Juan pointed with his chin to a place behind me. Without moving my feet, I began to turn my head over my left shoulder. But before I could see what he was pointing at, don Juan jumped and stopped me. The force of his leap and the speed with which he grabbed me made me lose my balance. As I fell on my back I had the sensation that my startled reaction had been to grab on to don Juan and consequently I dragged him with me to the ground. But when I looked up, the impressions of my tactile and visual senses were in total disaccord. I saw don Juan standing over me laughing, while my body felt the unmistakable weight and pressure of another body on top of me, almost pinning me down.

Don Juan extended his hand and helped me get up. My bodily sensation was that he was lifting two bodies. He smiled knowingly and whispered that one should never turn to one's left when facing the "nagual." He said that the "nagual" was deadly and there was no need to make the risks more dangerous than they already were. He then gently turned me around and made me face an enormous eucalyptus tree. It was perhaps the oldest tree around. Its trunk was nearly twice as thick as any of the others. He pointed with his eyes to the top. Don Genaro was perched on a branch. He was facing me. I could see his eyes like two huge mirrors reflecting light. I did not want to look but don Juan insisted that I should not move my eyes away. In a very forceful whisper he ordered me to blink, and not to succumb to fright or indulgence.

I noticed that if I blinked steadily don Genaro's eyes were not so awesome. It was only when I stared that the glare of his eyes became maddening.

He squatted on the branch for a long time. Then, without moving his body at all, he jumped to the ground and landed, in the same squatting position, a couple of yards from where I was. I witnessed the complete sequence of his jump, and I knew that I had perceived more than my eyes had allowed me to catch. Don Genaro had not really jumped. Something had pushed him as if from behind and had made him glide on a parabolic course. The branch where he had been perched was possibly a hundred feet high, and the tree was located about a hundred and fifty feet away from me; thus, his body had to trace a parabola to land where it did. But the force needed to cover that distance was not the product of don Genaro's muscles; his body was "blown" away from the branch to the ground. At one point I was able to see the soles of his shoes and his rear as his body described the parabola. Then he landed gently, although his weight crumbled the hard clumps of dried dirt and even raised a bit of dust.

Don Juan giggled behind me. Don Genaro stood up as if nothing had happened and tugged the sleeve of my shirt to give me a signal that we were leaving.

No one spoke on the way to don Genaro's house. I felt lucid and composed. A couple of times don Juan stopped and examined my eyes by staring into them. He seemed satisfied. As soon as we arrived, don Genaro went behind the house. It was still early in the morning. Don Juan sat on the floor by the door and pointed to a place for me to sit. I was exhausted. I lay down and went out like a light.

I woke up when don Juan shook me. I tried to look at the time. My watch was missing. Don Juan pulled it from his shirt pocket and handed it to me. It was around 1:00 P.M. I looked up and our eyes met.

"No. There's no explanation," he said, turning away from me. "The *nagual* is only for witnessing."

I went around the house looking for don Genaro; he was not there. I came back to the front. Don Juan had made me something to eat. After I had finished eating he began to talk.

"When one is dealing with the *nagual*, one should never look into it directly," he said. "You were peering at it this morning, and therefore you were sapped. The only way to look at the *nagual* is as if it were a common affair. One must blink in order to break the fixation. Our eyes are the eyes of the *tonal*, or perhaps it would be more accurate to say that our eyes have been trained by the *tonal*, therefore the *tonal* claims them. One of the sources of your bafflement and discomfort is that your *tonal* doesn't let go of your eyes. The day it does, your *nagual* will have won a great battle. Your obsession or, better yet, everyone's obsession is to arrange the world according to the *tonal*'s rules; so every time we are confronted with the *nagual*, we go out of our way to make our eyes stiff and intransigent. I must appeal to the part of your *tonal* which understands this dilemma and you must make an effort to free your eyes. The point is to convince the *tonal* that there are other worlds that can pass in front of the same windows. The *nagual* showed you that this morning. So, let your eyes be free; let them be true windows. The eyes can be the windows to peer into boredom or to peek into that infinity."

Don Juan made a sweeping arc with his left arm to point all around us. There was a glint in his eyes, and his smile was at once frightening and disarming.

"How can I do that?" I asked.

"I say that it is a very simple matter. Perhaps I say it is simple because I've been doing it for so long. All you have to do is to set up your intent as a customs house. Whenever you are in the world of the *tonal*, you should be an impeccable *tonal;* no time for irrational crap. But whenever you are in the world of the *nagual*, you should also be impeccable; no time for rational crap. For the warrior, intent is the gate in between. It closes completely behind him when he goes either way.

"Another thing one should do when facing the *nagual* is to shift the line of the eyes from time to time, in order to break the spell of the *nagual*. Changing the position of the eyes always eases the burden of the *tonal*. This morning I noticed that you were extremely vulnerable and I changed the position of your head. If you are in a pinch like that you should be able to shift by yourself. This shifting should be done only as a relief, though, not as another way of palisading yourself to safeguard the order of the *tonal*. My bet would be that you would strive to use this technique to hide the rationality of your *tonal* behind it, and thus believe that you're saving it from extinction. The flaw of your reasoning is that nobody wants or seeks the extinction of the *tonal*'s rationality. That fear is ill founded.

"There is nothing else I can tell you, except that you must follow every movement that Genaro makes, without draining yourself. You are testing now whether or not your *tonal* is crammed with nonessentials. If there are too many unnecessary items on your island you won't be able to sustain the encounter with the *nagual*."

"What would happen to me?"

"You may die. No one is capable of surviving a deliberate encounter with the *nagual* without a long training. It takes years to prepare the *tonal* for such an encounter. Ordinarily, if an average man comes face to face with the *nagual* the shock would be so great that he would die. The goal of a warrior's training then is not to teach him to hex or to charm, but to prepare his *tonal* not to crap out. A most difficult accomplishment. A warrior must be taught to be impeccable and thoroughly empty before he could even conceive witnessing the *nagual*.

"In your case, for instance, you have to stop calculating. What you were doing this morning was absurd. You call it explaining. I call it a sterile and boring insistence of the *tonal* to have everything under its control. Whenever it doesn't succeed, there is a moment of bafflement and then the *tonal* opens itself to death. What a prick! It would rather kill itself than relinquish control. And yet there is very little we can do to change that condition."

"How did you change it yourself, don Juan?"

"The island of the *tonal* has to be swept clean and maintained clean. That's the only alternative that a warrior has. A clean island offers no resistance; it is as if there were nothing there."

He went around the house and sat down on a big smooth rock. From there one could look into a deep ravine. He signaled me to sit down next to him.

"Can you tell me, don Juan, what else we are going to do today?" I asked.

"We aren't going to do anything. That is, you and I will only be the witnesses. Your benefactor is Genaro."

I thought I had misunderstood him in my eagerness to take notes. At the beginning stages of my apprenticeship, don Juan himself had introduced the term "benefactor." My impression had always been that he himself was my benefactor.

Don Juan had stopped talking and was staring at me. I made a quick assessment and my conclusion was that he must have meant that don Genaro was something like the star performer on that occasion. Don Juan giggled, as if he were reading my thoughts.

"Genaro is your benefactor," he repeated.

"But you are, aren't you?" I asked in a frantic tone.

"I'm the one who helped you sweep the island of the *tonal*," he said. "Genaro has two apprentices, Pablito and Nestor. He is helping them sweep the island; but I will show them the *nagual*. I will be their benefactor. Genaro is only their teacher. In these matters one can either talk or act; one cannot do both with the same person. One either takes the island of the *tonal* or one takes the *nagual*. In your case my duty has been to work with your *tonal*."

As don Juan spoke I had an attack of terror so intense that I was about to get ill. I had the feeling that he was going to leave me with don Genaro and that was a most dreadful scheme to me.

Don Juan laughed and laughed as I voiced my fears.

"The same thing happens to Pablito," he said. "The moment he sets eyes on me he gets ill. The other day he walked into the house when Genaro was gone. I was alone here and I had left my sombrero by the door. Pablito saw it and his *tonal* became so frightened that he actually shit in his pants."

I could easily understand and project into Pablito's feelings. When I considered the matter carefully, I had to admit that don Juan was terrifying. I had learned, however, to feel comfortable with him. I experienced with him a familiarity born out of our long association.

"I'm not going to leave you with Genaro," he said, still laughing. "I'm the one who takes care of your *tonal*. Without it you're dead."

"Has every apprentice a teacher and a benefactor?" I asked to ease my turmoil.

"No, not every apprentice. But some do."

"Why do some of them have both a teacher and a benefactor?"

"When an ordinary man is ready, power provides him with a teacher, and he becomes an apprentice. When the apprentice is ready, power provides him with a benefactor, and he becomes a sorcerer."

"What makes a man ready, so that power can provide him with a teacher?"

"No one knows that. We are only men. Some of us are men who

have learned to *see* and use the *nagual*, but nothing that we may have gained in the course of our lives can reveal to us the designs of power. Thus, not every apprentice has a benefactor. Power decides that."

I asked him if he himself had had a teacher and a benefactor, and for the first time in thirteen years he freely talked about them. He said that both his teacher and his benefactor were from central Mexico. I had always considered that information about don Juan to be of value for my anthropological research, but somehow at the moment of his revelation it did not matter.

Don Juan glanced at me. I though it was a look of concern. He then abruptly changed the subject and asked me to recount every detail of what I had experienced in the morning.

"A sudden fright always shrinks the *tonal*," he said as a comment on my description of how I felt when don Genaro screamed. "The problem here is not to let the *tonal* shrink itself out of the picture. A grave issue for a warrior is to know exactly when to allow his *tonal* to shrink and when to stop it. This is a great art. A warrior must struggle like a demon to shrink his *tonal*; and yet at the very moment the *tonal* shrinks, the warrior must reverse all that struggle to immediately halt that shrinking."

"But by doing that isn't he reverting back to what he already was?" I asked.

"No. After the *tonal* shrinks, the warrior is closing the gate from the other side. As long as his *tonal* is unchallenged and his eyes are tuned only for the *tonal*'s world, the warrior is on the safe side of the fence. He's on familiar ground and knows all the rules. But when his *tonal* shrinks, he is on the windy side, and that opening must be shut tight immediately, or he would be swept away. And this is not just a way of talking. Beyond the gate of the *tonal*'s eyes the wind rages. I mean a real wind. No metaphor. A wind that can blow one's life away. In fact, that is the wind that blows all living things on this earth. Years ago I acquainted you with that wind. You took it as a joke, though."

He was referring to a time when he had taken me to the mountains and explained certain properties of the wind. I had never thought it was a joke, however.

"It's not important whether you took it seriously or not," he said after listening to my protests. "As a rule the *tonal* must defend itself, at any cost, every time it is threatened; so it is of no real consequence how the *tonal* reacts in order to accomplish its defense. The only important matter is that the *tonal* of a warrior must become acquainted with other alternatives. What a teacher aims for, in this case, is the total weight of those possibilities. It is the weight of those new possibilities which helps to shrink the *tonal*. By the same token, it is the same weight which helps stop the *tonal* from shrinking out of the picture."

He signaled me to proceed with my narrative of the events of the morning, and he interrupted me when I came to the part where don Genaro slid back and forth from the tree trunk to the branch.

"The *nagual* can perform extraordinary things," he said. "Things that do not seem possible, things that are unthinkable for the *tonal*. But the extraordinary thing is that the performer has no way of knowing how those things happen. In other words, Genaro doesn't know how he does those things; he only knows that he does them. The secret of a sorcerer is that he knows how to get to the *nagual*, but once he gets there, your guess is as good as his as to what takes place."

"But what does one feel while doing those things?"

"One feels like one is doing something."

"Would don Genaro feel like he's walking up the trunk of a tree?"

Don Juan looked at me for a moment, then he turned his head away.

"No," he said in a forceful whisper. "Not in the way you mean it."

He did not say anything else. I was practically holding my breath, waiting for his explanation. Finally I had to ask, "But what does he feel?"

"I can't say, not because it is a personal matter, but because there is no way of describing it."

"Come on," I coaxed him. "There is nothing that one can't explain or elucidate with words. I believe that even if it's not possible to describe something directly, one can allude to it, beat around the bush."

Don Juan laughed. His laughter was friendly and kind. And yet there was a touch of mockery and sheer mischievousness in it.

"I have to change the subject," he said. "Suffice it to say that the *nagual* was aimed at you this morning. Whatever Genaro did was a mixture of you and him. His *nagual* was tempered by your *tonal*."

I insisted on probing and asked him, "When you're showing the *nagual* to Pablito, what do you feel?"

"I can't explain that," he said in a soft voice. "And not because I don't want to, but simply because I can't. My *tonal* stops there."

I did not want to press him any further. We remained silent for a while, then he began to talk again

"Let's say that a warrior learns to tune his *will*, to direct it to a pinpoint, to focus it wherever he wants. It is as if his *will*, which comes from the midsection of his body, is one single luminous fiber, a fiber that he can direct at any conceivable place. That fiber is the road to the *nagual*. Or I could also say that the warrior sinks into the *nagual* through that single fiber.

"Once he has sunk, the expression of the *nagual* is a matter of his personal temperament. If the warrior is funny the *nagual* is funny. If the warrior is morbid the *nagual* is morbid. If the warrior is mean the *nagual* is mean.

"Genaro always cracks me up because he's one of the most delightful creatures alive. I never know what he's going to come up with. That to me is the ultimate essence of sorcery. Genaro is such a fluid warrior that the slightest focusing of his *will* makes his *nagual* act in incredible ways."

"Did you yourself observe what don Genaro was doing in the trees?" I asked.

"No, I just knew, because I *saw*, that the *nagual* was in the trees. The rest of the show was for you alone."

"Do you mean, don Juan, that, like the time when you pushed me and I ended up in the market, you were not with me?"

"It was something like that. When one meets the *nagual* face to face, one always has to be alone. I was around only to protect your *tonal*. That is my charge."

Don Juan said that my "tonal" was nearly blasted to pieces when don Genaro descended from the tree; not so much because of any inherent quality of danger in the "nagual," but because my "tonal" indulged in its bewilderment. He said that one of the aims of the warrior's training was to cut the bewilderment of the "tonal," until the warrior was so fluid that he could admit everything without admitting anything.

When I described don Genaro's leap up to the tree and his leap down from it, don Juan said that the yell of a warrior was one of the most important issues of sorcery, and that don Genaro was capable of focusing on his yell, using it as a vehicle.

"You are right," he said. "Genaro was pulled partly by his yell and partly by the tree. That was true *seeing* on your part. That was a true picture of the *nagual*. Genaro's *will* was focused on the yell and his personal touch made the tree pull the *nagual*. The lines went both ways from Genaro to the tree and from the tree to Genaro.

"What you should have *seen* when Genaro jumped from the tree was that he was focusing on a spot in front of you and then the tree pushed him. But it only seemed to be a push; in essence it was more like being released by the tree. The tree released the *nagual* and the *nagual* came back to the world of the *tonal* on the spot he focused on.

"The second time that Genaro came down from the tree your *tonal* was not so bewildered; you were not indulging so hard and therefore you were not as sapped as you were the first time."

Around four in the afternoon don Juan stopped our conversation.

"We are going back to the eucalyptus trees," he said. "The *nagual* is waiting for us there."

"Aren't we risking being seen by people?" I asked.

"No. The *nagual* will keep everything suspended," he said.

THE WHISPERING OF THE NAGUAL

As we approached the eucalyptuses I saw don Genaro sitting on a tree stump. He waved his hand, smiling. We joined him.

There was a flock of crows in the trees. They were cawing as if something were frightening them. Don Genaro said that we had to remain motionless and quiet until the crows had calmed down.

Don Juan leaned his back against a tree and signaled me to do the same on a tree next to him a few feet away to his left. We were both facing don Genaro, who was three or four yards in front of us.

With a subtle movement of his eyes, don Juan gave me a cue to rearrange my feet. He was standing firmly, with his feet slightly apart, touching the tree trunk only with the upper part of his shoulder blades and with the very back of his head. His arms hung at his sides.

We stood like that for perhaps an hour. I kept a close vigil on both of them, especially on don Juan. At a given moment he slid gently down the tree trunk and sat down, still keeping the same areas of his body in contact with the tree. His knees were raised and he rested his arms on them. I imitated his movements. My legs had become extremely tired and the change of position made me feel quite comfortable.

The crows had stopped cawing by degrees, until there was not a single sound in the field. The silence was more unnerving to me than the noise of the crows.

Don Juan spoke to me in a quiet tone. He said that the twilight was my best hour. He looked at the sky. It must have been after six.

It had been an overcast day and I had had no way of checking the position of the sun. I heard the distant cries of geese and perhaps turkeys. But in the field with eucalyptus trees there was no noise. There had been no whistling of birds or sounds of large insects for a long time.

The bodies of don Juan and don Genaro had been in perfect immobility, as far as I could judge, except for a few seconds when they shifted their weight in order to rest.

After don Juan and I had slid to the ground, don Genaro made a sudden motion. He lifted his feet up and squatted on the stump. He then turned forty-five degrees, and I was looking at his left profile. I stared at don Juan in search of a clue. He jutted his chin; it was a command to look at don Genaro.

A monstrous agitation began to overtake me. I was incapable of containing myself. My bowels were loose. I could absolutely feel what Pablito must have felt when he saw don Juan's sombrero. I experienced such intestinal distress that I had to get up and run to the bushes. I heard them howling with laughter.

I did not dare to return to where they were. I hesitated for a while; I figured that the spell must have been broken by my sudden outburst. I did not have to ponder for too long; don Juan and don Genaro came over to where I was. They flanked me and we walked to another field. We stopped at the very center of it and I recognized that we had been there in the morning.

Don Juan spoke to me. He told me that I had to be fluid and silent and should stop my internal dialogue. I listened attentively. Don Genaro must have been aware that all my concentration was focused on don Juan's admonitions and he used that moment to do what he had done in the morning; he again let out his maddening scream. He caught me unaware but not unprepared. I almost immediately recuperated my balance by breathing. The jolt was terrifying, yet it did not have a prolonged effect on me and I was capable of following don Genaro's movements with my eyes. I saw him leap to a low branch on a tree. As I followed his course for a distance of eighty to ninety feet, my eyes experienced an extravagant distortion. It was not that he leaped by means of the spring action of his muscles; he rather glided through the air, catapulted in part by his formidable yell, and pulled by some vague lines emanating from the tree. It was as if the tree had sipped him through its lines.

Don Genaro stayed perched on the low branch for a moment. His left profile was turned to me. He began to perform a series of strange movements. His head wobbled, his body shivered. He hid his head various times in between his knees. The more he moved and fretted the more difficult it was for me to focus my eyes on his body. He seemed to be dissolving. I blinked desperately and then I shifted my line of vision by twisting my head to the right and to the left as don Juan had taught me. From my left perspective I saw don Genaro's body as I had never seen it before. It was as if he had put on a disguise. He had a furry suit on; the hair was the color of a Siamese cat, light buff-brown, with touches of dark chocolate brown on the legs and the back; it had a long thick tail. Don Genaro's costume made him look like a furry brown long-legged crocodile sitting on a branch. I could not see his head or his features.

I straightened my head to a normal position. The vision of don Genaro in disguise remained unchanged.

Don Genaro's arms shivered. He stood up on the branch, sort of stooped over, and leaped towards the ground. The branch was perhaps fifteen to twenty feet high. As far as I could judge, it was an ordinary leap of a man wearing a costume. I saw don Genaro's body almost touching the ground and then the thick tail of his costume vibrated and instead of landing he took off, as if powered with a silent jet engine. He went over the trees and then glided almost to the ground. He did that over and over. At times he would hold on to a branch and swing around a tree, or curl like an eel between branches. And then he would glide and circle around us, or flap his arms as he touched the very tops of the trees with his stomach.

Don Genaro's cavorting filled me with awe. My eyes followed him and two or three times I clearly perceived that he was using some brilliant lines, as if they were pulleys, to glide from one place to another. Then he went over the tops of the trees towards the south and disappeared behind them. I tried to anticipate the place where he would appear again, but he did not show up at all.

I noticed then that I was lying on my back and yet I had not been aware of a change in perspective. I had thought all along that I was looking at don Genaro from a standing position.

Don Juan helped me to sit up and then I saw don Genaro walking towards us with a nonchalant air. He smiled coyly and asked me if I had liked his flying. I attempted to say something but I was speechless.

Don Genaro exchanged a strange look with don Juan and adopted a squat position again. He leaned over and whispered something in my left ear. I heard him say, "Why don't you come and fly with me?" He repeated it five or six times.

Don Juan came towards me and whispered in my right ear, "Don't talk. Just follow Genaro."

Don Genaro made me squat and whispered to me again. I heard him with crystal clear precision. He repeated the statement perhaps ten times. He said, "Trust the *nagual*. The *nagual* will take you."

Then don Juan whispered in my right ear another statement. He said, "Change your feelings."

I could hear both of them talking to me at once, but I could also hear them individually. Every one of don Genaro's statements had to do with the general context of gliding through the air. The statements that he repeated dozens of times seemed to be those that became engraved in my memory. Don Juan's words, on the other hand, had to do with specific commands, which he repeated countless times. The effect of that dual whispering was most extraordinary. It was as if the sound of their individual words were splitting me in half. Finally the abyss between my two ears was so wide that I lost all sense of unity. There was something that was undoubtedly me, but it was not solid. It was rather like a glowing fog, a dark yellow mist that had feelings.

Don Juan told me that he was going to mold me for flying. The sensation I had then was that the words were like pliers that twisted and molded my "feelings."

Don Genaro's words were an invitation to follow him. I felt I wanted to, but I could not. The split was so great that I was incapacitated. Then I heard the same short statements repeated endlessly by both of them; things like "Look at that magnificent flying shape." "Leap, leap." "Your legs will reach the treetops." "The eucalyptuses are like green dots." "The worms are lights."

Something in me must have ceased at a given moment; perhaps my awareness of being talked to. I sensed that don Genaro was still with me, yet from the point of view of my perception I could only distinguish an enormous mass of the most extraordinary lights. At times their glare diminished and at times the lights became intense. I was also experiencing movement. The effect was like being pulled by a vacuum that never let me stop. Whenever my motion seemed to diminish and I could actually focus my awareness on the lights, the vacuum would pull me away again.

At one moment, between being pulled back and forth, I experienced the ultimate confusion. The world around me, whatever it was, was coming and going at the same time, thus the vacuumlike effect. I could see two separate worlds; one that was going away from me and the other that was coming closer to me. I did not realize this as one ordinarily would; that is, I did not become aware of it as something that had thus far been unrevealed. I rather had two realizations without the unifying conclusion.

After that my perceptions became dull. They either lacked precision, or they were too many and I had no way of sorting them. The next batch of discernible apperceptions were a series of sounds that happened at the end of a long tubelike formation. The tube was myself and the sounds were don Juan and don Genaro, again talking to me through each of my ears. The more they talked the shorter the tube became until the sounds were in a range I recognized. That is to say, the sounds of don Juan and don Genaro's words reached my normal range of perception; the sounds were first recognizable as noises, then as words yelled, and finally as words whispered in my ears.

I next noticed things of the familiar world. I was apparently lying face down. I could distinguish clumps of dirt, small rocks, dried leaves. And then I became aware of the field of eucalyptus trees.

Don Juan and don Genaro were standing by me. It was still light. I felt that I had to get into the water in order to consolidate myself. I walked to the river, took off my clothes and stayed in the cold water long enough to restore my perceptual balance.

Don Genaro left as soon as we arrived at his house. He casually patted me on the shoulder as he was leaving. I jumped away in a reflex reaction. I thought that his touch was going to be painful; to my amazement it was simply a gentle pat on the shoulder.

Don Juan and don Genaro laughed like two kids celebrating a prank.

"Don't be so jumpy," don Genaro said. "The *nagual* is not after you all the time."

He smacked his lips as though disapproving my overreaction, and with an air of candor and comradeship he extended his arms. I embraced him. He patted my back in a most friendly warm gesture.

"You must be concerned with the *nagual* only at certain moments," he said. "The rest of the time you and I are like all the other people on this earth."

He faced don Juan and smiled at him.

"Isn't it so, Juancho?" he asked, emphasizing the word Juancho, a funny nickname for Juan.

"That's so, Gerancho," don Juan answered, making up the word Gerancho.

They both had an explosion of laughter.

"I must warn you," don Juan said to me, "you have to exert the most demanding vigil to be sure when a man is a *nagual* and when a man is simply a man. You may die if you come into direct physical contact with the *nagual*."

Don Juan turned to don Genaro and with a beaming smile asked, "Isn't it so, Gerancho?"

"That's so, absolutely so, Juancho," don Genaro replied, and both of them laughed.

Their childlike mirth was very moving to me. The events of the day had been exhausting and I was very emotional. A wave of self-pity engulfed me. I was about to weep as I kept on repeating to myself that whatever they had done to me was irreversible and most likely injurious. Don Juan seemed to be reading my thoughts and shook his head in a gesture of disbelief. He chuckled. I made an effort to stop my internal dialogue, and my self-pity vanished.

"Genaro is very warm," don Juan commented when don Genaro had left. "The design of power was that you found a gentle benefactor."

I did not know what to say. The idea that don Genaro was my benefactor intrigued me no end. I wanted don Juan to tell me more about it. He did not seem inclined to talk. He looked at the sky and at the top of the dark silhouette of some trees at the side of the house. He sat down with his back against a thick forked pole, planted almost in front of the door, and told me to sit next to him to his left.

I sat by him. He pulled me closer by the arm until I was touching him. He said that that time of the night was dangerous for me, especially on that occasion. In a very calm voice he gave me a set of instructions: We were not to move from the spot until he saw fit to do so; we were to keep on talking, on an even keel, without long interruptions; and I had to breathe and blink as if I were facing the "nagual."

"Is the *nagual* around here?" I asked.

"Of course," he said and chuckled.

I practically huddled against don Juan. He began to talk and actually solicited any kind of question from me. He even handed me my notebook and pencil as if I could write in the darkness. His contention was that I needed to be as calm and normal as possible and there could be no better way of fortifying my "tonal" than through taking notes. He put the whole matter on a very compelling level; he said that if taking notes was my predilection, then I should be able to do it in complete darkness. There was a tone of challenge in his voice when he said that I could turn the taking of notes into a warrior's task, in which case the darkness would be no obstacle.

Somehow, he must have convinced me, for I managed to scribble down parts of our conversation. The main topic was don Genaro as my benefactor. I was curious to know when don Genaro had become my benefactor, and don Juan coaxed me to remember a supposedly extraordinary event that had happened the day I had met don Genaro, and which served as a proper omen. I could not recollect anything of the sort. I began to recount the experience; as far as I could remember it was a most unobtrusive and casual meeting, which took place in the spring of 1968. Don Juan stopped me.

"If you're dumb enough not to remember," he said, "we'd better leave it that way. A warrior follows the dictums of power. You will remember it when it becomes necessary."

Don Juan said that having a benefactor was a most difficult matter. He used as an example the case of his own apprentice Eligio, who had been with him for many years. He said that Eligio had been unable to find a benefactor. I asked him if Eligio would eventually find one; he answered that there was no way of predicting the quirks of power. He reminded me that once, years before, we had found a group of young Indians roaming around the desert in northern Mexico. He said that he "saw" that none of them had a benefactor, and that the general surroundings and the mood of the moment were just right for him to give them a hand, by showing them the "nagual." He was talking about one night when four young men sat by a fire while don Juan put on what I thought to be a spectacular show in which he apparently appeared to each of us in a different guise.

"Those guys knew a great deal," he said. "You were the only greenhorn among them."

"What happened to them afterwards?" I asked.

"Some of them found a benefactor," he replied.

Don Juan said that it was the duty of a benefactor to deliver his ward to power, and that the benefactor imparted to the neophyte his personal touch, as much if not more so than the teacher.

During a short pause in our talk I heard a strange rasping noise at the back of the house. Don Juan held me down; I had almost stood up as a reaction to it. Before the noise happened, our conversation had been a matter of course for me. But when the pause occurred, and there was a moment of silence, the strange noise popped through it. At that instant I had the certainty that our conversation was an extraordinary event. I had the sensation that the sound of don Juan's words and mine were like a sheet that broke, and that the rasping sound had been deliberately prowling, waiting for a chance to break through.

Don Juan commanded me to sit tight and not to pay attention to the surroundings. The rasping noise reminded me of the sound of a gopher clawing on hard dry ground. The moment I had thought of the simile I also had a visual image of a rodent, like the one don Juan had showed me on his palm. It was as if I were falling asleep and my thoughts were turning into visions or dreams.

I began the breathing exercise and held my stomach with my clasped hands. Don Juan kept on talking, but I was not listening to him. My attention was on the soft rustle of a snake-like thing slithering over small dry leaves. I had a moment of panic and physical revulsion at the thought of a snake crawling on me. I involuntarily put my feet under don Juan's legs and breathed and blinked frantically.

I heard the noise so close that it seemed to be only a couple of feet away. My panic mounted. Don Juan calmly said that the only way to fend off the "nagual" was to remain unaltered. He ordered me to stretch my legs and not to focus my attention on the noise. He imperatively demanded that I write or ask questions and make an effort not to succumb.

After a great struggle I asked him if don Genaro was making the noise. He said that it was the "nagual" and that I should not mix them; Genaro was the name of the "tonal." He then said something else, but I could not understand him. Something was circling around the house and I could not concentrate on our conversation. He commanded me to make a supreme effort. At one moment I found that I was babbling idiocies about my being unworthy. I had a jolt of fear and snapped into a state of great lucidity. Don Juan told me then that it was all right to listen. But there were no sounds.

"*The nagual* is gone," don Juan said and stood up and went inside.

He lit don Genaro's kerosene lantern and made some food. We ate in silence. I asked him if the "nagual" was coming back.

"No," he said with a serious expression. "It was just testing you. At this time of night, just after the twilight, you should always involve yourself in something. Anything would do. It is only for a short period, an hour perhaps, but in your case a most deadly hour.

"Tonight the *nagual* tried to make you stumble, but you were strong enough to ward off its assault. Once, you succumbed to it and I had to pour water over your body, this time you did fine."

I remarked that the word "assault" made the event sound very dangerous.

"Made it sound dangerous? That's a weird way of putting it," he said. "I'm not trying to scare you. The actions of the *nagual* are deadly. I've already told you that, and it is not that Genaro tries to hurt you; on the contrary, his concern for you is impeccable, but if you don't have enough power to parry the *nagual*'s onslaught, you're dead, regardless of my help or Genaro's concern."

After we finished eating, don Juan sat next to me and looked over my shoulder at my notes. I commented that it would probably take me years to assort everything that had happened to me during that day. I knew that I had been flooded with perceptions I could not ever hope to understand.

"If you cannot understand, you're in great shape," he said. "It is when you understand that you're in a mess. That's from the point of view of a sorcerer, of course. From the point of view of an average man, if you fail to understand you're sinking. In your case, I would say that an average man would think that you are disassociated, or you're beginning to become disassociated."

I laughed at his choice of words. I knew that he was throwing the concept of disassociation back at me; I had mentioned it to him some time back in connection with my fears. I assured him that this time I was not going to ask anything about what I had been through.

"I've never put a ban on talking," he said. "We can talk about the *nagual* to your heart's content, as long as you don't try to explain it. If you remember correctly, I said that the *nagual* is only for witnessing. So, we can talk about what we witnessed and about how we witnessed it. You want to take on the explanation of how it is all possible, though, and that is an abomination. You want to explain the *nagual* with the *tonal*. That is stupid, especially in your case, since you can no longer hide behind your ignorance. You know very well that we make sense in talking only because we stay within certain boundaries, and those boundaries are not applicable to the *nagual*."

I attempted to clarify the issue. It was not only that I wanted to explain everything from a rational point of view, but my need to explain stemmed from my necessity to maintain order throughout the tremendous onslaughts of chaotic stimuli and perceptions I had had.

Don Juan's comment was that I was trying to defend a point I did not agree with.

"You know damn well that you're indulging," he said. "To maintain order means to be a perfect *tonal*, and to be a perfect *tonal* means to be aware of everything that takes place on the island of the *tonal*. But you're not. So your argument about maintaining order has no truth in it. You only use it to win an argument."

I did not know what to say. Don Juan sort of consoled me by saying that it took a gigantic struggle to clean the island of the "tonal." Then he asked me to recount all I had perceived in my second session with the "nagual." When I had finished, he said that what I had witnessed as a furry crocodile was the epitome of don Genaro's sense of humor.

"It's a pity that you're still so heavy," he said. "You always get hooked by bewilderment and miss Genaro's real art."

"Were you aware of his appearance, don Juan?"

"No. The show was only for you."

"What did you *see?*"

"Today all I could *see* was the movement of the *nagual*, gliding through the trees and whirling around us. Anyone who *sees* can witness that."

"What about someone who doesn't *see?*"

"He would witness nothing, just the trees being blown by a wild wind perhaps. We interpret any unknown expression of the *nagual* as something we know; in this case the *nagual* might be interpreted as a breeze shaking the leaves, or even as some strange light, perhaps a lightning bug of unusual size. If a man who doesn't *see* is pressed, he would say that he thought he saw something but could not remember what. This is only natural. The man would be talking sense. After all, his eyes would have judged nothing extraordinary; being the eyes of the *tonal* they have to be limited to the *tonal*'s world, and in that world there is nothing staggeringly new, nothing which the eyes cannot apprehend and the *tonal* cannot explain."

I asked him about the uncharted perceptions that resulted from their whispering in my ears.

"That was the best part of the whole event," he said. "The rest could be dispensed with, but that was the crown of the day. The rule calls for the benefactor and the teacher to make that final trimming. The most difficult of all acts. Both the teacher and the benefactor must be impeccable warriors to even attempt the feat of splitting a man. You don't know this, because it still is beyond your realm, but power had been lenient with you again. Genaro is the most impeccable warrior there is."

"Why is the splitting of a man a great feat?"

"Because it is dangerous. You may have died like a little bug. Or worse yet, we may have never been able to put you back together, and you would have remained on that plateau of feeling."

"Why was it necessary to do it to me, don Juan?"

"There is a certain time when the *nagual* has to whisper in the ear of the apprentice and split him."

"What does that mean, don Juan?"

"In order to be an average *tonal* a man must have unity. His whole being must belong to the island of the *tonal*. Without that unity the man would go berserk; a sorcerer, however, has to break that unity, but without endangering his being. A sorcerer's goal is to last; that is, he doesn't take unnecessary risks, therefore he spends years sweeping his island until a moment when he could, in a manner of speaking, sneak off it. Splitting a man in two is the gate for such an escape.

"The splitting, which is the most dangerous thing you've ever gone through, was smooth and simple. The *nagual* was masterful in guiding you. Believe me, only an impeccable warrior can do that. I felt very good for you."

Don Juan put his hand on my shoulder and I had a gigantic urge to weep.

"Am I arriving at a point when you won't see me any more?" I asked.

He laughed and shook his head.

"You indulge like a son of a bitch," he said. "We all do that, though. We have different ways, that's all. Sometimes I indulge too. My way is to feel that I have pampered you and made you weak. I know that Genaro has the same feeling about Pablito. He pampers him like a child. But that is the way power set it up to be. Genaro gives Pablito everything he's capable of giving and one cannot wish he would do something else. One cannot criticize a warrior for doing his impeccable best."

He was quiet for a moment. I was too nervous to sit in silence.

"What do you think was happening to me when I felt like I was being sucked by a vacuum?" I asked.

"You were gliding," he said in a matter-of-fact tone.

"Through the air?"

"No. For the *nagual* there is no land, or air, or water. At this point you yourself can agree with that. Twice you were in that limbo and you were only at the door of the *nagual*. You've told me that everything you encountered was uncharted. So the *nagual* glides, or flies, or does whatever it may do, in *nagual*'s time, and that has nothing to do with *tonal*'s time. The two things don't jibe."

As don Juan spoke I felt a tremor in my body. My jaw dropped and my mouth opened involuntarily. My ears unplugged and I could hear a barely perceptible tingle or vibration. While I was describing my sensations to don Juan I noticed that when I talked it sounded as if someone else were talking. It was a complex sensation that amounted to my hearing what I was going to say before I said it.

My left ear was a source of extraordinary sensations. I felt that it was more powerful and more accurate than my right ear. There was something in it that had not been there before. When I turned around to face don Juan, who was to my right, I became aware that I had a range of clear auditory perception around that ear. It was a physical space, a range within which I could hear everything with incredible fidelity. By turning my head around I could scan the surroundings with my ear.

"The whispering of the *nagual* did that to you," don Juan said when I described my sensorial experience. "It'll come at times and then vanish. Don't be afraid of it, or of any unusual sensation that you may have from now on. But above all, don't indulge and become obsessed with those sensations. I know you will succeed. The time for your splitting was right. Power fixed all that. Now everything depends on you. If you are powerful enough you will sustain the great shock of being split. But if you're incapable of holding on, you will perish. You will begin to wither away, lose weight, become pale, absent-minded, irritable, quiet."

"Perhaps if you would have told me years ago," I said, "what you and don Genaro were doing, I would have enough . . ."

He raised his hand and did not let me finish.

"That's a meaningless statement," he said. "You once told me that if it wouldn't be for the fact that you're stubborn and given to rational explanations you would be a sorcerer by now. But to be a sorcerer in your case means that you have to overcome stubbornness and the need for rational explanations, which stand in your way. What's more, those shortcomings are your road to power. You can't say that power would flow to you if your life would be different.

"Genaro and I have to act the same way you do, within certain limits. Power sets up those limits and a warrior is, let's say, a prisoner of power; a prisoner who has one free choice: the choice to act either like an impeccable warrior, or to act like an ass. In the final analysis, perhaps the warrior is not a prisoner but a slave of power, because that choice is no longer a choice for him. Genaro cannot act in any other way but impeccably. To act like an ass would drain him and cause his demise.

"The reason why you're afraid of Genaro is because he has to use the avenue of fright to shrink your *tonal*. Your body knows that, although your *reason* may not, and thus your body wants to run away every time Genaro is around."

I mentioned that I was curious to know if don Genaro deliberately set out to scare me. He said that the "nagual" did strange things, things which were not foreseeable. He gave me, as an example, what had happened between us in the morning when he prevented my turning to my left to look at don Genaro in the tree. He said that he was aware of what his "nagual" had done although he had no way of knowing about it ahead of time. His explanation of the whole affair was that my sudden movement to the left was a step towards my death, which my "tonal" was deliberately taking as a suicidal plunge. That movement stirred his "nagual" and the result was that some part of him fell on top of me.

I made an involuntary gesture of perplexity.

"Your *reason* is telling you again that you're immortal," he said.

"What do you mean by that, don Juan?"

"An immortal being has all the time in the world for doubts and bewilderment and fears. A warrior, on the other hand, cannot cling to the meanings made under the *tonal*'s order, because he knows for a fact that the totality of himself has but a little time on this earth."

I wanted to make a serious point. My fears and doubts and bewilderment were not on a conscious level, and, no matter how hard I tried to control them, every time I was confronted with don Juan and don Genaro I felt helpless.

"A warrior cannot be helpless," he said. "Or bewildered or frightened, not under any circumstances. For a warrior there is time only for his impeccability; everything else drains his power, impeccability replenishes it."

"We're back again to my old question, don Juan. What's impeccability?"

"Yes, we're back again to your old question and consequently we're back again to my old answer: 'Impeccability is to do your best in whatever you're engaged in.'"

"But don Juan, my point is that I'm always under the impression I'm doing my best, and obviously I'm not."

"It's not as complicated as you make it appear. The key to all these matters of impeccability is the sense of having or not having time. As a rule of thumb, when you feel and act like an immortal being that has all the time in the world you are not impeccable; at those times you should turn, look around, and then you will realize that your feeling of having time is an idiocy. There are no survivors on this earth!"

THE WINGS OF PERCEPTION

Don Juan and I spent the whole day in the mountains. We left at dawn. He took me to four places of power and at each one of them he gave me specific instructions on how to proceed towards the fulfillment of the particular task that he had outlined years before as a life situation for me. We returned in the late afternoon. After eating, don Juan left don Genaro's house. He told me that I had to wait for Pablito, who was bringing some kerosene for the lantern, and that I should talk to him.

I became utterly absorbed in working on my notes and did not hear Pablito come in until he was next to me. Pablito's comment was that he had been practicing the "gait of power," and because of that I could not possibly have heard him unless I was capable of "seeing."

I had always liked Pablito. I had not, however, had very many opportunities in the past to be alone with him, although we were good friends. Pablito had always struck me as being a most charming person. His name, of course, was Pablo, but the diminutive, Pablito, suited him better. He was small-boned but wiry. Like don Genaro he was lean, unsuspectedly muscular, and strong. He was perhaps in his late twenties, but it seemed like he was eighteen. He was dark and of medium height. His brown eyes were clear and bright, and like don Genaro he had a winning smile with a touch of devilishness in it.

I asked him about his friend Nestor, don Genaro's other apprentice. In the past I had always seen them together, and they had always given me the impression of having an excellent rapport with each other; yet they were opposites in physical appearance and character. While Pablito was jovial and frank, Nestor was gloomy and withdrawn. He was also taller, heavier, darker, and much older.

Pablito said that Nestor had finally become involved in his work with don Genaro, and that he had changed into an altogether different person since the last time I had seen him. He did not want to elaborate any further on Nestor's work or change of personality and abruptly shifted the topic of conversation.

"I understand the *nagual* is biting your heels," he said.

I was surprised that he knew and I asked how he had found that out.

"Genaro tells me everything," he said.

I noticed that he did not speak of don Genaro in the same formal way I did. He simply called him Genaro in a familiar fashion. He said that don Genaro was like his brother, and that they were at ease around each other as though they were family. He openly professed that he loved don Genaro dearly. I was deeply moved by his simplicity and candor. In talking to him, I realized how close in temperament don Juan and I were; thus our relationship was formal and strict in comparison to don Genaro and Pablito's.

I asked Pablito why he was afraid of don Juan. His eyes flickered. It was as if the mere thought of don Juan made him wince. He did not answer. He seemed to be assessing me in some mysterious way.

"You're not afraid of him?" he asked.

I told him I was afraid of don Genaro and he laughed as if that were the last thing he expected to hear. He said that the difference between don Juan and don Genaro was like the difference between day and night. Don Genaro was the day; don Juan was the night, and as such he was the most frightening being on earth. Describing his fear for don Juan led Pablito to make some comments about his own condition as an apprentice.

"I'm in a most miserable state," he said. "If you could see what's in my house you would realize that I know too much for an ordinary man, and yet if you saw me with the *nagual*, you would realize that I don't know enough."

He quickly changed the subject and began to laugh at my taking notes. He said that don Genaro had provided hours of fun imitating me. He added that don Genaro liked me very much, in spite of the oddities of my person, and that he had expressed his delight in my being his "protegido."

This was the first time I had heard that term. It was congruous with another term introduced by don Juan at the beginning of our association. He had told me that I was his "escogido," the chosen one. The word "protegido" meant the protected one.

I asked Pablito about his meetings with the "nagual" and he told me the story of his first encounter with it. He said that once don Juan gave him a basket, which he took to be a gift of good will. He placed it on a hook over the door of his room, and since he could not conceive any use for it at that moment he forgot about it all day. He said that his idea was that the basket was a gift of power and had to be put to use with something very special.

During the early evening, which Pablito said was his deadly hour also, he walked into his room to get his jacket. He was alone in the house and was getting ready to go visit a friend. The room was dark. He grabbed the jacket and when he was about to reach the door the basket fell in front of him and rolled near his feet. Pablito said that he laughed his fright away as soon as he saw that it had only been the basket that had fallen from the hook. He leaned over to pick it up and got the jolt of his life. The basket jumped out of his reach and began to shake and squeak, as if someone were twisting and pressing down on it. Pablito said that there was enough light coming from the kitchen to clearly distinguish everything in the room. He stared at the basket for a moment, although he felt he should not do that. The basket began to convulse in the midst of some heavy, rasping and difficult breathing. Pablito maintained, in recounting his experience, that he actually saw and heard the basket breathing, and that it was alive and chased him around the room, blocking his exit. He said that the basket then began to swell, all the strips of bamboo came loose and turned into a giant ball, like a dry tumbleweed that rolled towards him. He fell backwards on the floor and the ball began to crawl onto his feet. Pablito said that by that time he was out of his mind, screaming hysterically. The ball had him trapped and moved on his legs like pins going through him. He tried to push it away and then noticed that the ball was the face of don Juan with his mouth open ready to devour him. At that point he could not stand the terror and lost consciousness.

Pablito, in a very frank and open manner, told me a series of terrifying encounters that he and other members of his household had had with the "nagual." We spent hours talking. He seemed to be in very much the same quandary that I was in, but was definitely more sensitive than I in handling himself within the sorcerers' frame of reference.

At one moment he got up and said that he felt don Juan was coming and did not want to be found there. He took off with incredible speed. It was as if something had pulled him out of the room. He left me in the middle of saying good-by.

Don Juan and don Genaro came back shortly. They were laughing.

"Pablito was running down the road like a soul chased by the devil," don Juan said. "I wonder why?"

"I think he got frightened when he saw Carlitos working his fingers to the bone," don Genaro said, mocking my writing.

He came closer to me.

"Hey! I've got an idea," he said almost in a whisper. "Since you like to write so much, why don't you learn to write with your finger instead of a pencil. That'll be a blast."

Don Juan and don Genaro sat by my side and laughed while they speculated about the possibility of writing with one's finger. Don Juan, in a serious tone, made a strange comment. He said, "There is no doubt that he could write with his finger, but would he be able to read it?"

Don Genaro doubled up with laughter and added, "I am confident that he can read anything." And then he began to tell a most disconcerting tale about a country bumpkin who became an important official during a time of political upheaval. Don Genaro said that the hero of his story was appointed minister, or governor, or perhaps even president, because there was no way of telling what people would do in their folly. Because of this appointment he came to believe that he was indeed important and learned to put on an act.

Don Genaro paused and examined me with the air of a ham actor overplaying his part. He winked at me and moved his eyebrows up and down. He said that the hero of the story was very good at public appearances and could whip up a speech with no difficulty at all, but that his position required that he read his speeches, and the man was illiterate. So he used his wits to outsmart everybody. He had a sheet of paper with something written on it and flashed it around whenever he gave a speech. And thus his efficiency and other good qualities were undeniable to all the country bumpkins. But one day a literate stranger came along and noticed that the hero was reading his speech while holding the sheet upside down. He began to laugh and pointed out the lie to everyone.

Don Genaro again paused for a moment and looked at me, squinting his eyes, and asked, "Do you think that the hero was caught? Not a chance. He faced everyone calmly and said, 'Upside down? Why should the position of the sheet matter if you know how to read?' And the bumpkins agreed with him."

Don Juan and don Genaro both exploded into laughter. Don Genaro patted me gently on the back. It was as if I were the hero of the story. I felt embarrassed and laughed nervously. I thought that perhaps there was a hidden meaning to it, but I did not dare ask.

Don Juan moved closer to me. He leaned over and whispered in my right ear, "Don't you think it's funny?" Don Genaro also leaned over towards me and whispered in my left ear, "What did he say?" I had an automatic reaction to both questions and made an involuntary synthesis.

"Yes. I thought he asked it's funny," I said.

They were obviously aware of the effect of their maneuvers; they laughed until tears rolled down their cheeks. Don Genaro, as usual, was more exaggerated than don Juan; he fell backwards and rolled on his back a few yards away from me. He lay on his stomach, extending his arms and legs out, and whirled around on the ground as though he were lying on a swivel. He whirled until he got close to me and his foot touched mine. He sat up abruptly and smiled sheepishly.

Don Juan was holding his sides. He was laughing very hard and it seemed that his stomach hurt.

After a while they both leaned over and kept on whispering into my ears. I tried to memorize the sequence of their utterances but after a futile effort I gave up. There were too many.

They whispered in my ears until I again had the sensation that I had been split in two. I became a mist, like the day before, a yellow glow that sensed everything directly. That is, I could "know" things. There were no thoughts involved; there were only certainties. And when I came into contact with a soft, spongy, bouncy feeling, which was outside of me and yet was part of me, I "knew" it was a tree. I sensed it was a tree by its odor. It did not smell like any specific tree I could remember, nonetheless something in me "knew" that that peculiar odor was the "essence" of tree. I did not have just the feeling that I knew, nor did I reason my knowledge out, or shuffle clues around. I simply knew that there was something there in contact with me, all around me, a friendly, warm, compelling smell emanating from something which was neither solid nor liquid but an undefined something else, which I "knew" was a tree. I felt that by "knowing" it in that manner I was tapping its essence. I was not repelled by it. It rather invited me to melt with it. It engulfed me or I engulfed it. There was a bond between us which was neither exquisite nor displeasing.

The next sensation I could recollect with clarity was a wave of wonder and exultation. All of me vibrated. It was as if charges of electricity were going through me. They were not painful. They were pleasing, but in such an undetermined form that there was no way of categorizing them. I knew, nevertheless, that whatever I was in contact with was the ground. Some part of me acknowledged with concise certainty that it was the ground. But the instant I tried to discern the infinitude of direct perceptions I was having, I lost all capacity to differentiate my perceptions.

Then all of a sudden I was myself again. I was thinking. It was such an abrupt transition that I thought I had woken up. Yet there was something in the way I felt that was not quite myself. I knew that there was indeed something missing before I fully opened my eyes. I looked around. I was still in a dream, or having a vision of some sort. My thought processes, however, were not only unimpaired but extraordinarily clear. I made a quick assessment. I had no doubt that don Juan and don Genaro had induced my dreamlike state for a specific purpose. I seemed to be on the verge of understanding what that purpose was when something extraneous to me forced me to pay attention to my surroundings. It took me a long moment to orient myself. I was actually lying on my stomach and what I was lying on was a most spectacular floor. As I examined it, I could not avoid a feeling of awe and wonder. I could not conceive what it was made of. Irregular slabs of some unknown substance had been placed in a most intricate yet simple fashion. They had been put together but were not stuck to the ground or to each other. They were elastic and gave when I attempted to pry them apart with my fingers, but once I released the tension they went right back to their original position.

I tried to get up and was seized by the most outlandish sensory distortion. I had no control over my body; in fact, my body did not seem to be my own. It was inert; I had no connection to any of its parts and when I tried to stand up I could not move my arms and I wobbled helplessly on my stomach, rolling on my side. The momentum of my wobbling almost made me do a complete turn onto my stomach again. My outstretched arms and legs prevented me from turning over and I came to rest on my back. In that position I caught a glimpse of two strangely shaped legs and the most distorted feet I had ever seen. It was my body! I seemed to be wrapped up in a tunic. The thought that came to my mind was that I was experiencing a scene of myself as a cripple or an invalid of some sort. I tried to curve my back and look at my legs but I could only jerk my body. I was looking directly at a yellow sky, a deep, rich lemon-yellow sky. It had grooves or canals of a deeper yellow tone and an endless number of protuberances that hung like drops of water. The total effect of that incredible sky was staggering. I could not determine if the protuberances were clouds. There were also areas of shadows and areas of different tones of yellow which I discovered as I moved my head from side to side.

Then something else attracted my attention: a sun at the very zenith of the yellow sky, right over my head, a mild sun — judging by the fact that I could stare into it — that cast a soothing, uniform whitish light.

Before I had had time to ponder upon all these unearthly sights, I was violently shaken; my head jerked and bobbed back and forth. I felt I was being lifted. I heard a shrill voice and giggling and I was confronted by a most astounding sight: a giant barefoot female. Her face was round and enormous. Her black hair was cut in pageboy fashion. Her arms and legs were gigantic. She picked me up and lifted me to her shoulders as if I were a doll. My body hung limp. I was looking down her strong back. She had a fine fuzz around her shoulders and down her spine. Looking down from her shoulder, I saw the magnificent floor again. I could hear it giving elastically under her enormous weight and I could see the pressure marks that her feet left on it.

She put me down on my stomach in front of a structure, some sort of building. I noticed then that there was something wrong with my depth perception. I could not figure out the size of the building by looking at it. At moments it seemed ridiculously small, but then after I seemingly adjusted my perception, I truly marveled at its monumental proportions.

The giant girl sat next to me and made the floor squeak. I was touching her enormous knee. She smelled like candy or strawberries. She talked to me and I understood everything she said; pointing to the structure, she told me that I was going to live there.

My prowess of observation seemed to increase as I got over the initial shock of finding myself there. I noticed then that the building had four exquisite dysfunctional columns. They did not support anything; they were on top of the building. Their shape was simplicity itself; they were long and graceful projections that seemed to be reaching for that awesome, incredibly yellow sky. The effect of those inverted columns was sheer beauty to me. I had a seizure of aesthetic rapture.

The columns seemed to have been made in one piece; I could not even conceive how. The two columns in front were joined by a slender beam, a monumentally long rod that I thought may have served as a railing of some sort, or a veranda overlooking the front.

The giant girl made me slide on my back into the structure. The roof was black and flat and was covered with symmetric holes that let the yellowish glare of the sky show through, creating the most intricate patterns. I was truly awed with the utter simplicity and beauty that had been achieved by those dots of yellow sky showing through those precise holes in the roof, and the patterns of shadows that they created on that magnificent and intricate floor. The structure was square, and outside of its poignant beauty it was incomprehensible to me.

My state of exultation was so intense at that moment that I wanted to weep, or stay there forever. But some force, or tension, or something undefinable began to pull me. Suddenly I found myself out of the structure, still lying on my back. The giant girl was there, but there was another being with her, a woman so big that she reached to the sky and eclipsed the sun. Compared to her the giant girl was just a little girl. The big woman was angry; she grabbed the structure by one of its columns, lifted it up, turned it upside down, and set it on the floor. It was a chair!

That realization was like a catalyst; it triggered some overwhelming perceptions. I went through a series of images that were disconnected but could be made to stand as a sequence. In successive flashes I saw or realized that the magnificent and incomprehensible floor was a straw mat; the yellow sky was the stucco ceiling of a room; the sun was a light bulb; the structure that had evoked such rapture in me was a chair that a child had turned upside down to play house.

I had one more coherent and sequential vision of another mysterious architectural structure of monumental proportions. It stood by itself. It looked almost like a shell of a pointed snail standing with its tail up. The walls were made of concave and convex plates of some strange purple material; each plate had grooves that seemed more functional than ornamental.

I examined the structure meticulously and in detail and found that it was, like in the case of the previous one, thoroughly incomprehensible. I expected to suddenly adjust my perception to disclose the "true" nature of the structure. But nothing of the sort happened. I then had a conglomerate of alien and inextricable "awarenesses," or "findings," about the building and its function, which did not make sense, because I had no frame of reference for them.

I regained my normal awareness all of a sudden. Don Juan and don Genaro were next to me. I was tired. I looked for my watch; it was gone. Don Juan and don Genaro giggled in unison. Don Juan said that I should not worry about time and that I should concentrate on following certain recommendations that don Genaro had made to me.

I turned to don Genaro and he made a joke. He said that the most important recommendation was that I should learn to write with my finger, to save on pencils and to show off.

They teased me about my notes for a while longer and then I went to sleep.

Don Juan and don Genaro listened to the detailed account of my experience, which I gave them at don Juan's request after I woke up the next day.

"Genaro feels that you've got enough for the time being," don Juan said after I finished talking.

Don Genaro assented with a nod.

"What was the meaning of what I experienced last night?" I asked.

"You caught a glimpse of the most important issue of sorcery," don Juan said. "Last night you peeked into the totality of yourself. But that's of course a meaningless statement for you at this moment. Obviously, arriving at the totality of oneself is not a matter of one's desire to agree, or of one's willingness to learn. Genaro thinks that your body needs time to let the whispering of the *nagual* sink into you."

Don Genaro nodded again.

"Plenty of time," he said, shaking his head up and down. "Twenty or thirty years perhaps."

I did not know how to react. I looked at don Juan for clues. They both had serious expressions.

"Do I really have twenty or thirty years?" I asked.

"Of course not!" don Genaro yelled and they broke into laughter.

Don Juan said that I should return whenever my inner voice told me to, and that in the meantime I should try to assemble all the suggestions that they had made while I was split.

"How do I do that?" I asked.

"By turning off your internal dialogue and letting something in you flow out and expand," don Juan said. "That something is your perception, but don't try to figure out what I mean. Just let the whispering of the *nagual* guide you."

Then he said that the night before I had had two sets of intrinsically different views. One was inexplicable, the other was perfectly natural, and the order in which they had happened pointed to a condition that was intrinsic to all of us.

"One view was the *nagual*, the other the *tonal*," don Genaro added.

I wanted him to explain his statement. He looked at me and patted me on the back.

Don Juan stepped in and said that the first two views were the "nagual," and that don Genaro had selected a tree and the ground as the points for emphasis. The other two were views of the "tonal" that he himself had selected; one of them was my perception of the world as an infant.

"It appeared to be an alien world to you, because your perception had not been trimmed yet to fit the desired mold," he said.

"Was that the way I really saw the world?" I asked.

"Certainly," he said. "That was your memory."

I asked don Juan whether the feeling of aesthetic appreciation that had enraptured me was also part of my memory.

"We go into those views as we are today," he said. "You were seeing that scene as you would see it now. Yet the exercise was one of perception. That was the scene of a time when the world became for you what it is now. A time when a chair became a chair."

He did not want to discuss the other scene.

"That wasn't a memory of my childhood," I said.

"That's right," he said. "It was something else."

"Was it something I will see in the future?" I asked.

"There's no future!" he exclaimed cuttingly. "The future is only a way of talking. For a sorcerer there is only the here and now."

He said that there was essentially nothing to say about it because the purpose of the exercise had been to open the wings of my perception, and that although I had not flown on those wings I had nonetheless touched four points which would be inconceivable to reach from the point of view of my ordinary perception.

I began to gather my things to leave. Don Genaro helped me pack my notebook; he put it in the bottom of my briefcase.

"It'll be warm and cozy there," he said and winked. "You can rest assured that it won't catch cold."

Then don Juan seemed to change his mind about my leaving and started to talk about my experience. I automatically tried to grab my briefcase from don Genaro's hands, but he dropped it to the floor before I touched it. Don Juan was talking with his back turned to me. I scooped up the briefcase and hurriedly searched for my notebook. Don Genaro had really packed it so tightly that I had a hellish time getting to it; finally I took it out and began to write. Don Juan and don Genaro were staring at me.

"You're in terrible shape," don Juan said, laughing. "You reach for your notebook as a drunkard reaches for the bottle."

"As a loving mother reaches for her child," don Genaro snapped.

"As a priest reaches for his crucifix," don Juan added.

"As a woman reaches for her panties," don Genaro yelled.

They went on and on presenting similes and howling with laughter as they walked me to my car.

PART THREE

The Sorcerers' Explanation

THREE WITNESSES TO THE NAGUAL

Upon returning home I was faced again with the task of organizing my field notes. What don Juan and don Genaro had made me experience became all the more poignant as I recapitulated the events. I noticed, however, that my usual reaction of indulging for months in bewilderment and awe over what I had gone through was not as intense as it had been in the past. Various times, I deliberately attempted to engage my feelings, as I had done before, in speculation and even in self-pity; but something was missing. I had also had the intention of writing down a number of questions to ask don Juan, don Genaro, or even Pablito. The project failed before I had begun it. There was something in me that prevented my entering into a mood of inquiry or perplexity.

I did not purposely seek to go back to don Juan and don Genaro, but neither did I shy away from the possibility. One day, however, without any premeditation on my part I simply felt that it was time to see them.

In the past, every time I was about to leave for Mexico, I had always had the feeling that there were thousands of important and pressing questions that I wanted to ask don Juan; this time there was nothing on my mind. It was as if after I had worked over my notes I had become emptied of the past and ready for the here and now of don Juan and don Genaro's world.

I had to wait only a few hours before don Juan "found" me in the market of a little town in the mountains of central Mexico. He greeted me with utmost affection and made a casual suggestion. He said that before we arrived at don Genaro's place, he would like to pay a visit to don Genaro's apprentices, Pablito and Nestor. As I turned off the highway he told me to keep a close watch for any unusual sight on the side of the road or on the road itself. I asked him to give me more precise clues about what he had in mind.

"I can't," he said. "The *nagual* doesn't need precise clues."

I slowed the car down in an automatic response to his reply. He laughed loudly and signaled me with a movement of his hand to keep on driving.

As we approached the town where Pablito and Nestor lived don Juan told me to stop my car. He moved his chin imperceptibly and pointed to a group of medium size boulders on the left side of the road.

"There's the *nagual*," he said in a whisper.

There was no one around. I had expected to see don Genaro. I looked at the boulders again and then I scanned the area around them. There was nothing in sight. I strained my eyes to distinguish anything, a small animal, an insect, a shadow, a strange formation of the rocks, anything unusual. I gave up after a moment and turned to face don Juan. He held my questioning gaze without smiling and then gently pushed my arm with the back of his hand to make me look at the boulders again. I stared at them, then don Juan got out of the car and told me to follow him and examine them.

We walked slowly on a gentle slope for about sixty or seventy yards to the base of the rocks. He stood there for a moment and whispered in my right ear that the "nagual" was waiting for me right at that place. I told him that no matter how hard I tried, all I could distinguish were the rocks and a few tufts of weeds and some cactuses. He insisted, however, that the "nagual" was there, waiting for me.

He ordered me to sit down, turn off my internal dialogue, and keep my unfocused eyes on the top of the boulders. He sat by me and, putting his mouth to my right ear, whispered that the "nagual" had seen me, that it was there although I could not visualize it, and that my problem was merely one of not being capable of completely shutting off my internal dialogue. I heard every word he said in a state of inner silence. I understood everything yet I was incapable of answering; the effort needed to think and talk would have been impossible. My reactions to his comments were not thoughts proper but rather complete units of feeling, which had all the innuendos of meaning that I usually associate with thinking.

He whispered that it was very difficult to start by oneself on the path towards the "nagual," and that I was indeed most fortunate to have been launched by the moth and its song. He said that by holding the memory of the "moth's call," I could bring it back to aid me.

His words were either an overpowering suggestion or perhaps I summoned that perceptual phenomenon he called the "moth's call," for no sooner had he whispered his words to me than the extraordinary sputtering sound became audible. Its richness of tone made me feel as if I were inside an echo chamber. As the sound grew in loudness or proximity, I also detected, in a dreamlike state, that something was moving on top of the boulders. The movement frightened me so intensely that I immediately regained my crystal clear awareness. My eyes focused on the boulders. Don Genaro was sitting on top of one of them! His feet were dangling; and with the heels of his shoes he was hammering the rock, producing a rhythmical sound that seemed to be synchronized with the "moth's call." He smiled and waved his hand at me. I wanted to think rationally. I had the feeling, the desire to figure out how he got there, or how I saw him there, but I could not involve my reason at all. All I could do, under the circumstances, was to look at him while he sat smiling, waving his hand.

After a moment he seemed to get ready to slide down the round boulder. I saw him stiffening his legs, preparing his feet for landing on the hard ground, and arching his back until he almost touched the surface of the rock in order to gain sliding momentum. But in the middle of his descent his body stopped. I had the impression he got stuck. He kicked a couple of times with both legs as if he were floating in water. He seemed to be trying to get loose from something that had trapped him by the seat of his pants. He rubbed the sides of his buttocks frantically with both hands. He actually gave me the impression of being painfully caught. I wanted to run to him and aid him, but don Juan held my arm. I heard him say to me, half choking with laughter, "Watch him! Watch him!"

Don Genaro kicked, contorted his body and wiggled from side to side as if he were loosening a nail; then I heard a loud pop and he glided, or was hurled, to where don Juan and I were standing. He landed four or five feet in front of me, on his feet. He rubbed his buttocks and jumped up and down in a dance of pain, yelling profanities.

"The rock didn't want to let me go and grabbed me by the ass," he said to me in a sheepish tone.

I experienced a sensation of unequaled joy. I laughed loudly. I noticed that my mirth was equal to my clarity of mind. I was engulfed at that moment in an overall state of great awareness. Everything around me was crystal clear. I had been drowsy or absent-minded before because of my inner silence. But then something in don Genaro's sudden appearance had created a state of great lucidity.

Don Genaro kept on rubbing his buttocks and jumping up and down for a while longer; then he limped to my car, opened the door and crawled into the back seat.

I automatically turned around to talk to don Juan. He was not anywhere in sight. I started to call him out loud. Don Genaro got out of the car and began to run around in circles also calling don Juan's name in a shrill, frantic tone. It was only then, as I watched him, that I realized he was mimicking me. I had had an attack of such an intense fear upon finding myself alone with don Genaro that I had run around the car three or four times in quite an unconscious manner, yelling don Juan's name.

Don Genaro said that we had to pick up Pablito and Nestor and that don Juan would be waiting for us somewhere along the way.

After I had overcome my initial fright, I told him that I was glad to see him. He teased me about my reaction. He said that don Juan was not like a father to me, but rather like a mother. He made some remarks and puns about "mothers" that were utterly funny. I was laughing so hard that I did not notice that we had arrived at Pablito's house. Don Genaro told me to stop and he got out of the car. Pablito was standing by the door of his house. He came running and got in the car and sat next to me in the front.

"Let's go to Nestor's place," he said as if he were in a hurry.

I turned to look for don Genaro. He was not around. Pablito urged me in a pleading voice to hurry.

We drove up to Nestor's house. He was also waiting by the door. We got out of the car. I had the feeling that the two of them knew what was going on.

"Where are we going?" I asked.

"Didn't Genaro tell you?" Pablito asked me with a tone of incredulity.

I assured them that neither don Juan nor don Genaro had mentioned anything to me.

"We're going to a power place," Pablito said.

"What are we going to do there?" I asked.

They both said in unison that they did not know. Nestor added that don Genaro had told him to guide me to the place.

"Did you come from Genaro's house?" Pablito asked.

I mentioned that I had been with don Juan and that we had found don Genaro on the way and that don Juan had left me with him.

"Where did don Genaro go?" I asked Pablito.

But Pablito did not know what I was talking about. He had not seen don Genaro in my car.

"He drove with me to your house," I said.

"I think you had the *nagual* in your car," Nestor said in a frightened tone.

He did not want to sit in the back and crammed next to Pablito in the front.

We drove in silence, except for Nestor's short commands to show the way.

I wanted to think about the events of that morning, but somehow I knew that any attempt to explain them was a fruitless indulging on my part. I tried to engage Nestor and Pablito in a conversation; they said that they were too nervous inside the car and could not talk. I enjoyed their candid reply and did not press them any further.

After more than an hour's drive, we parked the car on a side road and climbed up the side of a steep mountain. We walked in silence for another hour or so, with Nestor in the lead, and then we stopped at the bottom of a huge cliff, which was perhaps over two hundred feet high with a nearly vertical drop. With half-closed eyes Nestor scanned the ground, looking for a proper place to sit. I was painfully aware that he was clumsy in his scanning movements. Pablito, who was next to me, seemed at various times to be on the verge of stepping in and correcting him, but he restrained himself and relaxed. Then Nestor selected a place, after a moment's hesitation. Pablito sighed with relief. I knew that the place Nestor had selected was the proper one, but I could not figure out how I knew that. Thus I involved myself in the pseudo problem of imagining what place I would have selected myself if I had been leading them. I could not, however, even begin to speculate on the procedure I would have followed. Pablito was obviously aware of what I was doing.

"You can't do that," he whispered to me.

I laughed with embarrassment, as if he had caught me doing something illicit. Pablito laughed and said that don Genaro always walked around in the mountains with both of them and gave each of them the lead from time to time, so he knew that there was no way of imagining what would have been one's choice.

"Genaro says that the reason why there is no way to do that is because there are only right and wrong choices," he said. "If you make a wrong choice your body knows it, and so does the body of everyone else; but if you make a right choice the body knows that and relaxes and forgets right away that there was a choice. You reload your body, see, like a gun, for the next choice. If you want to use your body again for making the same choice, it doesn't work."

Nestor looked at me; he was apparently curious about my taking notes. He nodded affirmatively as if agreeing with Pablito and then smiled for the first time. Two of his upper teeth were crooked.

Pablito explained that Nestor was not mean or morbid but embarrassed by his teeth and that that was the reason he never smiled. Nestor laughed, covering his mouth. I told him that I could send him to a dentist to have his teeth straightened. They thought that my suggestion was a joke and laughed like two children.

"Genaro says that he has to overcome the feeling of shame by himself," Pablito said. "Besides, Genaro says that he's lucky; while everyone else bites the same way, Nestor can split a bone lengthwise with his strong crooked teeth and he can bite a hole through your finger like a nail."

Nestor opened his mouth and showed me his teeth. The left incisor and the canine had grown in sideways. He made his teeth clatter by biting on them and growled like a dog. He made two or three mock advances towards me. Pablito laughed.

I had never seen Nestor so light. The few times I had been with him in the past he had given me the impression of being a middle-aged man. As he sat there smiling with his crooked teeth I marveled at his youthful appearance. He looked like a young man in his early twenties.

Pablito again read my thoughts to perfection.

"He's losing his self-importance," he said. "That's why he's younger."

Nestor nodded affirmatively and without saying a word he let out a very loud fart. I was startled and dropped my pencil.

Pablito and Nestor nearly died laughing. When they had calmed down, Nestor came to my side and showed me a homemade contraption that made a peculiar sound when squeezed with the hand. He explained that don Genaro had showed him how to make it. It had a minute bellows, and the vibrator could be any kind of leaf that was placed in a slit between the two pieces of wood that were the compressors. Nestor said that the kind of sound it produced depended on the type of leaf that one used as a vibrator. He wanted me to try it and showed me how to squeeze the compressors to produce a certain type of sound, and how to open them in order to produce another.

"What do you use it for?" I asked.

They both exchanged a glance.

"That's his spirit catcher, you fool," Pablito said cuttingly.

His tone was peevish but his smile was friendly. They were both such a strange unnerving mixture of don Genaro and don Juan.

I became absorbed in a horrible thought. Were don Juan and don Genaro playing tricks on me? I had a moment of supreme terror. But something snapped inside of my stomach and I instantly became calm again. I knew that Pablito and Nestor were using don Genaro and don Juan as models for behavior. I myself had found that I also was behaving more and more like them.

Pablito said that Nestor was lucky to have a spirit catcher and that he did not have one himself.

"What shall we do here?" I asked Pablito.

Nestor answered as if I had addressed the question to him.

"Genaro told me that we have to wait here, and while we wait we should laugh and enjoy ourselves," he said.

"How long do you think we have to wait?" I asked.

He did not answer; he shook his head and looked at Pablito as if asking him.

"I have no idea," Pablito said.

We got involved then in a lively conversation about Pablito's sisters. Nestor teased him that his oldest sister had such a mean look that she could kill lice with her eyes. He said that Pablito was afraid of her because she was so strong that once in a fit of anger she plucked a handful of his hair as if it were chicken feathers.

Pablito conceded that his oldest sister had been a beast, but that the "nagual" had fixed her and brought her into line. After he had told me the story of how she was made to behave I realized that Pablito and Nestor never mentioned don Juan's name but referred to him as the "nagual." Apparently don Juan had intervened in Pablito's life and coerced all his sisters into leading a more harmonious life. Pablito said that after the "nagual" was through with them they were like saints.

Nestor wanted to know what I did with my notes. I explained my work to them. I had the weird sensation that they were genuinely interested in what I was saying and I ended up talking about anthropology and philosophy. I felt ludicrous and wanted to stop, but I found myself immersed in my elucidation and unable to cut it short. I had the unsettling sensation that both of them as a team were somehow forcing me into that lengthy explanation. Their eyes were fixed on me. They did not seemed to be bored or tired.

I was in the middle of a comment when I heard the faint sound of the "moth's call." My body stiffened and I never finished my sentence.

"The *nagual* is here," I said automatically.

Nestor and Pablito exchanged a look that I thought was sheer terror and jumped to my side and flanked me. Their mouths were open. They looked like frightened children.

I had an inconceivable sensory experience then. My left ear began to move. I felt it sort of wiggling by itself. It practically turned my head in a half circle until I was facing what I thought to be the east. My head tilted slightly to the right; in that position I was capable of detecting the rich sputtering sound of the "moth's call." It sounded as if it were far away, coming from the northeast. Once I had established the direction, my ear picked up an incredible amount of sounds. I had no way of knowing, however, whether they were memories of sounds I had heard before or actual sounds which were being produced then.

The place where we were was the rugged west slope of a mountain range. Towards the northeast there were groves of trees and patches of mountain shrubs. My ear seemed to pick up the sound of something heavy moving over rocks, coming from that direction.

Nestor and Pablito were either responding to my actions or they themselves were hearing the same sounds. I would have liked to ask them, but I did not dare; or perhaps I was incapable of interrupting my concentration.

Nestor and Pablito huddled against me, by my sides, when the sound became louder and closer. Nestor seemed to be the one who was most affected by it; his body shivered uncontrollably. At one moment my left arm began to shake; it raised without my volition until it was almost level with my face, and then it pointed to an area of shrubs. I heard a vibratory sound or a roar; it was a familiar sound to me. I had heard it many years before under the influence of a psychotropic plant. I detected in the shrubs a gigantic black shape. It was as if the shrubs themselves were becoming darker by degrees until they had changed into an ominous blackness. It had no definite form, but it moved. It seemed to breathe. I heard a chilling scream, which was mixed with the yells of terror of Pablito and Nestor; and the shrubs, or the black shape into which they had turned, flew up towards us.

I could not maintain my equanimity. Somehow something in me faltered. The shape first hovered over us, and then engulfed us. The light around us became opaque. It was as if the sun had set. Or as if all of a sudden it had become twilight. I felt Nestor and Pablito's heads under my armpits; I brought my arms down over their heads in an unconscious protective movement and I fell, spinning backwards.

I did not reach the rocky ground, however, for an instant later I found myself standing up flanked by Pablito and Nestor. Both of them, although taller than I, seemed to have shriveled; by arching their legs and backs they were actually shorter than I and fit under my arms.

Don Juan and don Genaro were standing in front of us. Don Genaro's eyes glittered like the eyes of a cat at night. Don Juan's eyes had the same glow. I had never seen don Juan look that way. He was truly awesome. More so than don Genaro. He seemed younger and stronger than usual. Looking at both of them, I had the maddening feeling that they were not men like myself.

Pablito and Nestor whined quietly. Then don Genaro said that we were the picture of the Trinity. I was the Father, Pablito was the Son, and Nestor the Holy Ghost. Don Juan and don Genaro laughed in a booming tone. Pablito and Nestor smiled meekly.

Don Genaro said that we had to disentangle ourselves, because embraces were permissible only between men and women, or between a man and his burro.

I realized then that I was standing on the same spot I had been before, and that obviously I had not spun backwards as I thought I had. In fact, Nestor and Pablito were also on the same spot they had been on.

Don Genaro signaled Pablito and Nestor with a movement of his head. Don Juan signaled me to follow them. Nestor took the lead and pointed out a sitting place for me and another one for Pablito. We sat in a straight line, about fifty yards from the place where don Juan and don Genaro stood motionless at the base of the cliff. As I kept on staring at them, my eyes went involuntarily out of focus. I knew I had definitely crossed them, because I was seeing four of them. Then my left eye image of don Juan became superimposed on the right eye image of don Genaro; the result of the merger was that I saw an iridescent being standing in between don Juan and don Genaro. It was not a man as I ordinarily see men. It was rather a ball of white fire; something like fibers of light covered it. I shook my head; the double image was dispelled, and yet the sight of don Juan and don Genaro as luminous beings persisted. I was seeing two strange elongated luminous objects. They looked like white iridescent footballs with fibers, fibers that had a light of their own.

The two luminous beings shivered; I actually saw their fibers shaking and then they whizzed out of sight. They were pulled up by a long filament, a cobweb that seemed to shoot out from the top of the cliff. The sensation I had was that a long beam of light or a luminous line had dropped from the rock and lifted them up. I perceived the sequence with my eyes and with my body.

I was also capable of noticing enormous disparities in my mode of perceiving, but I was incapable of speculating about them as I would have ordinarily done. Thus, I was aware that I was looking straight at the base of the cliff, and yet I was seeing don Juan and don Genaro on the top as if I had tilted my head up forty-five degrees.

I wanted to feel afraid, perhaps to cover my face and weep, or do something else within my normal range of responses. But I seemed to be locked. My desires were not thoughts, as I know thoughts, therefore they could not evoke the emotional response I was accustomed to eliciting in myself.

Don Juan and don Genaro plunged to the ground. I felt that they had done so judging by the consuming feeling of falling that I experienced in my stomach.

Don Genaro remained where he had landed, but don Juan walked towards us and sat down, behind me, to my right. Nestor was in a crouching position; his legs tucked in against his stomach; he was resting his chin on his cupped palms; his forearms served as supports by being propped against his thighs. Pablito was sitting with his body slightly bent forward, holding his hands against his stomach. I noticed then that I had placed my forearms across my umbilical region and I was holding myself by the skin on my sides. I had grabbed myself so hard that my sides ached.

Don Juan spoke in a dry murmur, addressing all of us.

"You must fix your gaze on the *nagual*," he said. "All thoughts and words must be washed away."

He repeated it five or six times. His voice was strange, unknown to me; it gave me the actual feeling of the scales on the skin of a lizard. That simile was a feeling, not a conscious thought. Each of his words peeled, like scales; there was such an eerie rhythm to them; they were muffled, dry, like soft coughing; a rhythmical murmur made into a command.

Don Genaro stood motionless. As I stared at him I could not keep my image conversion, and my eyes crossed involuntarily. In that state I noticed again a strange luminosity in don Genaro's body. My eyes were beginning to close, or to tear. Don Juan came to my rescue. I heard him giving a command not to cross the eyes. I felt a soft tap on my head. He had apparently hit me with a pebble. I saw the pebble bounce a couple of times on the rocks near me. He must have also hit Nestor and Pablito; I heard the sound of other pebbles as they bounced on the rocks.

Don Genaro adopted a strange dancing posture. His knees were bent, his arms were extended to his sides, his fingers outstretched. He seemed to be about to twirl; in fact, he half whirled around and then he was pulled up. I had the clear perception that he had been hoisted up by the line of a giant caterpillar that lifted his body to the very top of the cliff. My perception of the upward movement was a most weird mixture of visual and bodily sensations. I half saw and half felt his flight to the top. There was something that looked or felt like a line or an almost imperceptible thread of light pulling him up. I did not see his flight upward in the sense I would follow a bird in flight with my eyes. There was no linear sequence to his movement. I did not have to raise my head to keep him within my field of vision. I saw the line pulling him, then I felt his movement in my body, or with my body, and the next instant he was on the very top of the cliff, hundreds of feet up.

After a few minutes he plummeted down. I felt his falling and groaned involuntarily.

Don Genaro repeated his feat three more times. Each time, my perception was tuned. During his last upward leap I could actually distinguish a series of lines emanating from his midsection, and I knew when he was about to ascend or descend, judging by the way the lines of his body moved. When he was about to leap upward, the lines bent upward; the opposite happened when he was about to leap downward; the lines bent outward and down.

After his fourth leap don Genaro came to us and sat down behind Pablito and Nestor. Then don Juan moved to the front and stood where don Genaro had been. He stood motionless for a while. Don Genaro gave some brief instructions to Pablito and Nestor. I did not understand what he had said. I glanced at them and saw that he had made each one hold a rock and place it against the area of their navels. I was wondering whether I also had to do that, when he told me that the precaution did not apply to me but nonetheless I should have a rock within reach just in case I got ill. Don Genaro jutted his chin forward to indicate that I should gaze at don Juan, then he said something unintelligible; he repeated it, and although I did not understand his words, I knew that it was more or less the same formula that don Juan had voiced. The words did not really matter; it was the rhythm, the dryness of tone, the coughlike quality. I had the certainty that whatever language don Genaro was using was more appropriate than Spanish for the staccato quality of the rhythm.

Don Juan did exactly as don Genaro had initially done, but then instead of leaping upward he twirled around like a gymnast. In a semi-aware way I expected him to land on his feet again. He never did. His body kept on twirling a few feet above the ground. The circles were very rapid at first, then they slowed down. From where I was I could see don Juan's body hanging, like don Genaro's body had, from a threadlike light. He whirled slowly as if allowing us to fully view him. Then he began to ascend; he gained altitude until he reached the top of the cliff. Don Juan was actually floating as if he had no weight. His turns were slow and evoked the image of an astronaut in space whirling around in a state of weightlessness.

I got dizzy as I watched him. My feeling of getting ill seemed to trigger him and he began to whirl at a greater speed. He moved away from the cliff and as he gained speed I became utterly sick. I grabbed the rock and placed it on my stomach. I pressed it against my body as hard as I could. Its touch soothed me a bit. The act of reaching for the rock and holding it against me had allowed me a moment's break. Although I had not taken my eyes away from don Juan, I had nevertheless broken my concentration. Before I reached for the rock I felt that the speed which his floating body had gained was blurring his shape; he looked like a rotating disk and then a light that was spinning. After I had placed the rock against my body his speed diminished; he looked like a hat floating in the air, a kite that bobbed back and forth.

The movement of the kite was even more unsettling. I became uncontrollably ill. I heard the flapping of bird wings and after a moment of uncertainty I knew that the event had ended.

I felt so ill and exhausted that I lay down to sleep. I must have dozed off for a while. I opened my eyes when someone shook my arm. It was Pablito. He spoke to me in a frantic tone and said that I could not fall asleep, because if I did all of us would die. He insisted that we had to leave right away even if we had to drag ourselves on all fours. He also seemed to be physically exhausted. In fact, I had the idea that we should spend the night there. The prospect of walking to my car in the dark seemed most dreadful to me. I tried to convince Pablito, who was getting more frantic. Nestor was so ill that he was indifferent.

Pablito sat down in a state of total despair. I made an effort to organize my thoughts. It was quite dark by then, although there was still enough light to distinguish the rocks around us. The quietness was exquisite and soothing. I enjoyed the moment fully, but suddenly my body jumped; I heard the distant sound of a branch being cracked. I automatically turned to Pablito. He seemed to know what had happened to me. We grabbed Nestor by the armpits and practically lifted him up. We dragged him and ran. He apparently was the only one who knew the way. He gave us short commands from time to time.

I was not concerned with what we did. My attention was focused on my left ear, which seemed to be a unit independent from the rest of me. Some feeling in me forced me to stop every so often and scan the surroundings with my ear. I knew something was following us. It was something massive; it crushed small rocks as it advanced.

Nestor regained a degree of composure and walked by himself, holding on to Pablito's arm occasionally.

We arrived at a group of trees. By then it was completely dark. I heard a sudden and extremely loud cracking sound. It was like the cracking of a monstrous whip that lashed the tops of the trees. I could feel a wave of some sort rippling overhead.

Pablito and Nestor screamed and scrambled out of there at full speed. I wanted them to stop. I was not sure I could run in the dark. But at that instant I heard and felt a series of heavy exhalations right behind me. My fright was indescribable.

The three of us ran together until we reached the car. Nestor led us in some unknown way.

I thought that I should leave them at their houses and then go to a hotel in town. I would not have gone to don Genaro's place for anything in the world; but Nestor did not want to leave the car, neither did Pablito and neither did I. We ended up at Pablito's house. He sent Nestor to buy some beer and cola while his mother and sisters prepared food for us. Nestor made a joke and asked if he could be escorted by the oldest sister in case he was attacked by dogs or drunkards. Pablito laughed and told me that he had been entrusted with Nestor.

"Who has entrusted you with him?" I asked.

"Power, of course!" he replied. "At one time Nestor was older than me, but Genaro did something to him and now he's much younger. You saw that, didn't you?"

"What did don Genaro do?" I asked.

"You know, he made him a child again. He was too important and heavy. He would've died if he was not turned younger."

There was something truly candid and endearing about Pablito. The simplicity of his explanation was overwhelming to me. Nestor was indeed younger; not only did he look younger, but he acted like an innocent child. I knew without any doubt that he genuinely felt like one.

"I take care of him," Pablito continued. "Genaro says that it's an honor to look after a warrior. Nestor is a fine warrior."

His eyes shone, like don Genaro's. He patted me vigorously on the back and laughed.

"Wish him well, Carlitos," he said. "Wish him well."

I was very tired. I had a strange surge of happy sadness. I told him that I came from a place where people rarely if ever wish one another well.

"I know," he said. "The same thing happened to me. But I'm a warrior now and I can afford to wish him well."

THE STRATEGY OF A SORCERER

Don Juan was at don Genaro's house when I got there in the late morning. I greeted him.

"Hey, what happened to you? Genaro and I waited for you all night," he said.

I knew that he was joking. I felt light and happy. I had systematically refused to dwell on whatever I had witnessed the day before. At that moment, however, my curiosity was uncontrollable and I asked him about it.

"Oh, that was a simple demonstration of all the things that you should know before you get the sorcerers' explanation," he said. "What you did yesterday made Genaro feel that you have stored enough power to go for the real thing. You have obviously followed his suggestions. Yesterday you let the wings of your perception unfold. You were stiff but you still perceived all the comings and goings of the *nagual*; in other words, you *saw*. You also confirmed something which at this time is even more important than *seeing*, and that was the fact that you can now place your unwavering attention on the *nagual*. And that's what will decide the outcome of the last issue, the sorcerers' explanation.

"Pablito and you will go into it at the same time. It is a gift of power to be accompanied by such a fine warrior."

That seemed to be all he wanted to say. After a while I asked about don Genaro.

"He's around," he said. "He went into the bushes to make the mountains tremble."

I heard at that moment a distant rumble, like muffled thunder. Don Juan looked at me and laughed.

He made me sit down and asked if I had eaten. I had, so he handed me my notebook and led me to don Genaro's favorite spot, a large rock on the west side of the house, overlooking a deep ravine.

"Now is when I need your total attention," don Juan said. "Attention in the sense that warriors understand attention: a true pause, in order to allow the sorcerers' explanation to fully soak through you. We are at the end of our task; all the necessary instruction has been given to you and now you must stop, look back, and reconsider your steps. Sorcerers say that this is the only way to consolidate one's gains. I definitely would have preferred to tell you all this at your own place of power, but Genaro is your benefactor and his spot may be more beneficial to you in an instance like this."

What he was referring to as my "place of power" was a hilltop in the desert of northern Mexico, which he had shown me years before and had "given" to me as my own.

"Should I just listen to you without taking notes?" I asked.

"This is indeed a tricky maneuver," he said. "On the one hand, I need your total attention, and on the other, you need to be calm and self-assured. The only way for you to be at ease is to write, so this is the time to bring forth all your personal power and fulfill this impossible task of being yourself without being yourself."

He slapped his thigh and laughed.

"I've already told you that I am in charge of your *tonal* and that Genaro is in charge of your *nagual*," he went on. "It has been my duty to help you in every matter concerning your *tonal* and everything that I've done with you or to you was done to accomplish one single task, the task of cleaning and reordering your island of the *tonal*. That's my job as your teacher. Genaro's task as your benefactor is to give you undeniable demonstrations of the *nagual* and to show how to get to it."

"What do you mean by cleaning and reordering the island of the *tonal*?" I asked.

"I mean the total change which I've been telling you about from the first day we met," he said. "I've told you countless times that a most drastic change was needed if you wanted to succeed in the path of knowledge. That change is not a change of mood, or attitude, or outlook; that change entails the transformation of the island of the *tonal*. You have accomplished that task."

"Do you think that I've changed?" I asked.

He hesitated and then laughed loudly.

"You are as idiotic as ever," he said. "And yet you're not the same. See what I mean?"

He mocked my taking notes and said that he missed don Genaro, who would have enjoyed the absurdity of my writing down the sorcerers' explanation.

"At this precise point a teacher would usually say to his disciple that they have arrived at a final crossroad," he continued. "To say such a thing is misleading, though. In my opinion there is no final crossroad, no final step to anything. And since there is no final step to anything, there shouldn't be any secrecy about any part of our lot as luminous beings. Personal power decides who can or who cannot profit by a revelation; my experiences with my fellow men have proven to me that very, very few of them would be willing to listen; and of those few who listen even fewer would be willing to act on what they have listened to; and of those who are willing to act even fewer have enough personal power to profit by their acts. So, the matter of secrecy about the sorcerers' explanation boils down to a routine, perhaps a routine as empty as any other routine.

"At any rate, you know now about the *tonal* and the *nagual*, which are the core of the sorcerers' explanation. To know about them seems to be quite harmless. We are sitting here, talking innocently about them as if they were just an ordinary topic of conversation. You are calmly writing as you've done for years. The scenery around us is a picture of calmness. It is early afternoon, the day is beautiful, the mountains around us have made a protective cocoon for us. One doesn't have to be a sorcerer to realize that this place, which speaks of Genaro's power and impeccability, is the most appropriate background for opening the door; for that is what I'm doing today, opening the door for you. But before we venture beyond this point a fair warning is required; a teacher is supposed to speak in earnest terms and warn his disciple that the harmlessness and placidity of this moment are a mirage, that there is a bottomless abyss in front of him, and that once the door opens there is no way to close it again."

He paused for a moment.

I felt light and happy; from don Genaro's place of predilection I had a breathtaking view. Don Juan was right; the day and the scenery were more than beautiful. I wanted to worry about his admonitions and warnings, but somehow the tranquility around me screened out all my attempts and I found myself hoping that perhaps he was speaking only of metaphorical dangers.

Don Juan suddenly began to talk again.

"The years of hard training are only a preparation for the warrior's devastating encounter with . . ."

He paused again, looked at me with squinting eyes, and chuckled.

". . . with whatever lies out there, beyond this point," he said.

I asked him to explain his ominous statements.

"The sorcerers' explanation, which doesn't seem like an explanation at all, is lethal," he said. "It seems harmless and charming, but as soon as the warrior opens himself to it, it delivers a blow that no one can parry."

He broke into a loud laugh.

"So, be prepared for the worst, but don't hurry or panic," he proceeded. "You don't have any time, and yet you're surrounded by eternity. What a paradox for your *reason!*"

Don Juan stood up. He wiped off the debris on a smooth bowl-like depression and sat there comfortably, with his back against the rock, facing the northwest. He indicated another place for me where I too could sit comfortably. I was to his left, also facing the northwest. The rock was warm and gave me a feeling of serenity, of protection. It was a mild day; a soft wind made the heat of the afternoon sun very pleasant. I took off my hat but don Juan insisted that I should wear it.

"You're now facing in the direction of your own place of power," he said. "That is a prop that may protect you. Today you need all the props you can use. Your hat may be another one of them."

"Why are you warning me, don Juan? What's really going to happen?" I asked.

"What will happen here today depends on whether or not you have enough personal power to focus your unwavering attention on the wings of your perception," he said.

His eyes glittered. He seemed to be more excited than I had ever seen him before. I thought that there was something unusual in his voice, perhaps an unaccustomed nervousness.

He said that the occasion required that right there on my benefactor's place of predilection he recapitulate for me every step that he had taken in his struggle to help me clean and reorder my island of the "tonal." His recapitulation was meticulous and took him about five hours. In a brilliant and clear manner he gave me a succinct account of everything he had done to me since the day we met. It was as if a dam had been broken. His revelations caught me completely off guard. I had accustomed myself to be the aggressive prober; thus, to have don Juan — who was always the reluctant party — elucidating the points of his teachings in such an academic manner was as astounding as his wearing a suit in Mexico City. His control of the language, his dramatic timing, and his choice of words were so extraordinary that I had no way to explain them rationally. He said that at that point a teacher had to speak to the individual warrior in exclusive terms, that the way he was talking to me and the clarity of his explanation were part of his last trick, and that only at the end would everything that he was doing make sense to me. He talked without stopping, until he had finished presenting his recapitulation. And I wrote down everything he said without any conscious effort on my part.

"Let me begin by telling you that a teacher never seeks apprentices and no one can solicit the teachings," he said. "It's always an omen which points out an apprentice. A warrior who may be in the position of becoming a teacher must be alert in order to catch his cubic centimenter of chance. I *saw* you just before we met; you had a good *tonal*, like that girl we encountered in Mexico City. After I *saw* you I waited, very much like what we did with the girl that night in the park. The girl went by without paying attention to us. But you were brought to me by a man who ran away after babbling inanities. You were left there, facing me, also babbling inanities. I knew I had to act fast and hook you; you yourself would've had to do something of that sort if that girl would've talked to you. What I did was to grab you with my *will*."

Don Juan was alluding to the extraordinary way he had looked at me the day we met. He had fixed his gaze on me and I had had an inexplicable feeling of vacuity, or numbness. I could not find any logical explanation for my reaction and I have always believed that after our first meeting I went back to see him only because I had become obsessed with that look.

"That was my quickest way of hooking you," he said. "It was a direct blow to your *tonal*. I numbed it by focusing my *will* on it."

"How did you do that?" I asked.

"The warrior's gaze is placed on the right eye of the other person," he said. "And what it does is to stop the internal dialogue, then the *nagual* takes over; thus, the danger of that maneuver. Whenever the *nagual* prevails, even if it is only for an instant, there is no way of describing the feeling that the body experiences. I know that you have spent endless hours trying to figure out what you felt and that to this day you haven't been able to. I accomplished what I wanted, though. I hooked you."

I told him that I could still remember him staring at me.

"The gaze on the right eye is not a stare," he said. "It's rather a forceful grabbing that one does through the eye of the other person. In other words, one grabs something that is behind the eye. One has the actual physical sensation that one is holding something with the *will*."

He scratched his head, tilting his hat to the front, over his face.

"This is, naturally, only a way of talking," he continued. "A way of explaining weird physical sensations."

He ordered me to stop writing and look at him. He said that he was going to "grab" my "tonal" gently with his "will." The sensation I experienced was a repetition of what I had felt on that first day we had met and on other occasions when don Juan had made me feel that his eyes were actually touching me, in a physical sense.

"But, how do you make me feel you're touching me, don Juan? What do you actually do?" I asked.

"There's no way of exactly describing what one does," he said. "Something snaps forward from someplace below the stomach; that something has direction and can be focused on anything."

I again felt something like soft tweezers clasping some undefined part of me.

"It works only when the warrior learns to focus his *will*," don Juan explained after he moved his eyes away. "There's no way of practicing it, therefore I have not recommended or encouraged its use. At a given moment in the life of a warrior it simply happens. No one knows how."

He remained quiet for a while. I felt extremely apprehensive. Don Juan suddenly began to speak again.

"The secret is in the left eye," he said. "As a warrior progresses on the path of knowledge his left eye can clasp anything. Usually the left eye of a warrior has a strange appearance; sometimes it becomes permanently crossed, or it becomes smaller than the other, or larger, or different in some way."

He glanced at me and in a joking manner pretended to examine my left eye. He shook his head in mock disapproval and chuckled.

"Once the apprentice has been hooked, the instruction begins," he continued. "The first act of a teacher is to introduce the idea that the world we think we see is only a view, a description of the world. Every effort of a teacher is geared to prove this point to his apprentice. But accepting it seems to be one of the hardest things one can do; we are complacently caught in our particular view of the world, which compels us to feel and act as if we knew everything about the world. A teacher, from the very first act he performs, aims at stopping that view. Sorcerers call it stopping the internal dialogue, and they are convinced that it is the single most important technique that an apprentice can learn.

"In order to stop the view of the world which one has held since the cradle, it is not enough to just wish or make a resolution. One needs a practical task; that practical task is called the right way of walking. It seems harmless and nonsensical. As everything else which has power in itself or by itself, the right way of walking does not attract attention. You understood it and regarded it, at least for several years, as a curious way of behaving. It didn't dawn on you until very recently that that was the most effective way to stop your internal dialogue."

"How does the right way of walking stop the internal dialogue?" I asked.

"Walking in that specific manner saturates the *tonal*," he said. "It floods it. You see, the attention of the *tonal* has to be placed on its creations. In fact, it is that attention that creates the order of the world in the first place; so, the *tonal* must be attentive to the elements of its world in order to maintain it, and must, above all, uphold the view of the world as internal dialogue."

He said that the right way of walking was a subterfuge. The warrior, first by curling his fingers, drew attention to the arms; and then by looking, without focusing his eyes, at any point directly in front of him on the arc that started at the tip of his feet and ended above the horizon, he literally flooded his "tonal" with information. The "tonal," without its one-to-one relation with the elements of its description, was incapable of talking to itself, and thus one became silent.

Don Juan explained that the position of the fingers did not matter at all, that the only consideration was to draw attention to the arms by clasping the fingers in various unaccustomed ways, and that the important thing was the manner in which the eyes, by being kept unfocused, detected an enormous number of features of the world without being clear about them. He added that the eyes in that state were capable of picking out details which were too fleeting for normal vision.

"Together with the right way of walking," don Juan went on, "a teacher must teach his apprentice another possibility, which is even more subtle: the possibility of acting without believing, without expecting rewards—acting just for the hell of it. I wouldn't be exaggerating if I told you that the success of a teacher's enterprise depends on how well and how harmoniously he guides his apprentice in this specific respect."

I told don Juan that I did not remember him ever discussing "acting just for the hell of it" as a particular technique; all I could recollect were his constant but loose comments about it.

He laughed and said that his maneuver had been so subtle that it had bypassed me to that day. He then reminded me of all the nonsensical joking tasks that he used to give me every time I had been at his house. Absurd chores such as arranging firewood in patterns, encircling his house with an unbroken chain of concentric circles drawn in the dirt with my finger, sweeping debris from one place to another, and so forth. The tasks also included acts that I had to perform by myself at home, such as wearing a black cap, or tying my left shoe first, or fastening my belt from right to left.

The reason I had never taken them in any other vein except as jokes was that he would invariably tell me to forget about them after I had established them as regular routines.

As he recapitulated all the tasks he had given me I realized that by making me perform senseless routines he had indeed implanted in me the idea of acting without really expecting anything in return.

"Stopping the internal dialogue is, however, the key to the sorcerers' world," he said. "The rest of the activities are only props; all they do is accelerate the effect of stopping the internal dialogue."

He said that there were two major activities or techniques used to accelerate the stopping of the internal dialogue: erasing personal history and "dreaming." He reminded me that during the early stages of my apprenticeship he had given me a number of specific methods for changing my "personality." I had recorded them in my notes and had forgotten about them for years until I realized their importance. Those specific methods seemed at first to be highly idiosyncratic devices to coerce me into modifying my behavior.

He explained that the art of a teacher was to deviate the apprentice's attention from the main issues. A poignant example of that art was the fact that I had not realized until that day that he had actually tricked me into learning a most crucial point: to act without expecting rewards.

He said that in line with that rationale he had rallied my interest around the idea of "seeing," which, properly understood, was the act of dealing directly with the "nagual," an act that was an unavoidable end result of the teachings but an unattainable task as a task per se.

"What was the point of tricking me that way?" I asked.

"Sorcerers are convinced that all of us are a bunch of nincompoops," he said. "We can never relinquish our crummy control voluntarily, thus we have to be tricked."

His contention was that by making me focus my attention on a pseudo task, learning to "see," he had successfully accomplished two things. First he had outlined the direct encounter with the "nagual," without mentioning it, and second he had tricked me into considering the real issues of his teachings as inconsequential affairs. Erasing personal history and "dreaming" were never as important to me as "seeing." I regarded them as very entertaining activities. I even thought that they were the practices for which I had the greatest facility.

"Greatest facility," he said mockingly when he heard my comments. "A teacher must not leave anything to chance. I've told you that you were correct in feeling that you were being tricked. The problem was that you were convinced that that tricking was directed at fooling your *reason*. For me, tricking meant to distract your attention, or to trap it as the case required."

He looked at me with squinting eyes and pointed all around us with a sweeping gesture of his arm.

"The secret of all this is one's attention," he said.

"What do you mean, don Juan?"

"All of this exists only because of our attention. This very rock where we're sitting is a rock because we have been forced to give our attention to it as a rock."

I wanted him to explain that idea. He laughed and raised an accusing finger at me.

"This is a recapitulation," he said. "We'll get to that later."

He asserted that because of his decoy maneuver I became interested in erasing personal history and "dreaming." He said that the effects of those two techniques were ultimately devastating if they were exercised in their totality, and that then his concern was the concern of every teacher, not to let his apprentice do anything that would plunge him into aberration and morbidity.

"Erasing personal history and *dreaming* should only be a help," he said. "What any apprentice needs to buffer him is temperance and strength. That's why a teacher introduces the warrior's way, or living like a warrior. This is the glue that joins together everything in a sorcerer's world. Bit by bit a teacher must forge and develop it. Without the sturdiness and level-headedness of the warrior's way there is no possibility of withstanding the path of knowledge."

Don Juan said that learning the warrior's way was an instance when the apprentice's attention had to be trapped rather than deviated, and that he had trapped my attention by pushing me out of my ordinary circumstances every time I had gone to see him. Our roaming around the desert and the mountains had been the means to accomplish that.

The maneuver of altering the context of my ordinary world by taking me for hikes and hunting was another instance of his system that had bypassed me. Context disarrangement meant that I did not know the ropes and my attention had to be focused on everything don Juan did.

"What a trick! Uh?" he said and laughed.

I laughed with awe. I had never realized that he was so aware.

He then enumerated his steps in guiding and trapping my attention. When he had finished his account he added that a teacher had to take into consideration the personality of the apprentice, and that in my case he had to be careful because I was violent and would have thought nothing of killing myself out of despair.

"What a preposterous fellow you are, don Juan," I said in jest, and he exploded in a giant laugh.

He explained that in order to help erase personal history three other techniques were taught. They were: losing self-importance, assuming responsibility, and using death as an adviser. The idea was that, without the beneficial effect of those three techniques, erasing personal history would involve the apprentice in being shifty, evasive and unnecessarily dubious about himself and his actions.

Don Juan asked me to tell him what had been the most natural reaction I had had in moments of stress, frustration and disappointment before I became an apprentice. He said that his own reaction had been wrath. I told him that mine had been self-pity.

"Although you're not aware of it, you had to work your head off to make that feeling a natural one," he said. "By now there is no way for you to recollect the immense effort that you needed to establish self-pity as a feature of your island. Self-pity bore witness to everything you did. It was just at your fingertips, ready to advise you. Death is considered by a warrior to be a more amenable adviser, which can also be brought to bear witness on everything one does, just like self-pity, or wrath. Obviously, after an untold struggle you had learned to feel sorry for yourself. But you can also learn, in the same way, to feel your impending end, and thus you can learn to have the idea of your death at your fingertips. As an adviser, self-pity is nothing in comparison to death."

Don Juan pointed out then that there was seemingly a contradiction in the idea of change; on the one hand, the sorcerers' world called for a drastic transformation, and on the other, the sorcerers' explanation said that the island of the "tonal" was complete and not a single element of it could be removed. Change, then, did not mean obliterating anything but rather altering the use assigned to those elements.

"Take self-pity for instance," he said. "There is no way to get rid of it for good; it has a definite place and character in your island, a definite façade which is recognizable. Thus, every time the occasion arises, self-pity becomes active. It has history. If you then change the façade of self-pity, you would have shifted its place of prominence."

I asked him to explain the meaning of his metaphors, especially the idea of changing façades. I understood it as perhaps the act of playing more than one role at the same time.

"One changes the façade by altering the use of the elements of the island," he replied. "Take self-pity again. It was useful to you because you either felt important and deserving of better conditions, better treatment, or because you were unwilling to assume responsibility for the acts that brought you to the state that elicited self-pity, or because you were incapable of bringing the idea of your impending death to witness your acts and advise you.

"Erasing personal history and its three companion techniques are the sorcerers' means for changing the façade of the elements of the island. For instance, by erasing your personal history, you have denied use to self-pity; in order for self-pity to work you had to feel important, irresponsible, and immortal. When those feelings were altered in some way, it was no longer possible for you to feel sorry for yourself.

"The same was true with all the other elements which you've changed on your island. Without using those four techniques you never could've succeeded in changing them. But changing façades means only that one has assigned a secondary place to a formerly important element. Your self-pity is still a feature of your island; it will be there in the back in the same way that the idea of your impending death, or your humbleness, or your responsibility for your acts were there, without ever being used."

Don Juan said that once all those techniques had been presented, the apprentice arrived at a crossroad. Depending on his sensibility, the apprentice did one of two things. He either took the recommendations and suggestions made by his teacher at their face value, acting without expecting rewards; or he took everything as a joke or an aberration.

I remarked that in my own case I was confused by the word "techniques." I always expected a set of precise directions, but he had given me only vague suggestions; and I was incapable of taking them seriously or acting in accordance with his stipulations.

"That was your mistake," he said. "I had to decide then whether or not to use power plants. You could've used those four techniques to clean and reorder your island of the *tonal*. They would've led you to the *nagual*. But not all of us are capable of reacting to simple recommendations. You, and I for that matter, needed something else to shake us; we needed those power plants."

It had indeed taken me years to realize the importance of those early suggestions made by don Juan. The extraordinary effect that psychotropic plants had had on me was what gave me the bias that their use was the key feature of the teachings. I held on to that conviction and it was only in the later years of my apprenticeship that I realized that the meaningful transformations and findings of sorcerers were always done in states of sober consciousness.

"What would have happened if I had taken your recommendations seriously?" I asked.

"You would have gotten to the *nagual*," he replied.

"But would I have gotten to the *nagual* without a benefactor?"

"Power provides according to your impeccability," he said. "If you had seriously used those four techniques, you would've stored enough personal power to find a benefactor. You would've been impeccable and power would have opened all the necessary avenues. That is the rule."

"Why didn't you give me more time?" I asked.

"You had all the time you needed," he said. "Power showed me the way. One night I gave you a riddle to work out; you had to find your beneficial spot in front of the door of my house. That night you performed marvelously under pressure and in the morning you fell asleep over a very special rock that I had put there. Power showed me that you had to be pushed mercilessly or you wouldn't do a thing."

"Did the power plants help me?" I asked.

"Certainly," he said. "They opened you up by stopping your view of the world. In this respect power plants have the same effect on the *tonal* as the right way of walking. Both flood it with information and force the internal dialogue to come to a stop. The plants are excellent for that, but very costly. They cause untold damage to the body. This is their drawback, especially with the devil's weed."

"If you knew that they were so dangerous, why did you give me so many of them, so many times?" I asked.

He assured me that the details of the procedure were decided by power itself. He said that although the teachings were supposed to cover the same issues with all apprentices, the order was different for each one, and that he had gotten repeated indications that I needed a great deal of coercion in order to bother with anything.

"I was dealing with a sassy immortal being that had no respect for his life or his death," he said, laughing.

I brought up the fact that he had described and discussed those plants in terms of anthropomorphic qualities. His references to them were always as if the plants had personalities. He replied that that was a prescribed means for deviating the apprentice's attention away from the real issue, which was stopping the internal dialogue.

"If they are used only to stop the internal dialogue, what's their connection with the ally?" I asked.

"That's a difficult point to explain," he said. "Those plants lead the apprentice directly to the *nagual*, and the ally is an aspect of it. We function at the center of *reason* exclusively, regardless of who we are or where we come from. *Reason* can naturally account in one way or another for everything that happens within its view of the world. The ally is something which is outside of that view, outside the realm of *reason*. It can be witnessed only at the center of *will* at times when our ordinary view has stopped, therefore it is properly the *nagual*. Sorcerers, however, can learn to perceive the ally in a most intricate way, and in doing so they get too deeply immersed in a new view. So, in order to protect you from that fate, I did not emphasize the ally as sorcerers usually do. Sorcerers have learned after generations of using power plants to account in their views for everything that is accountable about them. I would say that sorcerers, by using their *will*, have succeeded in enlarging their views of the world. My teacher and benefactor were the clearest examples of that. They were men of great power, but they were not men of knowledge. They never broke the bounds of their enormous views and thus never arrived at the totality of themselves, yet they knew about it. It wasn't that they lived aberrant lives, claiming things beyond their reach; they knew that they had missed the boat and that only at their death would the total mystery be revealed to them. Sorcery had given them only a glimpse but never the real means to get to that evasive totality of oneself.

"I gave you enough of the sorcerers' view without letting you get hooked by it. I said that only if one pits two views against each other can one weasel between them to arrive at the real world. I meant that one can arrive at the totality of oneself only when one fully understands that the world is merely a view, regardless of whether that view belongs to an ordinary man or to a sorcerer.

"Here is where I varied from the tradition. After a lifelong struggle I know that what matters is not to learn a new description but to arrive at the totality of oneself. One should get to the *nagual* without maligning the *tonal*, and above all, without injuring one's body. You took those plants following the exact steps I followed myself. The only difference was that instead of plunging you into them I stopped when I judged that you had stored enough views of the *nagual*. That is the reason why I never wanted to discuss your encounters with power plants, or let you talk obsessively about them; there was no point in elaborating about the unspeakable. Those were true excursions into the *nagual*, the unknown."

I mentioned that my need to talk about my perceptions under the influence of psychotropic plants was due to an interest in elucidating a hypothesis of my own. I was convinced that with the aid of such plants he had provided me with memories of inconceivable ways of perceiving. Those memories, which at the time I experienced them may have seemed idiosyncratic and disconnected from anything meaningful, were later assembled into units of meaning. I knew that don Juan had artfully guided me each time, and that any assembling of meaning was made under his guidance.

"I don't want to emphasize those events, or explain them," he said dryly. "The act of dwelling on explanations will put us right back where we don't want to be; that is, we'll be thrown back into a view of the world, this time a much larger view."

Don Juan said that after the apprentice's internal dialogue has been stopped by the effect of power plants, an unavoidable impasse develops. The apprentice begins to have second thoughts about his whole apprenticeship. In don Juan's opinion, even the most willing apprentice at that point would suffer a serious loss of interest.

"Power plants shake the *tonal* and threaten the solidity of the whole island," he said. "It is at this time that the apprentice retreats, and wisely so; he wants to get out of the whole mess. It is also at this time that the teacher sets up his most artful trap, the worthy opponent. This trap has two purposes. First, it enables the teacher to hold his apprentice, and second, it enables the apprentice to have a point of reference for further use. The trap is a maneuver that brings forth a worthy opponent into the arena. Without the aid of a worthy opponent, who's not really an enemy but a thoroughly dedicated adversary, the apprentice has no possibility of continuing on the path of knowledge. The best of men would quit at this point if it were left up to them to decide. I brought to you as a worthy opponent the finest warrior one can find, la Catalina."

Don Juan was talking about a time, years before, when he had led me into a long-range battle with an Indian sorceress.

"I put you in bodily contact with her," he proceeded. "I chose a woman because you trust women. To disarrange that trust was very difficult for her. She confessed to me years later that she would've liked to quit, because she liked you. But she's a great warrior and in spite of her feelings she nearly blasted you off the planet. She disarranged your *tonal* so intensely that it was never the same again. She actually changed features on the face of your island so deeply that her acts sent you into another realm. One may say that she could've become your benefactor herself, had it not been that you were not cut out to be a sorcerer like she is. There was something amiss between you two. You were incapable of being afraid of her. You nearly lost your marbles one night when she accosted you, but in spite of that you were attracted to her. She was a desirable woman to you no matter how scared you were. She knew that. I caught you one day in town looking at her, shaking in your boots with fear and yet drooling at her.

"Because of the acts of a worthy opponent, then, an apprentice can be either blasted to pieces or changed radically. La Catalina's actions with you, since they did not kill you — not because she did not try hard enough but because you were durable — had a beneficial effect on you, and also provided you with a decision.

"The teacher uses the worthy opponent to force the apprentice into the choice of his life. The apprentice must choose between the warrior's world and his ordinary world. But no decision is possible unless the apprentice understands the choice; thus a teacher must have a thoroughly patient and understanding attitude and must lead his man with a sure hand to that choice, and above all he must make sure that his apprentice chooses the world and the life of a warrior. I accomplished this by asking you to help me overcome la Catalina. I told you she was about to kill me and that I needed your help to get rid of her. I gave you fair warning about the consequences of your choice and plenty of time to decide whether or not to make it."

I clearly remembered that don Juan had set me loose that day. He told me that if I did not want to help him I was free to leave and never come back. I felt at that moment that I was at liberty to choose my own course and had no further obligation to him.

I left his house and drove away with a mixture of sadness and happiness. I was sad to leave don Juan and yet I was happy to be through with all his disconcerting activities. I thought of Los Angeles and my friends and all the routines of my daily life which were waiting for me, those little routines that had always given me so much pleasure. For a while I felt euphoric. The weirdness of don Juan and his life was behind me and I was free.

My happy mood did not last long, however. My desire to leave don Juan's world was untenable. My routines had lost their power. I tried to think of something I wanted to do in Los Angeles, but there was nothing. Don Juan had once told me that I was afraid of people and had learned to defend myself by not wanting anything. He said that not wanting anything was a warrior's finest attainment. In my stupidity, however, I had enlarged the sensation of not wanting anything and made it lapse into not liking anything. Thus, my life was boring and empty.

He was right and as I zoomed north on the highway the full impact of my own unsuspected madness finally hit me. I began to realize the scope of my choice. I was actually leaving a magical world of continual renewal for my soft, boring life in Los Angeles. I began to recollect my empty days. I remembered one Sunday in particular. I had felt restless all day with nothing to do. No friends had come to visit me. No one had invited me to a party. The people I wanted to see were not home, and worst of all, I had seen all the movies in town. In the late afternoon, in ultimate despair, I searched the list of movies again and found one I had never wanted to see. It was being shown in a town thirty-five miles away. I went to see it, and hated it, but even that was better than having nothing to do.

Under the impact of don Juan's world, I had changed. For one thing, since I had met him I had not had time to be bored. That in itself was enough for me; don Juan had indeed made sure I would choose the warrior's world. I turned around and drove back to his house.

"What would have happened if I had chosen to go back to Los Angeles?" I asked.

"That would have been an impossibility," he said. "That choice didn't exist. All that was required of you was to allow your *tonal* to become aware of having decided to join the world of sorcerers. The *tonal* doesn't know that decisions are in the realm of the *nagual*. When we think we decide, all we're doing is acknowledging that something beyond our understanding has set up the frame of our so-called decision, and all we do is to acquiesce.

"In the life of a warrior there is only one thing, one issue alone which is really undecided: how far one can go on the path of knowledge and power. That is an issue which is open and no one can predict its outcome. I once told you that the freedom a warrior has is either to act impeccably or to act like a nincompoop. Impeccability is indeed the only act which is free and thus the true measure of a warrior's spirit."

Don Juan said that after the apprentice had made his decision to join the world of sorcerers, the teacher gave him a pragmatic chore, a task that he had to fulfill in his day-to-day life. He explained that the task, which is designed to fit the apprentice's personality, is usually a sort of farfetched life situation, which the apprentice is supposed to get into as a means of permanently affecting his view of the world. In my own case, I understood the task more as a lively joke than a serious life situation. As time passed, however, it finally dawned on me that I had to be earnest about it.

"After the apprentice has been given his sorcery task he's ready for another type of instruction," he proceeded. "He is a warrior then. In your case, since you were no longer an apprentice, I taught you the three techniques that help *dreaming*: disrupting the routines of life, the gait of power, and not-doing. You were very consistent, dumb as an apprentice and dumb as a warrior. You dutifully wrote down everything I said and everything that happened to you, but you did not act exactly as I had told you to. So I still had to blast you with power plants."

Don Juan then gave me a step-by-step rendition of how he had driven my attention away from "dreaming," making me believe that the important problem was a very difficult activity he had called not-doing, which consisted of a perceptual game of focusing attention on features of the world that were ordinarily overlooked, such as the shadows of things. Don Juan said that his strategy had been to set not-doing apart by imposing the most strict secrecy on it.

"Not-doing, like everything else, is a very important technique, but it was not the main issue," he said. "You fell for the secrecy. You, a blabbermouth, having to keep a secret!"

He laughed and said that he could imagine the troubles I must have gone through to keep my mouth shut.

He explained that disrupting routines, the gait of power, and not-doing were avenues for learning new ways of perceiving the world, and that they gave a warrior an inkling of incredible possibilities of action. Don Juan's idea was that the knowledge of a separate and pragmatic world of "dreaming" was made possible through the use of those three techniques.

"*Dreaming* is a practical aid devised by sorcerers," he said. "They were not fools; they knew what they were doing and sought the usefulness of the *nagual* by training their *tonal* to let go for a moment, so to speak, and then grab again. This statement doesn't make sense to you. But that's what you've been doing all along: training yourself to let go without losing your marbles. *Dreaming*, of course, is the crown of the sorcerers' efforts, the ultimate use of the *nagual*."

He went through all the exercises of not-doing that he had made me perform, the routines of my daily life that he had isolated for disrupting, and all the occasions when he had forced me to engage in the gait of power.

"We're coming to the end of my recapitulation," he said. "Now we have to talk about Genaro."

Don Juan said that there had been a very important omen the day I met don Genaro. I told him that I could not remember anything out of the ordinary. He reminded me that on that day we had been sitting on a bench in a park. He said that he had mentioned earlier to me that he was going to wait for a friend I had never met before, and then when the friend appeared I singled him out, without any hesitation, in the midst of a huge crowd. That was the omen that made them realize that don Genaro was my benefactor.

I remembered when he mentioned it that as we sat talking I had turned around and seen a small lean man who radiated an extraordinary vitality, or grace, or simple gusto; he had just turned a corner into the park. In a joking mood I told don Juan that his friend was approaching us, and that he was most certainly a sorcerer judging by the way he looked.

"Genaro recommended what to do with you from that day on," don Juan proceeded. "As your guide into the *nagual*, he gave you impeccable demonstrations, and every time he performed an act as a *nagual* you were left with a knowledge that defied and bypassed your *reason*. He disassembled your view of the world, although you are not aware of that yet. Again in this instance you behaved just like in the case of the power plants, you needed more than was necessary. A few of the *nagual*'s onslaughts should be enough to dismantle one's view; but even to this day, after all the *nagual*'s barrages, your view seems invulnerable. Oddly enough, that's your best feature.

"All in all, then, Genaro's job has been to lead you into the *nagual*. But here we have a strange question. What was being led into the *nagual*?"

He urged me with a movement of his eyes to answer the question.

"My *reason*?" I asked.

"No, *reason* is meaningless there," he replied. "*Reason* craps out in an instant when it is out of its safe narrow bounds."

"Then it was my *tonal*," I said.

"No, the *tonal* and the *nagual* are the two inherent parts of ourselves," he said dryly. "They cannot be led into each other."

"My perception?" I asked.

"You've got it," he yelled as if I were a child giving the right answer. "We're coming now to the sorcerers' explanation. I've warned you already that it won't explain anything and yet . . ."

He paused and looked at me with shiny eyes.

"This is another of the sorcerers' tricks," he said.

"What do you mean? What's the trick?" I asked with a touch of alarm.

"The sorcerers' explanation, of course," he replied. "You'll see that for yourself. But let's continue with it. Sorcerers say that we are inside a bubble. It is a bubble into which we are placed at the moment of our birth. At first the bubble is open, but then it begins to close until it has sealed us in. That bubble is our perception. We live inside that bubble all of our lives. And what we witness on its round walls is our own reflection."

He lowered his head and looked at me askance. He giggled.

"You're goofing," he said. "You're supposed to raise a point here."

I laughed. Somehow his warnings about the sorcerers' explanation plus the realization of the awesome range of his awareness had finally begun to take their toll on me.

"What was the point I was supposed to raise?" I asked.

"If what we witness on the walls is our own reflection, then the thing that's being reflected must be the real thing," he said, smiling.

"That's a good point," I said in a joking tone.

My reason could easily follow that argument.

"The thing reflected is our view of the world," he said. "That view is first a description, which is given to us from the moment of our birth until all our attention is caught by it and the description becomes a view.

"The teacher's task is to rearrange the view, to prepare the luminous being for the time when the benefactor opens the bubble from the outside."

He went into another studied pause and made another remark about my lack of attention judged by my incapacity to make an appropriate comment or question.

"What should've been my question?" I asked.

"Why should the bubble be opened?" he replied.

He laughed loudly and patted my back when I said, "That's a good question."

"Of course!" he exclaimed. "It has to be a good question for you, it's one of your own.

"The bubble is opened in order to allow the luminous being a view of his totality," he went on. "Naturally this business of calling it a bubble is only a way of talking, but in this case it is an accurate way.

"The delicate maneuver of leading a luminous being into the totality of himself requires that the teacher work from inside the bubble and the benefactor from outside. The teacher reorders the view of the world. I have called that view the island of the *tonal*. I've said that everything that we are is on that island. The sorcerers' explanation says that the island of the *tonal* is made by our perception, which has been trained to focus on certain elements; each of those elements and all of them together form our view of the world. The job of a teacher, insofar as the apprentice's perception is concerned, consists of reordering all the elements of the island on one half of the bubble. By now you must have realized that cleaning and reordering the island of the *tonal* means regrouping all its elements on the side of *reason*. My task has been to disarrange your ordinary view, not to destroy it but to force it to rally on the side of *reason*. You've done that better than anyone I know."

He drew an imaginary circle on the rock and divided it in two along a vertical diameter. He said that the art of a teacher was to force his disciple to group his view of the world on the right half of the bubble.

"Why the right half?" I asked.

"That's the side of the *tonal*," he said. "The teacher always addresses himself to that side, and by presenting his apprentice on the one hand with the warrior's way he forces him into reasonableness, and sobriety, and strength of character and body; and by presenting him on the other hand with unthinkable but real situations, which the apprentice cannot cope with, he forces him to realize that his *reason*, although it is a most wonderful affair, can only cover a small area. Once the warrior is confronted with his incapacity to reason everything out, he will go out of his way to bolster and defend his defeated *reason*, and to that effect he will rally everything he's got around it. The teacher sees to that by hammering him mercilessly until all his view of the world is on one half of the bubble. The other half of the bubble, the one that has been cleared, can then be claimed by something sorcerers call *will*.

"We can better explain this by saying that the task of the teacher is to wipe clean one half of the bubble and to reorder everything on the other half. The benefactor's task then is to open the bubble on the side that has been cleaned. Once the seal is broken, the warrior is never the same. He has then the command of his totality. Half of the bubble is the ultimate center of *reason*, the *tonal*. The other half is the ultimate center of *will*, the *nagual*. That is the order that should prevail; any other arrangement is nonsensical and petty, because it goes against our nature; it robs us of our magical heritage and reduces us to nothing."

Don Juan stood up and stretched his arms and back and walked around to loosen up his muscles. It was a bit cold by then.

I asked him if we were through.

"Why, the show hasn't even started yet!" he exclaimed and laughed. "That was only the beginning."

He looked at the sky and pointed to the west with a casual movement of his hand.

"In about an hour the *nagual* will be here," he said and smiled. He sat down again.

"We have one single issue left," he continued. "Sorcerers call it the secret of the luminous beings, and that is the fact that we are perceivers. We men and all the other luminous beings on earth are perceivers. That is our bubble, the bubble of perception. Our mistake is to believe that the only perception worthy of acknowledgment is what goes through our *reason*. Sorcerers believe that *reason* is only one center and that it shouldn't take so much for granted.

"Genaro and I have taught you about the eight points that make the totality of our bubble of perception. You know six points. Today Genaro and I will further clean your bubble of perception and after that you will know the two remaining points."

He abruptly changed the topic and asked me to give him a detailed account of my perceptions of the day before, starting from the point where I saw don Genaro sitting on a rock by the road. He did not make any comments or interrupt me at all. When I had finished, I added an observation of my own. I had talked to Nestor and Pablito in the morning and they had given me accounts of their perceptions, which were similar to mine. My point was that he himself had told me that the *nagual* was an individual experience which only the observer can witness. The day before there were three observers and all of us had witnessed more or less the same thing. The differences were expressed only in terms of how each of us felt or reacted to any specific instance of the whole phenomenon.

"What happened yesterday was a demonstration of the *nagual* for you, and for Nestor and Pablito. I'm their benefactor. Between Genaro and myself, we canceled out the center of *reason* in all three of you. Genaro and I had enough power to make you agree on what you were witnessing. Several years ago, you and I were with a bunch of apprentices one night, but I didn't have enough power by myself alone to make all of you witness the same thing."

He said that, judging by what I had told him I had perceived the day before and from what he had "seen" about me, his conclusion was that I was ready for the sorcerers' explanation. He added that so was Pablito, but he was uncertain about Nestor.

"To be ready for the sorcerers' explanation is a very difficult accomplishment," he said. "It shouldn't be, but we insist on indulging in our lifelong view of the world. In this respect you and Nestor and Pablito are alike. Nestor hides behind his shyness and gloom, Pablito behind his disarming charm; you hide behind your cockiness and words. All are views that seem to be unchallengeable; and as long as you three persist in using them, your bubbles of perception have not been cleared and the sorcerers' explanation will have no meaning."

In a spirit of jest I said that I had been obsessed with the famous sorcerers' explanation for a very long time, but the closer I got to it the further it seemed to be. I was going to add a joking comment when he took the words right out of my mouth.

"Wouldn't it be something if the sorcerers' explanation turns out to be a dud?" he asked in the midst of loud laughter.

He patted me on the back and seemed to be delighted, like a child anticipating a pleasant event.

"Genaro is a stickler for the rule," he said in a confiding tone. "There's nothing to this confounded explanation. If it would've been up to me I would have given it to you years ago. Don't put too much stock in it."

He looked up and examined the sky.

"Now you are ready," he said in a dramatic and solemn tone. "It's time to go. But before we leave this place I have to tell you one last thing: The mystery, or the secret, of the sorcerers' explanation is that it deals with unfolding the wings of perception."

He put his hand over my writing pad and said that I should go to the bushes and take care of my bodily functions and after that I should take off my clothes and leave them in a bundle right where we were. I looked at him questioningly and he explained that I had to be naked, but that I could keep my shoes and my hat on.

I insisted on knowing why I had to be naked. Don Juan laughed and said that the reason was rather personal and had to do with my own comfort, and that I myself had told him that that was the way I wanted it. His explanation baffled me. I felt that he was playing a joke on me or that, in conformity with what he had revealed to me, he was simply displacing my attention. I wanted to know why he was doing that.

He began to talk about an incident that had happened to me years before while we had been in the mountains of northern Mexico with don Genaro. On that occasion they were explaining to me that "reason" could not possibly account for everything that took place in the world. In order to give me an undeniable demonstration of it don Genaro performed a magnificent leap as a "nagual," and "elongated" himself to reach the top of some peaks ten or fifteen miles away. Don Juan said that I missed the issue, and that as far as convincing my "reason" was concerned, don Genaro's demonstration was a failure, but from the point of view of my bodily reaction it was a riot.

The bodily reaction that don Juan was referring to was something which was very vivid in my mind. I saw don Genaro disappear in front of my very eyes as if a wind had swished him away. His leap or whatever he had done had had such a profound effect on me that I felt as if his movement had ripped something in my intestines. My bowels became loose and I had to throw away my pants and shirt. My discomfort and embarrassment knew no limits; I had to walk naked, wearing only a hat, on a heavily trafficked highway until I got to my car. Don Juan reminded me that it was then that I had told him not to let me ruin my clothes again.

After I had taken my clothes off we walked a few hundred feet to a very large rock overlooking the same ravine. He made me look down. There was a drop of over a hundred feet. He then told me to turn off my internal dialogue and listen to the sounds around us.

After a few moments I heard the sound of a pebble bouncing from rock to rock on its way down to the bottom of the ravine. I heard every single bounce of the pebble with inconceivable clarity. Then I heard another pebble being thrown, and another one yet. I lifted my head to align my left ear to the direction of the sound and saw don Genaro sitting on top of the rock, twelve to fifteen feet from where we were. He was casually tossing pebbles down into the ravine.

He yelled and cackled when I saw him and he said that he had been hiding there waiting for me to discover him. I had a moment of bafflement. Don Juan whispered in my ear repeatedly that my "reason" was not invited to that event, and that I should give up the nagging desire to control everything. He said that the "nagual" was a perception only for me, and that that was the reason Pablito had not seen the "nagual" in my car. He added, as if reading my unvoiced feelings, that although the "nagual" was for me alone to witness, it still was don Genaro himself.

Don Juan took me by the arm and in a playful manner led me to where don Genaro was sitting. Don Genaro stood up and came closer to me. His body radiated a heat that I could see, a glow which dazzled me. He came to my side and without touching me he put his mouth close to my left ear and began to whisper. Don Juan also began whispering in my other ear. Their voices were synchronized. They were both repeating the same statements. They said that I should not be afraid, and that I had long powerful fibers, which were not there to protect me, for there was nothing to protect, or to be protected from, but that they were there to guide my "nagual's" perception in very much the same way my eyes guided my normal "tonal's" perception. They told me that my fibers were all around me, that through them I could perceive everything at once, and that one single fiber was enough for a leap from the rock into the ravine, or up from the ravine to the rock.

I had listened to everything they had whispered. Every word seemed to have had a unique connotation for me; I could retain every utterance and then play it back as if I were a tape recorder. They both urged me to leap to the bottom of the ravine. They said that I should first feel my fibers, then isolate one that went all the way down to the bottom of the ravine and follow it. As they spoke their commands I actually could match their words with adequate feelings. I sensed an itching all over me, especially a most peculiar sensation which was indiscernible in itself but approximated the sensation of a "long itching." My body could actually feel the bottom of the ravine and I sensed that feeling as an itching in some undefined area of my body.

Don Juan and don Genaro kept on coaxing me to slide through

that feeling, but I did not know how. I then heard don Genaro's voice alone.

He said that he was going to jump with me; he grabbed me, or pushed me, or embraced me, and plunged with me into the abyss. I had the ultimate sensation of physical anguish. It was as if my stomach was being chewed and devoured. It was a mixture of pain and pleasure of such intensity and duration that all I could do was to yell and yell at the top of my lungs. When the sensation subsided I saw an inextricable cluster of sparks and dark masses, beams of light and cloudlike formations. I could not tell whether my eyes were open or closed, or where my eyes were, or where my body was for that matter. Then I sensed the same physical anguish, although not as pronounced as the first time, and next I had the impression I had woken up and I found myself standing on the rock with don Juan and don Genaro.

Don Juan said that I had goofed again, that it was useless to leap if the perception of the leap was going to be chaotic. Both of them repeated countless times in my ears that the "nagual" by itself was of no use, that it had to be tempered by the "tonal." They said that I had to leap willingly and be aware of my act.

I hesitated, not so much because I was afraid but because I was reluctant. I felt my vacillation as if my body were swinging from side to side like a pendulum. Then some strange mood overtook me and I leaped with all my corporealness. I wanted to think as I took the plunge but I could not. I saw as if through a fog the walls of the narrow gorge and the jutting rocks at the bottom of the ravine. I did not have a sequential perception of my descent, I had instead the sensation that I was actually on the ground at the bottom; I distinguished every feature of the rocks in a short circle around me. I noticed that my view was not unidirectional and stereoscopic from the level of the eyes, but flat and all around me. After a moment I panicked and something pulled me up like a yo-yo.

Don Juan and don Genaro made me perform the leap over and over. After every jump don Juan urged me to be less reticent and unwilling. He said, time and time again, that the sorcerers' secret in using the "nagual" was in our perception, that leaping was simply an exercise in perception, and that it would end only after I had succeeded in perceiving, as a perfect "tonal," what was at the bottom of the ravine.

At one moment I had an inconceivable sensation. I was fully and soberly aware that I was standing on the edge of the rock with don Juan and don Genaro whispering in my ears, and then in the next instant I was looking at the bottom of the ravine. Everything was perfectly normal. It was almost dark by then, but there was still enough light to make everything absolutely recognizable as in the world of my everyday life. I was watching some bushes when I heard a sudden noise, a rock rolling down. I saw instantly a good size rock tumbling down the wall of the ravine towards me. In a flash I also saw don Genaro throwing it. I had an attack of panic and an instant later I had been pulled back to the site on top of the rock. I looked around; don Genaro was not there any more. Don Juan began to laugh and said that don Genaro had left because he could not stand my stench. I then had the embarrassing realization that I was truly a mess. Don Juan had been right in making me take my clothes off. He walked me to a stream nearby and washed me like a horse, scooping water with my hat and throwing it at me while he made hilarious comments about having saved my pants.

THE BUBBLE OF PERCEPTION

I spent the day by myself at don Genaro's house. I slept most of the time. Don Juan came back in the late afternoon and we hiked, in complete silence, to a nearby range of mountains. We stopped at dusk and sat on the edge of a deep gorge until it was almost dark. Then don Juan led me to another place close by, a monumental cliff with a sheer vertical rock wall. The cliff was unnoticeable from the trail that led to it; don Juan, however, had shown it to me several times before. He had made me look over the edge and had told me that the whole cliff was a place of power, especially the base of it, which was a canyon several hundred feet down. Every time I had looked into it I had had a discomforting chill; the canyon was always dark and menacing.

Before we reached the place, don Juan said that I had to go on by myself and meet Pablito on the edge of the cliff. He recommended that I should relax and perform the gait of power in order to wash away my nervous tiredness.

Don Juan stepped aside, to the left of the trail, and the darkness simply swallowed him. I wanted to stop and examine where he had gone, but my body did not obey. I began to jog although I was so tired that I could hardly keep on my feet.

When I reached the cliff I could not see anyone there and I went on jogging in place, breathing deeply. After a while I relaxed a bit; I stood motionless with my back against a rock, and I noticed then the shape of a man a few feet away from me. He was sitting, hiding his head in his arms. I had a moment of intense fright and recoiled, but then I explained to myself that the man must be Pablito, and without any hesitation I advanced towards him. I called Pablito's name out loud. I figured that he must have been uncertain of who I was and had become so scared that he had covered his head not to look. But before I reached him some inexplicable fear took possession of me. My body froze on the spot with my right arm already extended to touch him. The man lifted his head up. It was not Pablito! His eyes were two enormous mirrors, like a tiger's eyes. My body jumped backwards; my muscles tensed and then released the tension without the slightest influence of my volition, and I performed a backward leap, so fast and so far that under normal conditions I would have plunged into a grandiose speculation about it. As it was, however, my fright was so out of proportion that I had no inclination for pondering, and I would have run out of there had it not been that someone held my arm forcibly. The feeling that someone was holding me by the arm threw me into total panic; I screamed. My outburst, instead of being the shriek I thought it should have been, was a long chilling yell.

I turned to face my assailant. It was Pablito, who was shaking even more than me. My nervousness was at its peak. I could not talk, my teeth chattered and ripples went through my back, making me jerk involuntarily. I had to breathe through my mouth.

Pablito said, between chatters, that the "nagual" had been waiting for him, that he had barely gotten out of its clutches when he bumped into me, and that I had nearly killed him with my yell. I wanted to laugh and made the most weird sounds imaginable. When I regained my calmness I told Pablito that apparently the same thing had happened to me. The end result in my case had been that my fatigue had vanished; I felt instead an uncontainable surge of strength and well-being. Pablito seemed to be experiencing the same sensations; we began to giggle in a nervous silly way.

I heard the sound of soft and careful steps in the distance. I detected the sound before Pablito. He appeared to react to my stiffening. I had the certainty that someone was approaching the place where we were. We turned in the direction of the sound; a moment later the silhouettes of don Juan and don Genaro became visible. They were walking calmly and stopped four or five feet away from us; don Juan was facing me and don Genaro faced Pablito. I wanted to tell don Juan that something had scared me nearly out of my wits, but Pablito squeezed my arm. I knew what he meant. There was something strange about don Juan and don Genaro. As I looked at them my eyes began to get out of focus.

Don Genaro gave a sharp command. I did not understand what he had said, but I "knew" he had meant that we should not cross our eyes.

"The darkness has settled on the world," don Juan said, looking at the sky.

Don Genaro drew a half-moon on the hard ground. For a moment it seemed to me that he had used some iridescent chalk, but then I realized that he was not holding anything in his hands; I was perceiving the imaginary half-moon that he had drawn with his finger. He made Pablito and me sit on the inner curve of the convex edge, while he and don Juan sat cross-legged on the extreme ends of the half-moon, six or seven feet away from us.

Don Juan spoke first; he said that they were going to show us their allies. He told us that if we would gaze at their left sides, between their hips and their rib bones, we would "see" something like a rag or a handkerchief hanging from their belts. Don Genaro added that next to the rags on their belts there were two round buttonlike things, and that we should gaze at their belts until we "saw" the rags and the buttons.

Before don Genaro had spoken I had already noticed some flat item, like a piece of cloth, and one round pebble that hung from their belts. Don Juan's allies were darker and more menacing than don Genaro's. My reaction was a mixture of curiosity and fear. My reactions were experienced in my stomach and I was not judging anything in a rational manner.

Don Juan and don Genaro reached for their belts and seemed to unhook the dark pieces of cloth. They took them with their left hands; don Juan flung his in the air above his head, but don Genaro let his drop to the ground gently. The pieces of cloth stretched as if the hurling and the dropping had made them spread like perfectly smooth handkerchiefs; they descended slowly, bobbing like kites. The movement of don Juan's ally was the exact replica of what I had perceived him doing when he had whirled around days before. As the pieces of cloth got closer to the ground, they became solid, round and massive. They first curled as though they had fallen over a door knob, then they expanded. Don Juan's grew into a voluminous shadow. It took the lead and moved towards us, crushing small rocks and hard lumps of dirt. It came within four or five feet of us to the very dip of the half-moon, between don Juan and don Genaro. At one moment I thought it was going to roll over us and pulverize us. My terror at that instant was like a burning fire. The shadow in front of me was gigantic, perhaps fourteen feet high and six feet across. It moved as if it were feeling its way around with no eyes. It jerked and wobbled. I knew that it was looking for me. Pablito at that moment hid his head against my chest. The sensation that his movement produced in me dispelled some of the awesome attention that I had focused on the shadow. The shadow seemed to become disassociated, judging by its erratic jerks, and then it moved out of sight, merging with the darkness around.

I shook Pablito. He lifted his head and let out a muffled scream. I looked up. A strange man was staring at me. He seemed to have been right behind the shadow, perhaps hiding behind it. He was rather tall and lanky, he had a long face, no hair, and the left side of his head was covered by a rash or an eczema of some sort. His eyes were wild and shiny; his mouth was half open. He wore some strange pajama-like clothing; his pants were too short for him. I could not distinguish whether or not he had shoes on. He stood looking at us for what seemed to be a long time, as if waiting for an opening in order to lurch at us and tear us apart. There was so much intensity in his eyes. It was not hatred or violence but some sort of animal feeling of distrust. I could not stand the tension any longer. I wanted to adapt a fighting position that don Juan had taught me years before and I would have done so had it not been for Pablito, who whispered that the ally could not go over the line that don Genaro had drawn on the ground. I realized then that there was indeed a bright line that seemed to detain whatever was in front of us.

After a moment the man moved away to the left, just like the shadow before. I had the sensation that don Juan and don Genaro had called them both back.

There was a short quiet pause. I could not see don Juan or don Genaro any more; they were no longer sitting on the points of the half-moon. Suddenly I heard the sound of two small pebbles hitting the solid rock floor where we were sitting, and in a flash the area in front of us lit up as if a mellow yellowish light had been turned on. In front of us there was a ravenous beast, a giant nauseating-looking coyote or wolf. Its whole body was covered with a white secretion like perspiration or saliva. Its hair was raggedy and wet. Its eyes were wild. It growled with a blind fury that sent chills through me. Its jaw shivered and globs of saliva flew all over the place. It pawed the ground like a mad dog trying to get loose from a chain. Then it stood on its hind legs and moved its front paws and its jaws rabidly. All its fury seemed to be concentrated on breaking some barrier in front of us.

I became aware that my fear of that crazed animal was of a different sort than the fear of the two apparitions I had witnessed before. My dread of that beast was a physical revulsion and horror. I looked on in utter impotence at its rage. Suddenly it seemed to lose its wildness and trotted out of sight.

I heard then something else coming towards us, or perhaps I sensed it; all of a sudden the shape of a colossal feline loomed in front of us. I first saw its eyes in the darkness; they were huge and fixed like two pools of water reflecting light. It snorted and growled softly. It exhaled air and moved back and forth in front of us without taking its eyes away from us. It did not have the electric glow that the coyote had; I could not distinguish its features clearly, and yet its presence was infinitely more ominous than the other beast's. It seemed to be gathering strength; I felt that it was so daring that it would go beyond its limits. Pablito must have had a similar feeling, for he whispered that I should duck my head and lie almost flat against the ground. A second later the feline charged. It ran towards us and then it leaped with its paws extended forward. I closed my eyes and hid my head in my arms against the ground. I felt that the beast had ripped the protective line that don Genaro had drawn around us and was actually on top of us. I felt its weight pinning me down; the fur on its belly rubbed against my neck. It seemed that its forelegs were caught in something; it wriggled to set itself free. I felt its jerking and prodding and heard its diabolic puffing and hissing. I knew then that I was lost. I had a vague sense of a rational choice and I wanted to resign myself calmly to my fate of dying there, but I was afraid of the physical pain of dying under such awful circumstances. Then some strange force surged from my body; it was as if my body refused to die and pooled all its strength in one single point, my left arm and hand. I felt an indomitable surge coming through it. Something uncontrollable was taking possession of my body, something that forced me to push the massive malignant weight of that beast off of us. Pablito seemed to have reacted in the same fashion and we both stood up at once; there was so much energy created by both of us that the beast was flung like a rag doll.

The exertion had been supreme. I collapsed on the ground, panting for air. The muscles of my stomach were so tense that I could not breathe. I did not pay any attention to what Pablito was doing. I finally noticed that don Juan and don Genaro were helping me to sit up. I saw Pablito spread on the ground face down with his arms outstretched. He seemed to have fainted. After they had made me sit up, don Juan and don Genaro helped Pablito. Both of them rubbed his stomach and back. They made him stand up and after a while he could sit up by himself again.

Don Juan and don Genaro sat on the ends of the half-moon, and then they began to move in front of us as if a rail existed between the two points, a rail that they were using to shift their positions back and forth from one side to the other. Their movements made me dizzy. They finally stopped next to Pablito and began to whisper in his ear. After a moment they stood up, all three of them at once, and walked to the edge of the cliff. Don Genaro lifted Pablito as if he were a child. Pablito's body was stiff like a board; don Juan held Pablito by the ankles. He whirled him around, seemingly to gain momentum and force, and finally he let go of his legs and hurled his body out over the abyss away from the edge of the cliff.

I saw Pablito's body against the dark western sky. It described circles, just like don Juan's body had done days before; the circles were slow. Pablito seemed to be gaining altitude instead of falling down. Then the circling became accelerated; Pablito's body twirled like a disk for a moment and then it disintegrated. I perceived that it had vanished in thin air.

Don Juan and don Genaro came to my side, squatted by me and proceeded to whisper in my ears. Each said something different, yet I had no trouble in following their commands. It was as if I became "split" the instant they uttered their first words. I felt that they were doing with me what they had done with Pablito. Don Genaro made me whirl and then I had the thoroughly conscious sensation of spinning or floating for a moment. Next I was rushing through the air, plummeting down to the ground at a tremendous speed. I felt, as I was falling, that my clothes were ripping off, then my flesh fell off, and finally only my head remained. I had the very clear sensation that as my body became dismembered I lost my superfluous weight, and thus my falling lost its momentum and my speed decreased. My descent was no longer a vertigo. I began to move back and forth like a leaf. Then my head was stripped of its weight and all that was left of "me" was a square centimeter, a nugget, a tiny pebblelike residue. All my feeling was concentrated there; then the nugget seemed to burst and I was a thousand pieces. I knew, or something somewhere knew, that I was aware of the thousand pieces at once. I was the awareness itself.

Then some part of that awareness began to be stirred; it rose, grew. It became localized, and little by little I regained the sense of boundaries, consciousness or whatever, and suddenly the "me" I knew and was familiar with erupted into the most spectacular view of all the imaginable combinations of "beautiful" scenes; it was as if I were looking at thousands of pictures of the world, of people, of things.

The scenes then became blurry. I had the sensation that they were being passed in front of my eyes at a greater speed until I could not single out any of them for examination. Finally it was as if I were witnessing the organization of the world rolling past my eyes in an unbroken, endless chain.

I suddenly found myself standing on the cliff with don Juan and don Genaro. They whispered that they had pulled me back, and that I had witnessed the unknown that no one can talk about. They said that they were going to hurl me into it once more, and that I should let the wings of my perception unfold and touch the "tonal" and the "nagual" at once without being aware of going back and forth from one to the other.

I again had the sensations of being tossed, spinning, and falling down at a tremendous speed. Then I exploded. I disintegrated. Something in me gave out; it released something I had kept locked up all my life. I was thoroughly aware then that my secret reservoir had been tapped and that it poured out unrestrainedly. There was no longer the sweet unity I call "me." There was nothing and yet that nothing was filled. It was not light or darkness, hot or cold, pleasant or unpleasant. It was not that I moved or floated or was stationary, neither was I a single unit, a self, as I am accustomed to being. I was a myriad of selves which were all "me," a colony of separate units that had a special allegiance to one another and would join unavoidably to form one single awareness, my human awareness. It was not that I "knew" beyond the shadow of a doubt, because there was nothing I could have "known" with, but all my single awarenesses "knew" that the "I," the "me," of my familiar world was a colony, a conglomerate of separate and independent feelings that had an unbending solidarity to one another. The unbending solidarity of my countless awarenesses, the allegiance that those parts had for one another was my life force.

A way of describing that unified sensation would be to say that those nuggets of awareness were scattered; each of them was aware of itself and none was more predominant than the other. Then something would stir them, and they would join and emerge onto an area where all of them had to be pooled in one clump, the "me" I know. As "me" "myself" then I would witness a coherent scene of worldly activity, or a scene that pertained to other worlds and which I thought must have been pure imagination, or a scene that pertained to "pure thinking," that is, I had views of intellectual systems, or of ideas strung together as verbalizations. In some scenes I talked to myself to my heart's content. After every one of those coherent views the "me" would disintegrate and be nothing once more.

During one of those excursions into a coherent view I found myself on the cliff with don Juan. I instantly realized that I was then the total "me" I am familiar with. I felt my physicality as real. I was in the world rather than merely viewing it.

Don Juan hugged me like a child. He looked at me. His face was very close. I could see his eyes in the darkness. They were kind. They seemed to hold a question. I knew what it was. The unspeakable was truly unspeakable.

"Well?" he asked softly, as if he would need my reaffirmation.

I was speechless. The words "numb," "bewildered," "confused," and so on were not in any way appropriate descriptions of my feelings at that moment. I was not solid. I knew that don Juan had to grab me and keep me forcibly on the ground, otherwise I would have floated in the air and disappeared. I was not afraid of vanishing. I longed for the "unknown" where my awareness was not unified.

Don Juan walked me slowly, pushing down on both of my shoulders, to an area around don Genaro's house; he made me lie down and then covered me with soft dirt from a pile that he seemed to have prepared beforehand. He covered me up to my neck. With leaves he made a sort of pillow for my head to rest on and told me not to move or fall asleep at all. He said that he was going to sit and keep me company until the earth had again consolidated my form.

I felt very comfortable and had a nearly invincible desire to fall asleep, but don Juan would not let me. He demanded that I should talk about anything under the sun except what I had just experienced. I did not know what to talk about at first, then I asked about don Genaro. Don Juan said that don Genaro had taken Pablito and had buried him somewhere around there and was doing with him what he himself was doing with me.

I had the desire to sustain the conversation but something in me was incomplete; I had an unusual indifference, a tiredness that was more like boredom. Don Juan seemed to know how I felt. He began to talk about Pablito and how our fates were interlocked. He said that he became Pablito's benefactor at the same time that don Genaro became his teacher, and that power had paired Pablito and me step by step. He made the emphatic remark that the only difference between Pablito and me was that while Pablito's world as a warrior was governed by coercion and fear, mine was governed by affection and freedom. Don Juan explained that such a difference was due to the intrinsically different personalities of the benefactors. Don Genaro was sweet and affectionate and funny, while he himself was dry, authoritarian and direct. He said that my personality demanded a strong teacher but a tender benefactor, and that Pablito was the opposite; he needed a kind teacher and a stern benefactor.

We talked for a while longer and then it was morning. When the sun appeared over the mountains on the eastern horizon, he helped me to get up from under the dirt.

After I woke up in the early afternoon, don Juan and I sat by the door of don Genaro's house. Don Juan said that don Genaro was still with Pablito, preparing him for the last encounter.

"Tomorrow you and Pablito will go into the unknown," he said. "I must prepare you for it now. You will go into it by yourselves. Last night you two were like yo-yos being pulled back and forth; tomorrow you will be on your own."

I had then a rush of curiosity, and questions about my experiences of the night before just poured out of me. He was unruffled by my barrage.

"Today I have to accomplish a most crucial maneuver," he said. "I have to trick you for the last time. And you must fall for my tricking."

He laughed and slapped his thighs.

"What Genaro wanted to show you with the first exercise the other night was how sorcerers use the *nagual*," he went on. "There's no way to get to the sorcerers' explanation unless one has willingly used the *nagual*, or rather, unless one has willingly used the *tonal* to make sense out of one's actions in the *nagual*. Another way of making all this clear is to say that the view of the *tonal* must prevail if one is going to use the *nagual* the way sorcerers do."

I told him that I had found a blatant incongruity in what he had just said. On the one hand, he had given me, two days before, an incredible recapitulation of his studied acts over a period of years, acts designed to affect my view of the world; and on the other hand, he wanted that same view to prevail.

"One thing has nothing to do with the other," he said. "Order in our perception is the exclusive realm of the *tonal*; only there can our actions have a sequence; only there are they like stairways where one can count the steps. There is nothing of that sort in the *nagual*. Therefore, the view of the *tonal* is a tool, and as such it is not only the best tool but the only one we've got.

"Last night your bubble of perception opened and its wings unfolded. There is nothing else to say about it. It is impossible to explain what happened to you, so I'm not going to attempt to and you shouldn't try to either. It should be enough to say that the wings of your perception were made to touch your totality. Last night you went back and forth from the *nagual* to the *tonal* time and time again. You were hurled in twice so as to leave no possibility for mistakes. The second time you experienced the full impact of the journey into the unknown. And your perception unfolded its wings when something in you realized your true nature. You are a cluster.

"This is the sorcerers' explanation. The *nagual* is the unspeakable. All the possible feelings and beings and selves float in it like barges, peaceful, unaltered, forever. Then the glue of life binds some of them together. You yourself found that out last night, and so did Pablito, and so did Genaro the time he journeyed into the unknown, and so did I. When the glue of life binds those feelings together a being is created, a being that loses the sense of its true nature and becomes blinded by the glare and clamor of the area where beings hover, the *tonal*. The *tonal* is where all the unified organization exists. A being pops into the *tonal* once the force of life has bound all the needed feelings together. I said to you once that the *tonal* begins at birth and ends at death; I said that because I know that as soon as the force of life leaves the body all those single awarenesses disintegrate and go back again to where they came from, the *nagual*. What a warrior does in journeying into the unknown is very much like dying, except that his cluster of single feelings do not disintegrate but expand a bit without losing their togetherness. At death, however, they sink deeply and move independently as if they had never been a unit."

I wanted to tell him how completely homogeneous were his statements with my experience. But he did not let me talk.

"There is no way to refer to the unknown," he said. "One can only witness it. The sorcerers' explanation says that each of us has a center from which the *nagual* can be witnessed, the *will*. Thus, a warrior can venture into the *nagual* and let his cluster arrange and rearrange itself in any way possible. I've said to you that the expression of the *nagual* is a personal matter. I meant that it is up to the individual warrior himself to direct the arrangement and rearrangements of that cluster. The human form or human feeling is the original one, perhaps it is the sweetest form of them all to us; there are, however, an endless number of alternative forms which the cluster may adopt. I've said to you that a sorcerer can adopt any form he wants. That is true. A sorcerer who is in possession of the totality of himself can direct the parts of his cluster to join in any conceivable way. The force of life is what makes all that shuffling possible. Once the force of life is exhausted there is no way to reassemble that cluster.

"I have called that cluster the bubble of perception. I have also said that it is sealed, closed tightly, and that it never opens until the moment of our death. Yet it could be made to open. Sorcerers have obviously learned that secret, and although not all of them arrive at the totality of themselves, they know about the possibility of it. They know that the bubble opens only when one plunges into the *nagual*. Yesterday I gave you a recapitulation of all the steps that you have followed to arrive at that point."

He scrutinized me as if he were waiting for a comment or a question. What he had said was beyond comment. I understood then that it would have been of no consequence if he had told me everything fourteen years before, or if he would have told it to me at any point during my apprenticeship. What was important was the fact that I had experienced with or in my body the premises of his explanation.

"I'm waiting for your usual question," he said, voicing his words slowly.

"What question?" I asked.

"The one your *reason* is itching to voice."

"Today I relinquish all questions. I really don't have any, don Juan."

"That's not fair," he said, laughing. "There is one particular question that I need you to ask."

He said that if I would shut off my internal dialogue for just an instant I could discern what the question was. I had a sudden thought, a momentary insight, and I knew what he wanted.

"Where was my body while all that was happening to me, don Juan?" I asked and he broke into a belly laugh.

"This is the last of the sorcerers' tricks," he said. "Let's say that what I'm going to reveal to you is the last bit of the sorcerers' explanation. Up to this point your *reason* has haphazardly followed my doings. Your *reason* is willing to admit that the world is not as the description portrays it, that there is much more to it than what meets the eye. Your *reason* is almost willing and ready to admit that your perception went up and down that cliff, or that something in you or even all of you leaped to the bottom of the gorge and examined with the eyes of the *tonal* what was there, as if you had descended bodily with a rope and ladder. That act of examining the bottom of the gorge was the crown of all these years of training. You did it well. Genaro saw the cubic centimeter of chance when he threw a rock at the *you* that was at the bottom of the ravine. You *saw* everything. Genaro and I knew then without a doubt that you were ready to be hurled into the unknown. At that instant you not only *saw*, but you knew all about the double, the other."

I interrupted and told him that he was giving me undeserving credit for something that was beyond my understanding. His reply was that I needed time to let all those impressions settle down, and that once I had done that, answers would just pour out of me in the same manner that questions had poured out of me in the past.

"The secret of the double is in the bubble of perception, which in your case that night was at the top of the cliff and at the bottom of the gorge at the same time," he said. "The cluster of feelings can be made to assemble instantly anywhere. In other words, one can perceive the *here* and the *there* at once."

He urged me to think and remember a sequence of actions which he said were so ordinary that I had almost forgotten them.

I did not know what he was talking about. He coaxed me to try harder.

"Think about your hat," he said. "And think what Genaro did with it."

I had a shocking moment of realization. I had forgotten that don Genaro had actually wanted me to take off my hat because it kept on falling off, blown by the wind. But I did not want to let go of it. I had felt stupid being naked. Wearing a hat, which I ordinarily never do, gave me a sense of strangeness; I was not really myself, in which case being without clothes was not so embarrassing. Don Genaro had then attempted to change hats with me, but his was too small for my head. He made jokes about the size of my head and the proportions of my body, and finally he took my hat off and wrapped my head with an old poncho, like a turban.

I told don Juan that I had forgotten about that sequence, which I was sure had happened in between my so-called leaps. And yet the memory of those "leaps" stood as a unit which was uninterrupted.

"They certainly were an uninterrupted unit, and so was Genaro's cavorting with your hat," he said. "Those two memories cannot be made to go one after the other because they happened at the same time."

He made the fingers of his left hand move as if they could not fit into the spaces between the fingers of his right hand.

"Those leaps were only the beginning," he went on. "Then came your true excursion into the unknown; last night you experienced the unspeakable, the *nagual*. Your *reason* cannot fight the physical knowledge that you are a nameless cluster of feelings. Your *reason* at this point might even admit that there is another center of assemblage, the *will*, through which it is possible to judge or assess and use the extraordinary effects of the *nagual*. It has finally dawned on your *reason* that one can reflect the *nagual* through the *will*, although one can never explain it.

"But then comes your question, 'Where was I when all that was taking place? Where was my body?' The conviction that there is a real *you* is a result of the fact that you have rallied everything you've got around your *reason*. At this point your reason admits that the *nagual* is the indescribable, not because the evidence has convinced it, but because it is safe to admit that. Your *reason* is on safe ground, all the elements of the *tonal* are on its side."

Don Juan paused and examined me. His smile was kind.

"Let's go to Genaro's place of predilection," he said abruptly.

He stood up and we walked to the rock where we had talked two days before; we sat comfortably on the same spots with our backs against the rock.

"To make *reason* feel safe is always the task of the teacher," he said. "I've tricked your *reason* into believing that the *tonal* was accountable and predictable. Genaro and I have labored to give you the impression that only the *nagual* was beyond the scope of explanation; the proof that the tricking was successful is that at this moment it seems to you that in spite of everything you have gone through, there is still a core that you can claim as your own, your *reason*. That's a mirage. Your precious *reason* is only a center of assemblage, a mirror that reflects something which is outside of it. Last night you witnessed not only the indescribable *nagual* but also the indescribable *tonal*.

"The last piece of the sorcerers' explanation says that *reason* is merely reflecting an outside order, and that *reason* knows nothing about that order; it cannot explain it, in the same way it cannot explain the *nagual*. *Reason* can only witness the effects of the *tonal*, but never ever could it understand it, or unravel it. The very fact that we are thinking and talking points out an order that we follow without ever knowing how we do that, or what the order is."

I brought up then the idea of Western man's research into the workings of the brain as a possibility of explaining what that order was. He pointed out that all that that research did was to attest that something was happening.

"Sorcerers do the same thing with their *will*," he said. "They say that through the *will* they can witness the effects of the *nagual*. I can add now that through *reason*, no matter what we do with it, or how we do it, we are merely witnessing the effects of the *tonal*. In both cases there is no hope, ever, to understand or to explain what it is that we are witnessing.

"Last night was the first time that you flew on the wings of your perception. You were still very timid. You ventured only on the band of human perception. A sorcerer can use those wings to touch other sensibilities, a crow's for instance, a coyote's, a cricket's, or the order of other worlds in that infinite space."

"Do you mean other planets, don Juan?"

"Certainly. The wings of perception can take us to the most recondite confines of the *nagual* or to inconceivable worlds of the *tonal*."

"Can a sorcerer go to the moon, for instance?"

"Of course he can," he replied. "But he wouldn't be able to bring back a bag of rocks, though."

We laughed and joked about it but his statement had been made in ultimate seriousness.

"We have arrived at the last part of the sorcerers' explanation," he said. "Last night Genaro and I showed you the last two points that make the totality of man, the *nagual* and the *tonal*. I once told you that those two points were outside of oneself and yet they were not. That is the paradox of the luminous beings. The *tonal* of every one of us is but a reflection of that indescribable unknown filled with order; the *nagual* of every one of us is but a reflection of that indescribable void that contains everything.

"Now you should sit on Genaro's place of predilection until twilight; by then you should have pounded the sorcerers' explanation into place. As you sit here now, you have nothing except the force of your life that binds that cluster of feelings."

He stood up.

"Tomorrow's task is to plunge into the unknown by yourself while Genaro and I watch you without intervening," he said. "Sit here and turn off your internal dialogue. You may gather the power needed to unfold the wings of your perception and fly to that infinitude."

THE PREDILECTION OF TWO WARRIORS

Don Juan woke me up at the crack of dawn. He handed me a carrying gourd filled with water and a bag of dry meat. We walked in silence for a couple of miles to the place where I had left my car two days before.

"This journey is our last journey together," he said in a quiet voice when we arrived at my car.

I felt a strong jolt in my stomach. I knew what he meant.

He leaned against the back fender as I opened the passenger door and he looked at me with a feeling that had never been there before. We got in the car but before I started the motor he made some obscure remarks that I also understood to perfection; he said that we had a few minutes to sit in the car and touch again upon some feelings very personal and poignant.

I sat quietly but my spirit was restless. I wanted to say something to him, something that would have essentially soothed me. I searched in vain for the appropriate words, the formula that would have expressed the thing I "knew" without being told.

Don Juan talked about a little boy that I once knew, and about how my feelings for him would not change with the years or the distance. Don Juan said that he was certain that every time I thought of that little boy my spirit jumped joyfully and without a trace of selfishness or pettiness wished him the best.

He reminded me of a story that I had once told him about the little boy, a story which he had liked and had found to have a profound meaning. During one of our hikes in the mountains around Los

Angeles the little boy had gotten tired of walking, so I had let him ride on my shoulders. A wave of intense happiness engulfed us then and the little boy shouted his thanks to the sun and to the mountains.

"That was his way of saying good-by to you," don Juan said.

I felt the sting of anguish in my throat.

"There are many ways of saying farewell," he said. "The best way is perhaps by holding a particular memory of joyfulness. For instance, if you live like a warrior, the warmth you felt when the little boy rode on your shoulders will be fresh and cutting for as long as you live. That is a warrior's way of saying farewell."

I hurriedly turned on the motor and drove faster than usual on the hard-packed rocky ground until we got onto the unpaved road.

We drove a short distance and then we walked the rest of the way. After about an hour we came to a grove of trees. Don Genaro, Pablito, and Nestor were there waiting for us. I greeted them. All of them appeared to be so happy and vigorous. As I looked at them and at don Juan I was overcome by a feeling of profound empathy for all of them. Don Genaro embraced me and patted me affectionately on the back. He told Nestor and Pablito that I had had a fine performance leaping into the bottom of a ravine. With his hand still on my shoulder he addressed them in a loud voice.

"Yes sir," he said, looking at them. "I'm his benefactor and I know that that was quite an achievement. That was the crown of years of living like a warrior."

He turned to me and placed his other hand on my shoulder. His eyes were shiny and peaceful.

"There's nothing I can say to you, Carlitos," he said, voicing his words slowly. "Except that you had an extraordinary amount of excrement in your bowels."

With that he and don Juan howled with laughter until they seemed about to pass out. Pablito and Nestor giggled nervously, not knowing exactly what to do.

When don Juan and don Genaro had quieted down, Pablito said to me that he was unsure of his capability of going into the "unknown" by himself.

"I really don't have the faintest idea of how to do it," he said.

"Genaro says that one needs nothing except impeccability. What do you think?"

I told him that I knew even less than he did. Nestor sighed and seemed truly concerned; he moved his hands and his mouth nervously as if he were on the verge of saying something important and did not know how.

"Genaro says that you two will make it," he finally said.

Don Genaro signaled with his hand that we were leaving. He and don Juan walked together, a few yards ahead of us. We followed the same mountain trail nearly all day. We walked in complete silence and never stopped. All of us had a provision of dry meat and a gourd of water, and it was understood that we would eat as we walked. At a certain point the trail definitely became a road. It curved around the side of a mountain and suddenly the view of a valley opened up in front of us. It was a breath-taking sight, a long green valley glimmering in sunlight; there were two magnificent rainbows over it and patches of rain all over the surrounding hills.

Don Juan stopped walking and jutted his chin to point out something down in the valley to don Genaro. Don Genaro shook his head. It was not an affirmative or negative gesture; it was more like a jerk of his head. They both stood motionless peering into the valley for a long time.

We left the road there and took what seemed to be a short cut. We began to descend via a more narrow and hazardous path that led to the northern part of the valley.

When we reached the flatland, it was midafternoon. The strong scent of river willows and moist dirt enveloped me. For a moment the rain was like a soft green rumble on the nearby trees to my left, then it was only a quivering in the reeds. I heard the rustling of a stream. I stopped for a moment to listen. I looked at the top of the trees; the high cirrus clouds on the western horizon looked like puffs of cotton scattered in the sky. I stood there watching the clouds long enough for everyone else to get quite a bit ahead of me. I ran after them.

Don Juan and don Genaro stopped and turned around in unison; their eyes moved and focused on me with such uniformity and precision that they seemed to be one single person. It was a brief stupendous glance that sent chills through my back. Then don Genaro laughed and said that I ran thumping, like a three-hundred-pound flat-footed Mexican.

"Why a Mexican?" don Juan asked.

"A flat-footed three-hundred-pound Indian doesn't run," don Genaro said in an explanatory tone.

"Oh," don Juan said as if don Genaro had really explained something.

We crossed the narrow lush green valley and climbed into the mountains to the east. By late afternoon we finally came to a halt on top of a flat barren mesa that overlooked a high valley towards the south. The vegetation had changed drastically. There were round eroded mountains all around. The land in the valley and on the sides of the hills was parceled and cultivated and yet the entire scene gave me the feeling of barrenness.

The sun was already low on the southwest horizon. Don Juan and don Genaro called us to the northern edge of the mesa. From that point the view was sublime. There were endless valleys and mountains towards the north and a range of high sierras towards the west. The sunlight reflecting on the distant northern mountains made them look orange, like the color of the banks of clouds over the west. The scenery, in spite of its beauty, was sad and lonely.

Don Juan handed me my writing pad, but I did not feel like taking notes. We sat in a half circle with don Juan and don Genaro at the ends.

"You started on the path of knowledge writing, and you will finish the same way," don Juan said.

All of them urged me to write, as if my writing were essential.

"You're at the very edge, Carlitos," don Genaro said suddenly. "You and Pablito both."

His voice was soft. Without his joking tone, he sounded kind and worried.

"Other warriors journeying into the unknown have stood on this very spot," he went on. "They all wish you two very well."

I felt a ripple around me as if the air had been half solid and something had created a wave that rippled through it.

"All of us here wish you two well," he said.

Nestor embraced Pablito and me and then he sat apart from us.

"We still have some time," don Genaro said, looking at the sky. And then turning to Nestor, he asked, "What should we do in the meantime?"

"We should laugh and enjoy ourselves," Nestor answered briskly.

I told don Juan that I was afraid of what was waiting for me, and that I had most certainly been tricked into all that; I who had not even imagined that situations like the one Pablito and I were living existed. I said that something truly awesome had taken possession of me and little by little had pushed me until I was facing something perhaps worse than death.

"You're complaining," don Juan said dryly. "You're feeling sorry for yourself to the last minute."

They all laughed. He was right. What an invincible urge! And I thought I had vanquished it from my life. I begged all of them to forgive my idiocy.

"Don't apologize," don Juan said to me. "Apologies are nonsense. What really matters is being an impeccable warrior in this unique place of power. This place has harbored the finest warriors. Be as fine as they were."

Then he addressed both Pablito and me.

"You already know that this is the last task in which we will be together," he said. "You will enter into the *nagual* and the *tonal* by the force of your personal power alone. Genaro and I are here only to bid you farewell. Power has determined that Nestor should be a witness. So be it.

"This will also be the last crossroad of yours which Genaro and I will attend. Once you have entered the unknown by yourselves you cannot depend on us to bring you back, so a decision is mandatory; you must decide whether or not to return. We are confident that you two have the strength to return if you choose to do so. The other night you were perfectly capable, in unison or separately, to throw off the ally that otherwise would have crushed you to death. That was a test of your strength.

"I must also add that few warriors survive the encounter with the unknown that you are about to have; not so much because it is hard, but because the *nagual* is enticing beyond any statement, and warriors who are journeying into it find that to return to the *tonal*, or to the world of order and noise and pain, is a most unappealing affair.

"The decision to stay or to return is done by something in us which is neither our *reason* nor our desire, but our *will*, so there is no way of knowing the outcome of it beforehand.

"If you choose not to return you will disappear as if the earth had swallowed you. But if you choose to return to this earth you must wait like true warriors until your particular tasks are finished. Once they are finished, either in success or defeat, you will have the command over the totality of yourselves."

Don Juan paused for a moment. Don Genaro looked at me and winked.

"Carlitos wants to know what it means to have command over the totality of oneself," he said, and everybody laughed.

He was right. Under other circumstances I would have asked about it; the situation, however, was too solemn for questions.

"It means that the warrior has finally encountered power," don Juan said. "No one can tell what each warrior would do with it; perhaps you two will roam peacefully and unnoticed on the face of the earth, or perhaps you will turn out to be hateful men, or perhaps notorious, or kind. All that depends on the impeccability and the freedom of your spirit.

"The important thing, however, is your task. That is the bestowal made by a teacher and a benefactor to their apprentices. I pray that you two will succeed in bringing your tasks to a culmination."

"Waiting to fulfill that task is a very special waiting," don Genaro said all of a sudden. "And I'm going to tell you the story of a band of warriors who lived in another time on the mountains, somewhere in that direction."

He casually pointed to the east, but then, after a moment's hesitation, he seemed to change his mind and stood up and pointed to the distant northern mountains.

"No. They lived in that direction," he said, looking at me and smiling with an air of erudition. "Exactly one hundred and thirty-five kilometers from here."

Don Genaro was perhaps imitating me. His mouth and forehead were contracted, his hands were tightly clasped against his chest holding some imaginary object that he may have intended to be a notebook. He maintained a most ridiculous posture. I had once met a German scholar, a Sinologist, who looked exactly like that. The thought that all along I might have been unconsciously imitating the grimaces of a German Sinologist was utterly funny to me. I laughed by myself. It seemed to be a joke just for me.

Don Genaro sat down again and proceeded with his story.

"Whenever a member of that band of warriors was thought to have committed an act which was against their rules, his fate was put to the decision of all of them. The culprit had to explain his reasons for having done what he did. His comrades had to listen to him; and then they either disbanded because they had found his reasons convincing, or they lined up with their weapons at the very edge of a flat mountain very much like this mountain where we are sitting now, ready to carry out his death sentence because they had found his reasons to be unacceptable. In that case the condemned warrior had to say good-by to his old comrades, and his execution began."

Don Genaro looked at me and Pablito as if waiting for a sign from us. Then he turned to Nestor.

"Perhaps the witness here could tell us what the story has to do with these two," he said to Nestor.

Nestor smiled shyly and seemed to immerse himself deep in thought for a moment.

"The witness has no idea," he said and broke up into a nervous giggle.

Don Genaro asked everyone to stand up and go with him to look over the west edge of the mesa.

There was a mild slope down to the bottom of the land formation, then there was a narrow flat strip of land ending in a crevice that seemed to be a natural channel for the runoff of rain water.

"Right where that ditch is, there was a row of trees on the mountain in the story," he said. "Beyond that point there was a thick forest.

"After saying good-by to his comrades, the condemned warrior was supposed to begin walking down the slope towards the trees. His comrades then cocked their weapons and aimed at him. If no one shot, or if the warrior survived his wounds and reached the edge of the trees, he was free."

We went back to the place where we had been sitting.

"How about now, witness?" he asked Nestor. "Can you tell?"

Nestor was the epitome of nervousness. He took off his hat and scratched his head. He then hid his face in his hands.

"How can the poor witness know?" he finally retorted in a challenging tone and laughed with everybody else.

"They say that there were men who pulled through unharmed," don Genaro continued. "Let's say that their personal power affected their comrades. A wave went through them as they were aiming at him and no one dared to use his weapon. Or perhaps they were in awe of his bravery and could not harm him."

Don Genaro looked at me and then at Pablito.

"There was a condition set up for that walk to the edge of the trees," he went on. "The warrior had to walk calmly, unaffected. His steps had to be sure and firm, his eyes looking straight ahead, peacefully. He had to go down without stumbling, without turning to look back, and above all without running."

Don Genaro paused; Pablito assented to his words by nodding.

"If you two decide to return to this earth," he said, "you will have to wait like true warriors until your tasks are fulfilled. That waiting is very much like the walk of the warrior in the story. You see, the warrior had run out of human time and so have you. The only difference is in who is aiming at you. Those who were aiming at the warrior were his warrior comrades. But what's aiming at you two is the unknown. Your only chance is your impeccability. You must wait without looking back. You must wait without expecting rewards. And you must aim all of your personal power at fulfilling your tasks.

"If you don't act impeccably, if you begin to fret and get impatient and desperate, you'll be cut down mercilessly by the sharpshooters from the unknown.

"If, on the other hand, your impeccability and personal power are such that you are capable of fulfilling your tasks, you will then achieve the promise of power. And what's that promise? you may ask. It is a promise that power makes to men as luminous beings. Each warrior has a different fate, so there is no way of telling what that promise will be for either of you."

The sun was about to set. The light orange color on the distant northern mountains had become darker. The scenery gave me the feeling of a windswept lonely world.

"You have learned that the backbone of a warrior is to be humble and efficient," don Genaro said and his voice made me jump. "You have learned to act without expecting anything in return. Now I tell you that in order to withstand what lies ahead of you beyond this day, you'll need your ultimate forbearance."

I experienced a shock in my stomach. Pablito began to shiver quietly.

"A warrior must be always ready," he said. "The fate of all of us here has been to know that we are the prisoners of power. No one knows why us in particular, but what a great fortune!"

Don Genaro stopped talking and lowered his head as if he were exhausted. That had been the first time that I had heard him speak in such terms.

"It is mandatory here that a warrior says good-by to all those present and to all those he leaves behind," don Juan said suddenly. "He must do this in his own words and loudly, so his voice will remain here forever in this place of power."

Don Juan's voice brought forth another dimension to my state of being at that moment. Our conversation in the car became all the more poignant. How right he was when he had said that the serenity of the scenery around us was only a mirage and that the sorcerers' explanation delivered a blow that no one could parry. I had heard the sorcerers' explanation and I had experienced its premises; and there I was, more naked and more helpless than ever in my entire life.

Nothing that I had ever done, nothing that I had ever imagined, could even compare to the anguish and the loneliness of that moment. The sorcerers' explanation had stripped me even of my "reason." Don Juan was right again when he said that a warrior could not avoid pain and grief but only the indulging in them. At that moment my sadness was uncontainable. I could not stand to say good-by to those who had shared with me the turns of my fate. I told don Juan and don Genaro that I had made a pact with someone to die together and that my spirit could not bear to leave alone.

"We are all alone, Carlitos," don Genaro said softly. "That's our condition."

I felt in my throat the anguish of my passion for life and for those close to me; I refused to say good-by to them.

"We are alone," don Juan said. "But to die alone is not to die in loneliness."

His voice sounded muffled and dry, like coughing.

Pablito wept quietly. Then he stood up and spoke. It was not a harangue or a testimonial. In a clear voice he thanked don Genaro and don Juan for their kindness. He turned to Nestor and thanked him for having given him the opportunity to take care of him. He wiped his eyes with his sleeve.

"What a wonderful thing it was to be in this beautiful world! In this marvelous time!" he exclaimed and sighed.

His mood was overwhelming.

"If I don't return I beg you as an ultimate favor to help those who have shared my fate," he said to don Genaro.

He then turned towards the west in the direction of his home. His lean body convulsed with tears. He ran towards the edge of the mesa with outstretched arms as if he were running to embrace someone. His lips moved, he seemed to be talking in a low voice.

I turned my head away. I did not want to hear what Pablito was saying.

He came back to where we were sitting, slumped down next to me, and lowered his head.

I was incapable of saying a thing. But then an outside force seemed to take over and made me stand up, and I too spoke my thanks and my sadness.

We were quiet again. A north wind hissed softly, blowing in my face. Don Juan looked at me. I had never seen so much kindness in his eyes. He said to me that a warrior said farewell by thanking all those who had had a gesture of kindness or concern for him, and that I had to voice my gratitude not only to them but also to those who had taken care of me and had helped me on my way.

I faced the northwest, towards Los Angeles, and all the sentimentality of my spirit poured out. What a purifying release it was to voice my thanks!

I sat down again. No one looked at me.

"A warrior acknowledges his pain but he doesn't indulge in it," don Juan said. "Thus the mood of a warrior who enters into the unknown is not one of sadness; on the contrary, he's joyful because he feels humbled by his great fortune, confident that his spirit is impeccable, and above all, fully aware of his efficiency. A warrior's joyfulness comes from having accepted his fate, and from having truthfully assessed what lies ahead of him."

There was a long pause. My sadness was paramount. I wanted to do something to get out of such oppressiveness.

"Witness, please squeeze your spirit catcher," don Genaro said to Nestor.

I heard the loud, most ludicrous sound of Nestor's contraption.

Pablito nearly got hysterical laughing, and so did don Juan and don Genaro. I noticed a peculiar smell and realized then that Nestor had farted. What was horrendously funny was the expression of ultimate seriousness on his face. He had farted not as a joke but because he did not have his spirit catcher with him. He was being helpful in the best way he could.

All of them laughed with abandon. What facility they had for shifting from sublime situations to utterly ludicrous ones.

Pablito turned to me suddenly. He wanted to know if I was a poet, but before I could answer his question don Genaro made a rhyme.

"Carlitos is really cool; he's got a bit of a poet, a nut and a fool," he said.

They all had another outburst of laughter.

"That's a better mood," don Juan said. "And now, before Genaro and I say good-by to you, you two may say anything you please. It might be the last time you utter a word, ever."

Pablito shook his head negatively, but I had something to say. I wanted to express my admiration, my awe for the exquisite temper of don Juan and don Genaro's warrior spirit. But I became entangled in my words and ended up saying nothing; or even worse yet, I ended up sounding as if I were complaining again.

Don Juan shook his head and smacked his lips in mock disapproval. I laughed involuntarily; it did not matter, however, that I had flubbed my chance to tell them of my admiration. A very intriguing sensation began to take possession of me. I had a sense of exhilaration and joy, an exquisite freedom that made me laugh. I told don Juan and don Genaro that I did not give a fig about the outcome of my encounter with the "unknown," that I was happy and complete, and that whether I lived or died was of no importance to me at that moment.

Don Juan and don Genaro seemed to enjoy my assertions even more than I did. Don Juan slapped his thigh and laughed. Don Genaro threw his hat on the floor and yelled as if he were riding a wild horse.

"We have enjoyed ourselves and laughed while waiting, just as the witness recommended," don Genaro said all of a sudden. "But it is the natural condition of order that it should always come to an end."

He looked at the sky.

"It's almost time for us to disband like the warriors in the story," he said. "But before we go our separate ways I must tell you two one last thing. I am going to disclose to you a warrior's secret. Perhaps you can call it a warrior's predilection."

He addressed me in particular and said that once I had told him that the life of a warrior was cold and lonely and devoid of feelings. He even added that at that precise moment I was convinced that it was so.

"The life of a warrior cannot possibly be cold and lonely and without feelings," he said, "because it is based on his affection, his devotion, his dedication to his beloved. And who, you may ask, is his beloved? I will show you now."

Don Genaro stood up and walked slowly to a perfectly flat area right in front of us, ten or twelve feet away. He made a strange gesture there. He moved his hands as if he were sweeping dust from his chest and his stomach. Then an odd thing happened. A flash of an almost imperceptible light went through him; it came from the ground and seemed to kindle his entire body. He did a sort of backward pirouette, a backward dive more properly speaking, and landed on his chest and arms. His movement had been executed with such precision and skill that he seemed to be a weightless being, a wormlike creature that had turned on itself. When he was on the ground he performed a series of unearthly movements. He glided just a few inches above the ground, or rolled on it as if he were lying on ball bearings; or he swam on it describing circles and turning with the swiftness and agility of an eel swimming in the ocean.

My eyes began to cross at one moment and then without any transition I was watching a ball of luminosity sliding back and forth on something that appeared to be the floor of an ice-skating rink with a thousand lights shining on it.

The sight was sublime. Then the ball of fire came to rest and stayed motionless. A voice shook me and dispelled my attention. It was don Juan talking. I could not understand at first what he was saying. I looked again at the ball of fire; I could distinguish only don Genaro lying on the ground with his arms and legs spread out.

Don Juan's voice was very clear. It seemed to trigger something in me and I began to write.

"Genaro's love is the world," he said. "He was just now embracing this enormous earth but since he's so little all he can do is swim in it. But the earth knows that Genaro loves it and it bestows on him its care. That's why Genaro's life is filled to the brim and his state, wherever he'll be, will be plentiful. Genaro roams on the paths of his love and, wherever he is, he is complete."

Don Juan squatted in front of us. He caressed the ground gently.

"This is the predilection of two warriors," he said. "This earth, this world. For a warrior there can be no greater love."

Don Genaro stood up and squatted next to don Juan for a moment while both of them peered fixedly at us, then they sat in unison, cross-legged.

"Only if one loves this earth with unbending passion can one release one's sadness," don Juan said. "A warrior is always joyful because his love is unalterable and his beloved, the earth, embraces him and bestows upon him inconceivable gifts. The sadness belongs only to those who hate the very thing that gives shelter to their beings."

Don Juan again caressed the ground with tenderness.

"This lovely being, which is alive to its last recesses and understands every feeling, soothed me, it cured me of my pains, and finally when I had fully understood my love for it, it taught me freedom."

He paused. The silence around us was frightening. The wind hissed softly and then I heard the distant barking of a lone dog.

"Listen to that barking," don Juan went on. "That is the way my beloved earth is helping me now to bring this last point to you. That barking is the saddest thing one can hear."

We were quiet for a moment. The barking of that lone dog was so sad and the stillness around us so intense that I experienced a numbing anguish. It made me think of my own life, my sadness, my not knowing where to go, what to do.

"That dog's barking is the nocturnal voice of a man," don Juan said. "It comes from a house in that valley towards the south. A man is shouting through his dog, since they are companion slaves for life, his sadness, his boredom. He's begging his death to come and release him from the dull and dreary chains of his life."

Don Juan's words had caught a most disturbing line in me. I felt he was speaking directly to me.

"That barking, and the loneliness it creates, speaks of the feelings of men," he went on. "Men for whom an entire life was like one Sunday afternoon, an afternoon which was not altogether miserable, but rather hot and dull and uncomfortable. They sweated and fussed a great deal. They didn't know where to go, or what to do. That afternoon left them only with the memory of petty annoyances and te-dium, and then suddenly it was over; it was already night."

He recounted a story I had once told him about a seventy-two-year-old man who complained that his life had been so short that it seemed to him that it was only the day before that he was a boy. The man had said to me, "I remember the pajamas I used to wear when I was ten years old. It seems that only one day has passed. Where did the time go?"

"The antidote that kills that poison is here," don Juan said, caress-ing the ground. "The sorcerers' explanation cannot at all liberate the spirit. Look at you two. You have gotten to the sorcerers' explana-tion, but it doesn't make any difference that you know it. You're more alone than ever, because without an unwavering love for the being that gives you shelter, aloneness is loneliness.

"Only the love for this splendorous being can give freedom to a warrior's spirit; and freedom is joy, efficiency, and abandon in the face of any odds. That is the last lesson. It is always left for the very last moment, for the moment of ultimate solitude when a man faces his death and his aloneness. Only then does it make sense."

Don Juan and don Genaro stood up and stretched their arms and arched their backs, as if sitting had made their bodies stiff. My heart began to pound fast. They made Pablito and me stand up.

"The twilight is the crack between the worlds," don Juan said. "It is the door to the unknown."

He pointed with a sweeping movement of his hand to the mesa where we were standing.

"This is the plateau in front of that door."

He pointed then to the northern edge of the mesa.

"There is the door. Beyond, there is an abyss and beyond that abyss is the unknown."

Don Juan and don Genaro then turned to Pablito and said good-by to him. Pablito's eyes were dilated and fixed; tears were rolling down his cheeks.

I heard don Genaro's voice saying good-by to me, but I did not hear don Juan's.

Don Juan and don Genaro moved towards Pablito and whispered briefly in his ears. Then they came to me. But before they had whispered anything I already had that peculiar feeling of being split.

"We will now be like dust on the road," don Genaro said. "Perhaps it will get in your eyes again, someday."

Don Juan and don Genaro stepped back and seemed to merge with the darkness. Pablito held my forearm and we said good-by to each other. Then a strange urge, a force, made me run with him to the northern edge of the mesa. I felt his arm holding me as we jumped and then I was alone.